D1061450

Transformative Learning in Practice

Transformative Learning in Practice

Insights from Community, Workplace, and Higher Education

Jack Mezirow
Edward W. Taylor
and Associates

JOSSEY-BASS
A Wiley Imprint
www.josseybass.com

Copyright © 2009 by John Wiley & Sons, Inc. All rights reserved.

Published by Jossey-Bass
A Wiley Imprint
989 Market Street, San Francisco, CA 94103-1741—www.josseybass.com

No part of this publication may be reproduced, stored in a retrieval system, or transmitted in any form or by any means, electronic, mechanical, photocopying, recording, scanning, or otherwise, except as permitted under Section 107 or 108 of the 1976 United States Copyright Act, without either the prior written permission of the publisher, or authorization through payment of the appropriate per-copy fee to the Copyright Clearance Center, Inc., 222 Rosewood Drive, Danvers, MA 01923, 978-750-8400, fax 978-646-8600, or on the Web at www.copyright.com. Requests to the publisher for permission should be addressed to the Permissions Department, John Wiley & Sons, Inc., 111 River Street, Hoboken, NJ 07030, 201-748-6011, fax 201-748-6008, or online at www.wiley.com/go/permissions.

Readers should be aware that Internet Web sites offered as citations and/or sources for further information may have changed or disappeared between the time this was written and when it is read.

Limit of Liability/Disclaimer of Warranty: While the publisher and author have used their best efforts in preparing this book, they make no representations or warranties with respect to the accuracy or completeness of the contents of this book and specifically disclaim any implied warranties of merchantability or fitness for a particular purpose. No warranty may be created or extended by sales representatives or written sales materials. The advice and strategies contained herein may not be suitable for your situation. You should consult with a professional where appropriate. Neither the publisher nor author shall be liable for any loss of profit or any other commercial damages, including but not limited to special, incidental, consequential, or other damages.

Jossey-Bass books and products are available through most bookstores. To contact Jossey-Bass directly call our Customer Care Department within the U.S. at 800-956-7739, outside the U.S. at 317-572-3986, or fax 317-572-4002.

Jossey-Bass also publishes its books in a variety of electronic formats. Some content that appears in print may not be available in electronic books.

Library of Congress Cataloging-in-Publication Data
Mezirow, Jack, 1923-
 Transformative learning in practice : insights from community, workplace, and higher education / Jack Mezirow, Edward W. Taylor, and Associates.—1st ed.
   p. cm.
 Includes index.
 ISBN 978-0-470-25790-6 (cloth)
 1. Transformative learning—Cross-cultural studies.   I. Taylor, Edward W. II. Title.
 LC1100.M49 2010
 370.11′5—dc22
                          2009021652

Printed in the United States of America
FIRST EDITION

HB Printing   10 9 8 7 6 5 4 3 2

The Jossey-Bass Higher Education Series

CONTENTS

PREFACE

In the past decade, interest has been growing in the field of adult education and higher education about the practice of transformative learning: an approach to teaching based on promoting change, where educators challenge learners to critically question and assess the integrity of their deeply held assumptions about how they relate to the world around them.

Transformative learning has become the dominant teaching paradigm discussed within the field of adult education. It has interested scholars and educators to such an extent that it is no longer just an adult education teaching construct. Rather, it is becoming a standard of practice in a variety of disciplines and educational settings: higher education, professional education, organizational development, international education, and community education. For example, transformative learning guides instruction in a first-year sociology course at a Canadian university, where it provides a framework for facilitating critical refection in the workplace; it is used to promote female empowerment in Senegal for those who are fighting the practice of female genital cutting; it provides guidance in promoting community among online learners; and it guides the instruction for medical students in palliative care. These settings, as well as many others, begin to shed light on the broad reach that transformative learning offers higher and adult education as a viable and responsive practice.

Research about transformative learning also continues to grow exponentially, to the point that a national conference, held every couple of years, is devoted to this topic. Published research continues to grow as well. A recent review of this research shows that much of the focus is on fostering transformative learning. In other words, it is about understanding, identifying, and making sense of transformative learning as a practice in the classroom and other settings. Nevertheless, despite its growing presence as an area of research and a means of practice in a variety of settings, there is still much we do not know about the practice of transformative learning.

Many questions remain unanswered or inadequately understood. How are educators conceptualizing the purpose and practice of fostering transformative learning? What are effective practices for promoting transformative learning in formal and informal settings? What is it about transformative learning that is most helpful in informing practice? How does the teaching setting shape the practice of transformative learning? What are the successes, strengths, and outcomes of fostering transformative learning? What are the risks, challenges, and caveats when practicing it?

These questions and others form the foundation of this book, which seeks to bring to life the practice of transformative learning and its application within varied educational settings. The chapters in this book, written by a cadre of talented scholars and practitioners from a variety of adult and higher education contexts, reveal an in-depth and personal perspective about the everyday practice of fostering transformative learning within unique educational settings.

The contributors represent a diverse and experienced group of scholar-practitioners who are actively engaged in the work of transformative learning in a variety of national and international settings, among them higher education, corporations, and communities. Readers will be able to glean from these chapters strategies, methods, and caveats from experienced educators who deeply believe in the practice of transformative learning and who respect its challenges and appreciate its rewards.

ABOUT THIS BOOK

Compiling this book required a process of sorting through a variety of resources in an effort to identify individuals who could provide an informative chapter on the practice of transformative learning. The central source for this book was the conference proceedings of seven International Transformative Learning Conferences conducted from 1998 to 2007, along with a review of published journal articles on fostering transformative learning (Taylor, 2000, 2007). Seven collaboratively planned conferences were held from 1998 and 2007: three were conducted in New York, and the others in California, Ontario, Michigan, and New Mexico. Each produced a comprehensive publication of peer-selected papers, accepted for presentation at the conference and included in conference proceedings.

These proceedings provided an invaluable resource ensuring diverse per-spectives of fostering transformative learning. The breadth of application of transformative learning in each conference is reflected, for example, in the Proceedings of the Sixth Conference in Michigan, which contained thirty-two presentations, including addressing applications of transformative learning in education, organizations, religion, diversity, spirituality, gender, critical humility, transformation theory, disability, race, conflict resolution, research, popular education, community development, cross-cultural learning, autobi-ography, diversity, health, online education creativity, faculty development, films, democratic citizenship, and art. In addition to the proceedings, published research studies about fostering transformative learning were reviewed as well.

As book editors, we went through all the conference proceedings and published literature reviews relevant to fostering transformative learning. Our goal was to identify a host of contributors who provide a diverse approach to practice transformative learning within a variety of settings.

ORGANIZATION OF THE BOOK

The chapters are organized into five parts. Part One consists of two chapters that set the context for the book by providing an introduction to the practice of fostering transformative learning and to the theory of transformative learning. The next three parts, the heart of the book, contain twenty-two chapters that provide insight into the practice of fostering transformative learning in various settings: in higher education (nine chapters), workplace education (six chapters), and community and social change education (seven chapters). The one chapter in Part Five serves as a reflective analysis of all the chapters, identifying what they reveal as a whole about the practice of transformative learning.

The emphasis of reflection on practice is central to the entire book. Teaching is often a tacit and unreflective activity, with educators rarely writing up their ideas of practice for others to read. In response to this concern and in keeping with the idea of promoting a reflexive practice, we asked the contributors to look back and discuss what new insights and challenges they learned from this experience that would better inform interested practitioners about fostering transformative learning.

In addition, each contributor was asked to develop his or her chapter with an instrumental emphasis and less theoretical analysis concerning transforma-tive learning. The intent was to provide practical and concrete instructional guidance to interested practitioners. We hope that the readers of this book will find new insights into practice and gain a greater appreciation of the challenges associated with fostering transformative learning regardless of the setting. We also hope readers will explore and take risks in their classrooms and informal educational settings, always pushing the limits of what is known about transformative education.

ACKNOWLEDGMENTS

A book of such breadth and depth does not come together without the hard work of dedicated individuals. We thank the contributors to this book particularly for their creative and thoughtful insights into fostering transformative learning, their promptness in submitting their chapters and turning around revisions in a timely manner, and their patience with our editorial comments. Furthermore, we acknowledge the invaluable contribution by Jodi Jarecke, a graduate assistant at Penn State University in Harrisburg. She spent many, many hours overseeing the administration of the book, editing, and providing insightful comments about the individual chapters. It was our good fortune to have her as part of the editorial team and as a contributor to the final chapter of the book.

September 2009

Jack Mezirow
Edward W. Taylor

REFERENCES

Taylor, E. W. (2000). Fostering Mezirow's transformative learning theory in the adult education classroom: A critical review. *Canadian Journal of the Study of Adult Education, 14,* 1–28.

Taylor, E. W. (2007). An update of transformative learning theory: A critical review of the empirical research (1999–2005). *International Journal of Lifelong Education, 26,* 173–191.

ABOUT THE AUTHORS

Lucia Alcántara is a seasoned consultant with expertise in organizational capacity building and development. Her career spans over ten years of working with executives and work groups in private and public corporations. She has cofacilitated several cooperative inquiry projects and is completing doctoral research on knowledge creation from inquiry groups at Columbia University's Teachers College. The results of her research have been published in international conference journals for the Association for Human Resources Development and the Academy of Management's Research Methods Division. As an educational facilitator she has taught management and multicultural relations at Cornell University and Russell Sage College, respectively. Alcántara holds a bachelor's degree from the Maxwell School at Syracuse University and a master's in public administration from Baruch College.

Stephen Brookfield is Distinguished University Professor at the University of St. Thomas in Minneapolis-St. Paul, Minnesota. Since beginning his teaching career in 1970, he has worked in England, Canada, Australia, and the United States, teaching in a variety of college settings, including ten years as a professor of higher and adult education at Columbia University in New York. He has written ten books on adult learning, teaching, critical thinking, discussion methods, and critical theory, four of which have won the Cyril O. Houle World

Award for Literature in Adult Education (in 1986, 1989, 1996, and 2005). He also won the 1986 Imogene Okes Award for Outstanding Research in Adult Education. His work has been translated into German, Finnish, and Chinese. In 1991, he was awarded an honorary doctor of letters degree from the University System of New Hampshire for his contributions to understanding adult learning. In 2001, he received the Leadership Award from the Association for Continuing Higher Education for "extraordinary contributions to the general field of continuing education on a national and international level." He currently serves on the editorial boards of educational journals in Britain, Canada, and Australia, as well as in the United States. During 2002, he was a visiting professor at Harvard University. In 2003, he was awarded an honorary doctor of letters degree from Concordia University (St. Paul).

⚭

Shauna Butterwick is associate professor of adult education in the Department of Educational Studies at the University of British Columbia, Vancouver, Canada. She teaches foundations of adult education, community-based adult education, and feminist theory in the diploma and graduate adult education programs, as well as teaching in the educational leadership and policy doctoral program. Much of her research focuses on women's learning, including learning in social movements, as well as women's educational experiences in welfare programs and life skills training. Her scholarship also focuses on the policy context of adult education programs. She has experience with community-based, participatory research and a strong interest in the value and contribution of arts-based teaching and research. Among her publications is "Embodied Metaphors: Telling Feminist Coalition Stories Through Popular Theatre," *New Zealand Journal of Adult Learning* (2005).

⚭

Patricia Cranton is a visiting professor of adult education at Penn State University in Harrisburg, Pennsylvania. Her primary research interests have been in the areas of teaching and learning in higher education, transformative learning, and, most recently, authenticity and individuation. Her most recent books include a second edition of *Planning Instruction for Adult Learners* (2000), *Becoming an Authentic Teacher* (2001), *Finding Our Way: A Guide for Adult Educators* (2003), and the second edition of *Understanding and Promoting Transformative Learning* (2006). She received her Ph.D. degree in 1976 from the University of Toronto.

⚭

Deborah Davidson teaches in the Department of Sociology at York University in Toronto, Canada. While her primary research is in health and family, it was her love of teaching that brought her to research in the area of pedagogy. Her independently and coauthored refereed publications thus far include four articles in journals, three as book chapters, and one in a conference proceeding. She has been nominated for two teaching awards, has reviewed for the journal *Excellence in Education,* and has been invited to apply for board membership of the *Open Education Journal.* She received her M.A. and Ph.D. in sociology from York University in Toronto, Canada.

৵

John M. Dirkx is professor of higher, adult, and lifelong education and director of the Michigan Center for Education and Work at Michigan State University. He teaches courses on adult learning, transformative learning, program planning, teaching methods, training and professional development, group dynamics, and qualitative research. His primary research interests focus on the emotional, psychosocial, transformative, and spiritual dimensions of teaching and learning in adult and higher education. He is the coauthor of *A Guide to Planning and Implementing Instruction for Adults: A Theme-Based Approach* (1997) and numerous book chapters and journal articles on adult learning.

৵

Joe F. Donaldson is professor of higher and continuing education and assistant director of the Statewide Cooperative Ed.D. Program in Educational Leadership in the Department of Educational Leadership and Policy Analysis at the University of Missouri-Columbia. His current research and writing focus on adult undergraduate students in higher education and education in the professions. His work has been published in the *Adult Education Quarterly, Review of Higher Education, Medical Education,* and *Journal of Higher Education,* among others. Donaldson is a consulting editor for the *Adult Education Quarterly* and is on the editorial board of the *Journal of Continuing Higher Education.* He has received numerous awards for his research and publications, including the 2002 Research and Scholarship Award from the University Continuing Education Association and the 2007 Marlowe Force award from the Association of Continuing Higher Education. Donaldson holds a B.S. and M.S. from the University of Tennessee-Knoxville and a Ph.D. in continuing education from the University of Wisconsin-Madison.

৵

Deborah Duveskog is an agronomist currently pursuing a Ph.D. at the Swedish University of Agricultural Sciences with her doctoral research relating to analysis of the learning process and impact of change and transformation in Farmer Field Schools in East Africa. She has also been working for the U.N. Food and Agricultural Organization in the East Africa region for eight years, where she has managed a range of empowerment, extension, and community-development-related programs and supported the development of a participatory monitoring and evaluation system for community interventions. She has published a range of practitioner-oriented publications on the Farmer Field School approach and participatory monitory and education.

ళ

Peter Easton is associate professor of adult and international education at Florida State University, where he teaches courses in international development education, multicultural education, adult learning, and participatory methodologies. He has worked extensively in Africa and the Caribbean and is particularly interested in problems of education and employment and methods of adult learning. His recent publications include "Social Policy from the Bottom Up: Abandoning FGC in Sub-Saharan Africa" (with Karen Monkman and Rebecca Miles) in *Development in Practice* (2003); "Education and Indigenous Knowledge" in Rainer Wrote et al. *Indigenous Knowledge: Local Pathways to Global Development* (2004); and "Adult Education and Social Sustainability: Harnessing the Red Queen Effect," in *Convergence* (2007). He received his Ph.D. from Florida State University.

ళ

Tony Egan is a psychologist and senior teaching fellow in the Department of the Dean, Dunedin School of Medicine, New Zealand. He has worked on curriculum development and evaluation in medical education for twenty years and sits on school and faculty committees responsible for development of the undergraduate medical course. He has researched and published on a wide range of topics, and his current preoccupations are the role of the hidden curriculum in medical education and learning and assessing how to achieve safe and effective clinical outcomes. He has a long-term affiliation with general practice (GP), coordinating continuing education for local GPs and contributing to the development of undergraduate programs in primary care and rural health. In 2003, he was elected to honorary fellowship of the Royal New Zealand College of General Practitioners. He is an enthusiastic contributor to ANZAME, the Australasian association for health professional education, editor of its journal, *Focus on Health Professional Education,* and serves as a reviewer for a number of journals.

∽

The European-American Collaborative Challenging Whiteness fosters learning and research about white supremacist consciousness. It is a group of six white adult education practitioner-scholars who, as individuals, practice in a variety of institutional and community settings. They have been working together since 1998 to support each other in efforts to change their awareness about privilege, race, and racism and to become more effective as change agents in their professional and personal lives. Members, who came together through a cultural consciousness project at the California Institute of Integral Studies in San Francisco, are Carole Balas, Elizabeth Karl, Alec MacLeod, Doug Paxton, Penny Rosenwasser, and Linda Sartor. They use a collective name because it reflects their beliefs about how knowledge is constructed. Inquiries about the collaborative's work can be addressed to collaborative@eccw.org. Further information is available at http://www.iconoclastic.net/eccw/.

∽

Beth Fisher-Yoshida is on the faculty in the Social and Organizational Psychology Program at Teachers College, Columbia University, and is also the associate director of the International Center for Cooperation and Conflict Resolution, where she oversees the education and practice functions of the center and conducts participatory action research. She also consults globally to corporate and nonprofit organizations, supporting them in their change efforts through organization development, strategic initiatives, team effectiveness, conflict resolution, and leadership development. A Certified Clinical Sociologist, she received her Ph.D. in human and organizational systems and M.A. in organization development from Fielding Graduate University; an M.A. in special education from Teachers College, Columbia University; and a B.S. in special education and B.A. in art from Buffalo State College.

∽

Esbern Friis-Hansen works as a senior researcher with the Politics and Governance Group at the Danish Institute for International Studies. He holds a Ph.D. in geography and has twenty-five years of experience with social science development research and consultancies, primarily in East and southern Africa. His ongoing studies are in farmer empowerment and rural institutions in East and southern Africa; impact assessment of Farmer Field Schools in East Africa;

and local governance of agricultural advisory services and social change in Soroti District, Uganda. He has published widely on agrarian issues in Africa and has contributed to agricultural policy formulating processes.

∽

Sarah Gravett is professor of higher and adult education and dean of the faculty of education at the University of Johannesburg (UJ) in South Africa. Prior to taking up this position, she was deputy dean and the chair of the Department of Higher and Adult Education at UJ. Her research focus implies an interest in the cognitive and social dynamics of teaching and learning. More specifically, she has focused on teaching as a learning-centered endeavor with the explicit intent to guide, foster, advance, and support deep and meaningful learning. A main thrust of this research is the notion that deep and meaningful learning is best facilitated through educational dialogue. She is the author or coauthor of numerous books and articles on this and related themes.

∽

Catherine A. Hansman is professor of adult learning and development at Cleveland State University and teaches master's and doctoral courses in adult education and qualitative research. She is a recipient of a Cyril O. Houle Scholarship in Adult and Continuing Education for emerging scholars. She holds a bachelor of music from the University of Cincinnati College-Conservatory of Music, a master's of education from Indiana University, and a doctorate in adult and community education from Ball State University. Her writings have been published in books, chapters, and journals such as *Adult Basic Education, Adult Learning,* and the *Adult Education Quarterly.*

∽

Sandra Hayes is a lecturer at Teachers College, Columbia University, where she has taught collaborative negotiation, leadership, and action research. She also teaches conflict resolution and organizational communication at Fairleigh Dickinson University. As an organizational development consultant who specializes in collaborative negotiation strategies, team building, and leadership development, her experience includes designing, conducting, and facilitating meetings and training workshops for a host of profit and nonprofit institutions including the United Nations, Unicef, New York City Health and Hospital, Reuters, Praxair, Citibank, American Express, Lucent Technologies, New York City Board of Education, Association for the Help of Retarded Children, and New York University Wagner School of Public Service. Hayes is also a doctoral candidate in adult learning and leadership at Teachers College, Columbia University, where her research interest in adult learning and development has been bolstered by an ongoing interest in and study of the various ways adults can learn through inquiry.

༄

Lee Herman has been a mentor at the State University of New York, Empire State College since 1979. He has won college and university awards for teaching and mentoring. He is cofounder of the Empire State College Mentoring Institute. With Alan Mandell, he has authored many articles and chapters, as well as the book *From Teaching to Mentoring: Principle and Practice, Dialogue and Life in Adult Education* (2004).

༄

Barbara P. Heuer is assistant professor at Fordham University's Graduate School of Education in New York City. She holds an M.L.S. from Rutgers University and an Ed.D. from the University of Georgia. With a background in information science and community service, she teaches in the master's program in adult education and human resource development. Her research interests are in informal and online learning, information literacy, and adult development.

༄

Jodi Jarecke is a graduate fellow and doctoral candidate in the Adult Education Department at Penn State Harrisburg. She received her M.P.H. from Northern Illinois University in 2005 and her B.A. from Rutgers University in 2000. She has developed educational programs and materials for community sustainability and preparedness initiatives through her work with local health departments and the AmeriCorps VISTA program. She has also worked on the development of medical education programs with the American Academy of Pediatrics, serving as managing editor for program materials for Pediatric First Aid for Caregivers and Teachers and the Pediatric Education for Prehospital Professionals. Her primary research interests include medical education and teaching and learning in the clinical environment.

༄

Kathleen P. King, Ed.D., is professor of adult education at Fordham University's Graduate School of Education in New York City. King's major areas of research have been transformative learning, professional development, distance learning, and instructional technology. Her experience in adult learning has spanned these fields in varied organizations, including community-based organizations, business, higher education, career and technical education, and numerous partnerships. She continues to explore and develop learning innovations and opportunities to address equity, access, and international issues. She is the author of eleven books and numerous articles. In addition to receiving numerous academic and professional awards in the field of adult learning, her coedited book about distance education, *Harnessing Innovations Technologies in Higher Education,* received the Frandson Book Award from the University Continuing Education Association in 2007. King is the coeditor of *Perspectives: The New York Journal of Adult Learning,* and an editorial board member for several national and international academic journals.

∽

Debra Langan is an assistant professor in the Criminology Program at Wilfrid Laurier University, Brantford, Ontario, Canada. She received her Ph.D. in sociology from York University. She is the recipient of the 2001 York Sociology Undergraduate Student Association's John O'Neill Award for Teaching Excellence. Her research focuses on the scholarship of teaching and learning, families and intimate relations, qualitative methodology, and critical social psychology. Her publications can be accessed at www.arts.yorku.ca/soci/dlangan and include "Using Mothering at Work: Embracing the Contradictions in Pedagogy and Praxis," *Journal of the Association for Research on Mothering* (2004); "Critical Pedagogy and Personal Struggles: Feminist Scholarship Outside Women's Studies" (with Deborah Davidson), *Feminist Teacher* (2005); and "The Political Is Personal: TAs on the Front Lines of the Critical Consciousness Campaign" (with Marcia Oliver and Laurel Atkinson), *Radical Pedagogy* (2007).

∽

Elizabeth A. Lange, Ph.D., M.Ed., B.Ed., is assistant professor of adult education in educational policy studies at the University of Alberta, Canada. Her research focuses on the theory and practice of transformative and restorative learning in adult education, adult sustainability and environmental education, social movement learning, socioenvironmental responsibility and work, participatory action research, and pedagogy for social change. She has over twenty-five years of experience as an educator and facilitator in formal education and community and international settings. She was honored with the Graduate Research Award by the Thirty-Seventh Adult Education Research Conference. She is currently working on several transformative learning projects with the immigrant and refugee community, as well as the social work community. Her other publications can be found on her Web page as part of the University of Alberta Web site.

∽

Randee Lipson Lawrence, Ed.D, is an associate professor in adult education at National-Louis University in Chicago. Her research interests include extrarational ways of knowing and learning through the arts. She is the editor of *Artistic Ways of Knowing: Expanded Opportunities for Teaching and Learning* (2005) and the author of several publications that exemplify her practice of incorporating affective, cognitive, somatic, and spiritual dimensions into teaching and learning. She also works with students to use these processes in their research. Among her other research interests and commitments are feminist pedagogy, collaborative inquiry, experiential and transformative learning, arts-based research, dreamwork, photography, and painting.

∽

Rod MacLeod is medical director of Hibiscus Coast Hospice; prior to that he was district medical director of palliative care (Waitemata DHB). He is Honorary Clinical Professor in General Practice and Primary Health Care, University of Auckland, and adjunct professor in the Departments of General Practice and Medical and Surgical Sciences at University of Otago, Dunedin School of Medicine. He was previously South Link Health Professor in Palliative Care at the Dunedin School of Medicine, University of Otago, and director of palliative care at the Otago Community Hospice. He was associate dean (academic and curriculum) and chair of the Medical Education Group. Prior to this, he was director of palliative care at Mary Potter Hospice in Wellington. He has a long-standing interest in education in palliative care, completing his Ph.D. work in 2002 with a dissertation entitled, "Changing the Way That Doctors Learn to Care for People Who Are Dying." He has published widely in the area of palliative care in national and international peer-reviewed journals. He is the author of *Snapshots on the Journey: An Anthology of Poems Through Death and Remembrance* (2002).

∽

Terrence E. Maltbia is faculty director of the Columbia Coaching Certification Program, a strategic partnership between the Columbia Business School's Executive Education Division and the Corporate Learning Solutions Group at Teachers College, Columbia University. He also teaches in the Adult Learning and Leadership Program, Department of Organization at Teachers College. He completed his doctorate at Teachers College. His current research is focused on strategic learning, leadership, organizational and executive coaching, and cultural competence. He recently coauthored *A Leader's Guide to Leveraging Diversity* (2009) with Anne Power. Prior to joining Teachers College, he held positions in sales, sales management, corporate employment, organization development, and consulting.

Alan Mandell is College Professor of Adult Learning and Mentoring at the State University of New York, Empire State College, where he has been faculty mentor, administrator, and director of the Mentoring Institute for more than thirty years. With colleague Lee Herman, he has written articles and chapters, and the book *From Teaching to Mentoring: Principles and Practice, Dialogue and Life in Adult Education* (2004). He is also the coauthor (with Elana Michelson) of *Portfolio Development and the Assessment of Prior Learning: Perspectives, Models and Practices* (2004).

Victoria J. Marsick is codirector of the J.M. Huber Institute for Learning in Organizations and professor of adult and organizational learning in the Department of Organization and Leadership, Teachers College, Columbia University. She holds a Ph.D. from the University of California, Berkeley. Her current research, speaking, and consulting are on organizational learning, informal learning, and action learning. She has collaborated with Martha Gephart in developing a framework and instruments to guide system-level learning and change; developed a diagnostic tool for organizational learning with Karen Watkins that has been used in private and nonprofit settings; and worked with Kathleen Dechant and Elizabeth Kasl on a model and diagnostic tool to improve team learning. She recently coauthored *Understanding Action Learning* (2007) with Judy O'Neil; book chapters and journal articles on informal and incidental learning with Karen Watkins; and *Strategic Organizational Learning* (forthcoming) with Martha Gephart.

Susan R. Meyer, president of Life-Work Coach and Susan R. Meyer Coaching and Consulting, focuses on transformative change in individuals and organizations. She works with individuals at midlife, leaders in transition, women seeking empowerment, executive development programs, and change initiatives. Meyer holds a B.A. in English from the State University of New York at Albany, master's degrees in educational and counseling psychology from New York University, and a doctorate in adult learning from Teachers College, Columbia University. She has written about journaling, coaching, and transformative learning for the Third and Fifth and Sixth International Transformative Learning Conferences. Recent articles include (with Loretta Donovan and Steve Fitzgerald) "Transformative Learning and Appreciative Inquiry: Incorporating Coaching and Action for Deep Organizational Change" in the *International Journal for Coaching in Organizations*, and (with Loretta Donovan) "Transformative Appreciative Inquiry: The Spiral Architecture of Appreciative Inquiry and Transformative Learning" in *Appreciative Inquiry Practitioner*.

⟳

Jack Mezirow is Emeritus Professor of Adult and Continuing Education, Teachers College, Columbia University. He introduced the concept of transformative learning to the field of adult education in 1978 in "Perspective Transformation," published in *Adult Education Quarterly*. The research base for this concept evolved out of a comprehensive national study of women returning to college. Among his books are *Learning as Transformation* (with Associates, 2000), *Transformative Dimensions of Adult Learning* (1991), and *Fostering Critical Reflection in Adulthood* (with Associates, 1990), all published by Jossey-Bass. Mezirow has written several other books, chapters, and articles, and his books on transformative learning have been translated into Greek, German, French, Italian, and Finnish.

⟳

Rebecca Miles is an associate professor in the urban and regional planning program at Florida State University. She has written extensively on environments and health, planning and health and safety, and development and social policy, publishing in social science and public health journals. Her interests range from the sociology of international development (gender, education, and work; empowerment processes at the local and regional scale), to the social and spatial context of health and health behavior, to policy issues in housing and environmental health. She has special interests in the health consequences of substandard housing and poor-quality housing environments; in how social and built environments can enhance quality of life, with a particular focus on low-income communities; and how urban change and development processes affect men and women differently, especially those living in poverty.

Her research also evaluates interventions to address gender inequalities in population health and development.

༄

Karen Monkman, associate professor at DePaul University, teaches courses in comparative education, social and cultural foundations in education, and qualitative research methods. Her interests span pre-K through university levels, as well as formal, nonformal, and informal education. She writes on social justice and transformation, gender and immigration, and contextual dynamics such as globalization. Her recent publications include, with Pauline Lipman, "Globalization and Social Justice in Education" in William Ayres, Therese Quinn, and David Stovall's edited *Handbook of Social Justice in Education* (2008); *Globalization and Education: Integration and Contestation Across Cultures* (coedited with Nelly P. Stromquist, 2000); "NGOs and Their Impact on Gendered Education," in Barbara J. Bank, *Gender and Education: An Encyclopedia* (2007); with Rebecca Miles and Peter Easton, "The Transformatory Potential of a Village Empowerment Program: The Tostan Replication in Mali," *Women's Studies International Forum* (2007); and "Tostan's Participatory Education Program in Mali," in Mary Ann Maslak's *Structure and Agency: Engendering Educational Policies, Practices and Programs* (2008). She received her Ph.D. from the University of Southern California.

༄

Nadine Petersen is senior lecturer on the Faculty of Education at the University of Johannesburg in South Africa. Her current research focuses on initial professional education of teachers and service-learning, within a social justice framework. She has published widely in national and international journals and read papers at various national and international conferences in the areas of teaching and learning in higher education, academic staff development, transformative learning, community service in higher education, and service-learning. She is currently coleader of a nationally funded research niche area project, Learning to Be a Teacher, which investigates teacher learning histories and how their histories relate to their practice.

༄

Ron Sheese is an associate professor of psychology at York University in Toronto, Canada, and associated with the Centre for Academic Writing and the Centre for the Support of Teaching, both of which he has served as director. He received his M.A. and Ph.D. in psychology from the University of Illinois.

He is a recipient of the Ontario Confederation of University Faculty Associations Provincial Teaching Award and the Canadian 3M Teaching Fellowship. His research focuses on educational applications of cognitive developmental theory, and he is one of the authors of the book *Cognitive Development: Neo-Piagetian Perspectives* (2007).

‰

Regina O. Smith is an assistant professor of adult and continuing education leadership and higher education at the University of Wisconsin at Milwaukee. She teaches courses on adult learning and development, program planning, organizational learning, administrative leadership, serving multicultural and special needs adults, the history and foundations of the Wisconsin Technical College System, the community college, educational dimensions of practice with older adults, urban adult education, administrative leadership, and international adult education. Her primary research interests focus on the psychodynamic aspects of group dynamics, problem-based learning, online learning, and epistemological beliefs. She is also the author of several articles and book chapters on the same topics.

‰

Edward W. Taylor is an associate professor of adult education at Penn State University-Harrisburg. He received his Ed.D. in adult education from the University of Georgia. His research interests include adult cognition and learning (transformative learning), nonformal education, and medical education. His work has appeared in *Adult Education Quarterly, International Journal of Lifelong Education, Studies in the Education of Adults,* and other scholarly journals. He recently published an edited book, *Teaching for Change: Fostering Transformative Learning in the Classroom.* He has been a coeditor of the *Adult Education Quarterly* since 2006 and an active member of the planning committee for several International Transformative Learning Conferences. Prior to joining the faculty at Penn State, he was a core faculty member at Antioch University for six years. Before his venture into higher education he worked for Eckerd Family Youth Alternatives as a training specialist in Clearwater, Florida.

‰

Elizabeth J. Tisdell is an associate professor of adult education at Pennsylvania State University, Harrisburg. She received her Ed.D. in adult education from the University of Georgia, an M.A. in religion from Fordham University, and a B.A.

in mathematics from the University of Maine. Her research interests include spirituality and culture in adult development and adult learning, critical and feminist pedagogy, multicultural issues, and critical media literacy in teaching for diversity in adult education. Her scholarly work has appeared in numerous journals and edited books. Tisdell is the author of *Exploring Spirituality and Culture in Adult and Higher Education,* based on a research study of a diverse group of adult educators, and is the coeditor and a contributing chapter author of two edited books, *Team Teaching and Learning* (2000) and *Popular Culture, Entertainment Media, and Adult Education* (2007). She is currently the coeditor of the journal *Adult Education Quarterly.* Prior to joining the faculty at Penn State, Tisdell was associate professor of adult and continuing education at National-Louis University in Chicago and on the faculty at Antioch University, Seattle. She worked as a campus minister for the Catholic church from 1979 to 1989 at Central Michigan University and Loyola University, New Orleans.

∽

Derise E. Tolliver is an associate professor and a member of the resident faculty at DePaul University's School for New Learning (SNL). She is also the Chicago director of the SNL B.A. Program at Tangaza College in Kenya. Prior to 1995, she was an assistant professor in the Psychology Department and served as the director of assessment and staff psychologist at the DePaul University Community Mental Health Center. As a resident faculty member at SNL, Tolliver functions as a faculty mentor to adult students, advising them and assessing their work as they pursue their individualized competency-based academic programs. In addition, she brings revolutionary activism to her courses by encouraging students to broaden their perspectives and decenter from Eurocentric ways of knowing. Her teaching and scholarship interests include African-centered psychology, spirituality and culture in adult learning, teaching practice, personal and social transformation, travel study, and internationalization of the curriculum. She received her Ph.D. and M.A. in clinical psychology from Duke University and her B.A. in psychology from Wellesley College. She is licensed as a clinical psychologist in the state of Illinois.

∽

Jo A. Tyler is assistant professor at Pennsylvania State University, Harrisburg, where she teaches in the M.Ed. program in training and development. A corporate practitioner for twenty-five years, most recently as a vice president of organization and management development at Armstrong World industries, she now consults with organizations interested in the influence and interplay of their stories, storytelling, and organizational narratives. She has published articles and book chapters on storytelling in organizational settings and other topics related to organizational development. She received her Ed.D. from Columbia University in adult education and leadership.

∽

Judith Kollins Wright is the cultural competency integration specialist at Planned Parenthood of Northeast Ohio in Cleveland, Ohio. She earned a B.S. in education and social policy at Northwestern University and completed an M.Ed. in adult learning and Development at Cleveland State University. With an interest in ethnographic research, she has conducted field research in Chicago, Mexico, Cleveland, and Bolivia. Her research on popular education in Cochabamba, Bolivia, in 2002 has served as the basis for several published articles and presentations.

∽

Lyle Yorks is associate professor of adult and organizational learning, Teachers College, Columbia University, where he teaches courses in human resource development, strategy development and strategic learning, and research. He is also director of the AEGIS (Adult Education Guided Intensive Study) doctoral program. Yorks has researched and consulted on action learning, collaborative inquiry, staff and executive development issues, and learning transfer with companies around the world. His recent authored and coauthored publications have appeared in the *Academy of Management Learning and Education, Adult Education Quarterly, Journal of Applied Behavioral Science, Human Resource Development Quarterly, New Directions for Adult and Continuing Education, Teachers College Record,* and other professional journals. His recent books include *Strategic Human Resource Development* (2004) and *Collaborative Inquiry in Practice* (2000). He has earned master's degrees at Vanderbilt University and Columbia University and his doctoral degree at Columbia.

Transformative Learning in Practice

PART ONE

INTRODUCTION

The two chapters in Part One set the context for this book by providing an overview of transformative learning theory and a discussion of current research on the practice of fostering transformative learning. In Chapter One, Edward Taylor presents an overview of what is known about fostering transformative learning and identifies its core elements: experience, critical reflection, dialogue, holistic orientation, appreciation for context, and authentic relationships. In Chapter Two, Jack Mezirow offers a general introduction to transformative learning theory with a discussion of key concepts, historical influences, varying theoretical perspectives, and current issues. Readers will find a good deal of consistency of what is being reported in the literature and what is discussed in practice in the chapters that follow.

CHAPTER ONE

Fostering Transformative Learning

Edward W. Taylor

Fostering transformative learning is seen as teaching for change—a practice of education that is "predicated on the idea that students are seriously challenged to assess their value system and worldview and are subsequently changed by the experience" (Quinnan, 1997, p. 42). It involves the most significant learning in adulthood, that of communicative learning, which entails the identification of problematic ideas, beliefs, values, and feelings; critically assessing their underlying assumptions; testing their justification through rational discourse; and striving for decisions through consensus building (Mezirow, 1995; Mezirow & Associates, 2000).

Despite this understanding, the practice of fostering transformative learning is illusive and an ever-shifting approach to teaching, and much about it remains unknown or poorly understood. Like any other educational approach, it is rooted in ideals, and when the realities of practice are explored, it becomes difficult to get a handle on how it plays out in the classroom. It is also laced with contradictions and oversights. For example, how does an educator foster a change in perspective among learners within a theoretical orientation that advocates a learner-centered approach to teaching, free of coercion, and assumes "the educational experience is never value neutral" (Ettling, 2006, p. 60)? This question is further complicated when layered with the lens of positionality, a concept overlooked in Mezirow's conception of transformative learning.

3

Another factor often not discussed or given much consideration is the varied contexts in which educators engage transformative learning and how these contexts shape practice. Although most of the research on incorporating transformative learning practices has taken place in higher education settings, recent research has demonstrated transformative learning in human resources and training, cooperative extension, faculty development programs, and distance education, to mention just a few. Little is known about the unique challenges that emerge in these contexts and how transformative learning is conceptualized in both purpose and practice (Taylor, 2007).

In response to these challenges and unanswered questions, my goal in this chapter is to identify what I see as the core elements of fostering transformative learning that have emerged from the empirical literature. This discussion helps set the stage for the rest of the book, providing a backdrop to what is known about fostering transformative learning as readers reflect on the various settings and practices illustrated in each chapter.

CORE ELEMENTS

Core elements are the essential components that frame a transformative approach to teaching. These elements, based on the literature, seem to be part of most transformative educational experiences. Originally three such elements were identified: individual experience, critical reflection, and dialogue (Taylor, 1998). However, as the study of transformative learning has evolved, other elements have emerged as equally significant: a holistic orientation, awareness of context, and an authentic practice. Moreover, the conceptualizations of some of the original elements have evolved as well. For example, while critical reflection was at one time predominantly seen as a rational approach to learning, research has revealed that it is the affective ways of knowing that prioritize experience and identify for the learner what is personally most significant in the process of reflection.

It is important to note that these elements have an interdependent relationship; they do not stand alone. For example, without individual experience, there is little or nothing to engage in critical reflection. Similarly, developing an authentic practice is significant for fostering trusting relationships between learners and teacher, which often provides the safe environment for learners to engage in critical reflection, ultimately allowing transformative learning to take place.

In addition, it is important to recognize that these elements are not a series of decontextualized teaching techniques or strategies that can be applied arbitrarily without an appreciation for their connection to a larger theoretical framework of transformative learning theory. These elements are rooted in deeply held assumptions about the nature of adult learning and purposes of teaching for change. Those assumptions and the nature of that change are part and parcel of an educator's transformative theoretical orientation. It is the reciprocal relationship between the core elements and the theoretical orientation of transformative learning that provides a lens for making meaning and guiding a transformative practice. To engage in the application of these core elements without some awareness of a larger theoretical orientation and its underlying purpose is not transformative learning. It is rudderless teaching, with no clear goal or purpose.

Developing an awareness of a theoretical orientation to transformative learning is therefore important. Further challenging the educator is the existence of multiple theoretical orientations to transformative learning beyond Mezirow's original conception. These orientations tend to fall loosely into two theoretical frameworks (Taylor, 2008). One framework, espoused by Jack Mezirow, Laurent Daloz, John Dirkx, Robert Kegan, and Patricia Cranton, among others, involves a collection of theoretical orientations that emphasize personal transformation and growth, where the unit of analysis is primarily the individual, with little attention given to the role of context and social change in the transformative experience. Core elements in this orientation, such as critical reflection, emphasize self-critique of deeply held assumptions, which leads to greater personal awareness in relationship to others. The second framework of theoretical orientations, espoused, for example, by Paulo Freire, Elizabeth Tisdell, Juanita Johnson-Bailey, and Mary Alfred, sees fostering transformative learning as being as much about social change as personal transformation, where individual and social transformation are inherently linked. Critical reflection in this orientation is more about ideological critique, where learners develop an awareness of power and greater agency (political consciousness) to transform society and their own reality. All that being said, how these elements are interpreted and engaged in the classroom is therefore significantly shaped by the theoretical orientation of the educator (Taylor, 2008).

Finally, it is important to note that this discussion of core elements is an evolving process, and the elements identified are a continual work of progress, particularly as more research comes forth. The identification of these elements emerges from a series of literature reviews of empirical studies on transformative learning completed over the past decade. Each of the elements is discussed in relationship to empirical literature about fostering transformative learning.

Individual Experience

Individual experience, the primary medium of transformative learning, consists of what each learner brings (prior experiences) and also what he or she experiences within the "classroom" itself. It "constitutes a starting point for discourse leading to critical examination of normative assumptions underpinning the learner's...value judgments or normative expectations'' (Mezirow & Associates, 2000, p. 31). Experience is also what educators stimulate and create through classroom activities and learners and teachers reflect on as they learn new ideas about themselves and their world. It is seen as socially constructed, so that it can be deconstructed and acted on through a process of dialogue and self-reflection. Although an understanding of the nature of experience in relationship to transformative learning is limited, research offers some insight into both prior experience and classroom-created experience.

Of significance seems to be the degree of life experience when fostering transformative learning. A greater life experience provides a deeper well from which to draw on and react to as individuals engage in dialogue and reflection. For example, Cragg, Plotnikoff, Hugo, and Casey (2001), in a study exploring transformation of professional values among graduate students enrolled in R.N. and B.S.N. nursing programs in a variety of settings (distance, hybrid, generic), found that ''nurses with more experience are more likely to internalize the new points of view to which their education exposes them'' (p. 6). Furthermore, it is also important to recognize what learners are experiencing in their life as they enter the classroom. It is the nature of the experiences that offer the means for fostering transformative learning. For example, Lange (2004), in a study on revitalizing citizen action, found that students who were participating in a continuing education certificate program were experiencing disillusionment and fragmentation in their lives. Educators saw these experiences as ''pedagogical entry points'' (p. 129) that offered opportunities for engaging a learner's personal dilemma as a potentially transformative experience.

In addition to prior experience, it is also important to consider what kind of individual and group experiences educators attempt to create in the classroom in order to foster transformative learning. Research has revealed that value-laden course content and intense experiential activities offer experiences that can be a catalyst for critical reflection and can provide an opportunity to promote transformative learning. Value-laden course content can both provoke and provide a process for facilitating change. For example, content about AIDS, abortion, wellness, spirituality, death, and dying have been found to encourage learners to reflect on both their personal and professional values, which at times can be in conflict with each other (Taylor, 2000). Also, content found in the medium of text can provide a catalyst for reflection, resulting in not only a greater understanding of the text but also greater personal insight (Kritskaya & Dirkx, 1999). For example, romantic fiction has been used as a means to help women question traditional conceptions of romantic relationships and redefine power located in relationships. Jarvis (2003) found that ''narrative organization and point of view may lead readers to identify with characteristics, whose values and actions are in opposition to their own. Reflection on this identification may challenge existing meaning perspectives at the personal or sociocultural level" (p. 265).

Along with value-laden course content is the application of intense experiential activities within the classroom. These activities help provoke meaning making among the participants by acting as triggers or disorienting dilemmas, provoking critical reflection, and facilitating transformative learning, allowing learners to experience learning more directly and holistically. For example, in order to develop an awareness of the African American struggles for civil rights among preservice teachers, Herber (1998) developed a series of experiential activities designed to initiate and facilitate the transformative process. One activity included a tour of the National Civil Rights Museum in Memphis, Tennessee, with the objective of documenting the ongoing struggle for equality in a diverse society. She found that the museum tour served as a catalyst for the transformative process for several of the learners. More important, she learned "that adult learners can confront a difficult and painful social issue, they can become aware of perceptual distortions about race, they can move to a more inclusive permeable perspective through experiential learning, reflection, and discussion in a context that supports the questioning of assumptions" (p. 158). Similarly, an educational program for medical students on palliative care requires students to spend time with a dying patient and family members "hearing their stories and exploring issues of importance to them" (MacLeod, Parkin, Pullon, & Robertson, 2003, p. 58). A consequence of this direct and intense experience is often an emotional one, prompting critical reflection and in this case leading to empathy—both knowing what the patient and family have experienced and a recognition of the emotions generated by that experience.

As these findings suggest, both prior experiences and those created in the classroom through activities, readings, and relationships with other learners provide the gist for critical reflection and classroom dialogue. It is this interdependent relationship between experience and critical reflection that potentially leads to a new perspective.

Promoting Critical Reflection

The second core element of fostering transformative learning is the promotion of critical reflection among learners. Critical reflection, a distinguishing characteristic of adult learning, refers to questioning the integrity of deeply held assumptions and beliefs based on prior experience. It is often prompted in response to an awareness of conflicting thoughts, feelings, and actions and at times can lead to a perspective transformation (Mezirow, 2000). There are three forms of reflection in the transformation of meaning perspectives: content (reflecting on what we perceive, think, feel, and act), process (reflecting on how we perform the functions of perceiving), and premise (an awareness of why we perceive). Premise reflection, the least common of the three and the basis for critical reflection, refers to examining the presuppositions underlying our knowledge of the world. Recently premise reflection has been purported as a form of reflection that needs to be engaged sooner and more often, particularly among those who have greater experience (Kreber, 2004).

Learning to be critically reflective is seen by some to rest on "mature cognitive development" (Merriam, 2004, p. 65). For example, in a longitudinal study, Liimatainen, Poskiparta, Karhila, and Sjögren (2001) explored the development of reflective learning and found differences among nursing students in reaching critical consciousness during their education program. Some students evolved to become "critical reflectors," where their "schemas indicated communicative and transformative learning and features of an empowerment approach to health promotion" (p. 656). Other students, both nonreflectors and reflectors, demonstrated less development during their time in the program and stayed at a level of reflection indicative of schemata that emphasized technical rationality.

In another example, Kreber (2004) looked at the levels of reflection using categories developed by Mezirow, such as content, process, and premise, in relationship to three domains of teaching knowledge: instructional (design and processes), pedagogical (student learning), and curricular (goals and purposes of courses). She found that premise reflection was the least common among participants of any of domains of teaching knowledge, although more experienced staff found knowing through process and premise reflection within certain forms of knowledge (for example, pedagogical and instructional) more relevant than their younger counterparts did. She concluded that when learning about teaching, teachers need to begin with premise reflection in "order to be more meaningful" (p. 41), that is, more concerned with why they teach than with how or what to teach.

To assist educators in recognizing the development of critical reflection among learners, there are indicators that assess levels of reflection (Boyer, Maher, & Kirkman, 2006; Kreber, 2004; Liimatainen et al., 2001). Such indicators as levels, a repertory grid, and coding schemas lend a hand in categorizing reflection, offer examples for learners, and demonstrate how previous research has often been too arbitrary in identifying critical reflection. For example, one coding schema identified eight levels of reflection, from thoughtful action without reflection (level 0) to theoretical reflectivity (level 7), which is an "awareness that routine or taken-for-granted practice may not be the complete answer, obvious learning from experience or change [in] perspective" (Liimatainen et al., p. 654).

In addition to recognizing the development of critical reflection, recent research has identified instructional aids that assist in its maturation, such as writing both online and in reflective journals (Boyer, Maher, & Kirkman, 2006; Chimera, 2006; Kitchenham, 2006; Ziegler, Paulus, & Woodside, 2006).

The written format potentially strengthens the reflective experience by creating artifacts of ideas of the mind. It requires learners to externalize their reflective experience, taking the "discussion away from the merely affective and/or psychological domains and forces a kind of reconciliation with the material-inherently perspective altering, socio-communicative activity" (Burke, 2006, p. 85). Writing helps address a limitation of making sense of reflection, that which challenges learners to both recall from memory and verbally articulate reflective moments during their teaching practice, particularly about a phenomenon (teaching) that often operates at a tacit level. Writing provides a means for both reflecting and recording previous thoughts that can be shared with others and returned to and reflected on when most relevant.

Dialogue

Building on the importance of critical reflection is the engagement in dialogue with the self and others. Dialogue is the essential medium through which transformation is promoted and developed. However, in contrast to everyday discussions, it is used most often in transformative learning "when we have reason to question the comprehensibility, truth, appropriateness (in relation to norms), or authenticity (in relation to feelings) of what is being asserted or to question the credibility of the person making the statement" (Mezirow, 1991, p. 77).

It is within the arena of dialogue that experience and critical reflection play out. Dialogue becomes the medium for critical reflection to be put into action, where experience is reflected on, assumptions and beliefs are questioned, and habits of mind are ultimately transformed. The dialogue is not so much analytical, point-counterpoint dialogue, but dialogue emphasizing relational and trustful communication, often at times "highly personal and self-disclosing" (Carter, 2002, p. 82). Again, the emphasis (personal or social transformation) is framed by educators' theoretical orientation to transformative learning. Although research is limited in this area concerning transformative learning, social interaction and dialogue have been found to lead to consensual validation (valid by the process of discussing it) among learners. This validation helps learners who, for example, were diagnosed HIV-positive and realized "they were not alone on this transformational journey" (Baumgartner, 2002, pp. 56–57).

Ideal conditions for participants to engage in reflective dialogue include the importance of providing "the most accurate and complete information"; ensuring "freedom from coercion and distorting self-deception; encouraging an openness to alternative points of view"; demonstrating "empathy and concern about how others think and feel; developing an ability to weigh evidence and assess arguments objectively"; developing "greater awareness of the context of ideas and more critically reflective [sic] of assumptions"; ensuring "an equal opportunity to participate in various roles of the discourse"; and "encouraging a willingness to seek understanding and agreement to accept a resulting best judgment as a test of validity until new perspectives, evidence, or arguments are encountered and validated through discourse as yielding a better judgment" (Mezirow & Associates, 2000, pp. 13–14).

In addition, it is important not only to create positive conditions for productive dialogue, but also to pay mind to the nature of the dialogue—what the participants are actually discussing. Research has revealed that dialogue helps identify the learner's "edge of meaning," a transitional zone, of knowing and meaning making. "It is this liminal space that we can come to terms with the limitations of our knowing and thus begin to stretch those limits" (Berger, 2004, p. 338). This edge of meaning was revealed in dialogue among graduate students in a master's in education program who at times had difficulty articulating ideas and coherent thoughts when discussing ontological issues about their personal lives—the way they make sense of their world. Also, the emotions of the students varied widely, from frightened and uncomfortable feelings to excitement and joy.

This study and others remind educators that engaging in dialogue is much more than having an analytical conversation; it involves an acute awareness of learners' attitudes, feelings, personalities, and preferences over time, and as signs of change and instability begin to emerge, educators can respond accordingly. It also means developing a sense of trust in the process of dialogue with others, creating a setting that helps learners live with some discomfort while on the edge of knowing, in the process of gaining new insights and understandings. A less analytical perspective of dialogue requires a more holistic orientation or approach to transformative learning, where the learner and the educator engage in other ways of knowing.

Holistic Orientation

A third essential component to fostering transformative learning is the emphasis on a holistic orientation to teaching. This orientation encourages the engagement with other ways of knowing—the affective and relational. Past research has demonstrated that often too much emphasis is given to rational discourse and critical reflection in the fostering of transformative learning and not enough recognition of the role of the affective and other ways of knowing (Taylor, 1998). As Brown (2006) concludes, learners rarely change through a rational process (analyze-think-change). Instead they "are more likely to change in a see-feel-change sequence" (p. 732). Affective knowing—developing an awareness of feelings and emotions in the reflective process—is inherent in critical reflection. There is an interdependent relationship between the physiological process of cognition and emotion. Emotions are inherently cognitive; they "anticipate future needs, prepare for actions, and even prepare for thinking certain types of thoughts" (Parrott &

Schulkin, 1993, p. 56). They often act as a trigger for the reflective process, prompting the learner to question deeply held assumptions.

Until recently, there had been little guidance provided to educators in how to engage in a holistic approach to transformative learning in the classroom, particularly the affective component. Along with didactic pedagogies, it means including opportunities for learners to experience presentational ways of knowing, such as "engagement with music, all the plastic arts, dance, movement, and mime, as well as all forms of myth, fable, allegory, and drama" (Davis-Manigualte, Yorks, & Kasl, 2006, p. 27). Other examples include the use of the arts (Berger, 2004; Hanlin-Rowney et al., 2006; Patteson, 2002), online group meditation (Hanlin-Rowney et al., 2006), and cultural autobiographies (Brown, 2006). Presentational or expressive ways of knowing are "about inviting 'the whole person' into the classroom environment, we mean the person in fullness of being: as an affective, intuitive, thinking, physical, spiritual self" (Yorks & Kasl, 2006, p. 46). The affective domain of a holistic approach reveals much about the psycho- and sociocultural dynamics of the individual and the group within the classroom. Engaging emotions in the classroom provides "an opportunity for establishing a dialogue with those unconscious aspects of ourselves seeking expression through various images, feelings, and behaviors within the learning setting" (Dirkx, 2006, p. 22). Furthermore, by exploring emotional issues with students, the educator can address the dynamics that contribute to a resistance in learning, as well as potentially initiate a process of individuation—that of "a deeper understanding, realization, and appreciation of who he or she is" (p. 18).

To successfully engage expressive ways of knowing in the classroom, educators have to be prepared to work on their own holistic awareness, creating a learning environment conducive to whole person learning (for example, by adopting rituals or creating community) and modeling emphatic connections of learners' experiences through expressive activities, for example, by storytelling and cooperative inquiry. Furthermore, expressive ways of knowing provide the means to evoke experiences for greater exploration, help learners become more aware of their feelings and their relationship to sense making, and help concretize an experience allowing the learner to reexperience the learning experience through expressive representation (Taylor, 2006).

Awareness of Context

Developing an awareness of context when fostering transformative learning is developing a deeper appreciation and understanding of the personal and sociocultural factors that play an influencing role in the process of transformative learning. These factors include the surroundings of the immediate learning event, the personal and professional situation of the learners at the time (their prior experience), and the background context that is shaping society.

As previously discussed, the prior experience of learners potentially has a significant influence on practice. Insight into this experience reveals that some learners may have a greater predisposition for change. Early research demonstrated that participants with recent experiences of critical incidences in their lives seemed more predisposed to change. "The disturbing events in the participants' lives...create a fertile ground for perspective transformation" (Pierce, 1986, p. 296). The same is true of "pedagogical entry points" (Lange, 2004, p. 129) and when learners are in the transitional zone of meaning making (Berger, 2004).

The lack of or resistance to change can also be explained from a contextual perspective, particularly in terms of barriers that are in place or inhibit what is necessary for transformative learning—for example, rules and sanctions imposed on welfare women returning to work in a family empowerment project (Christopher, Dunnagan, Duncan, & Paul, 2001); the downside of cohort experiences where there is often an unequal distribution of group responsibilities and an emphasis on task completion instead of reflective dialogue (Scribner & Donaldson, 2001); rigid role assignments and the need for both the teachers and program developers to be deliberate at times for transformative learning to occur in educational programming (Taylor, 2003); and a culture of resistance to technology (Whitelaw, Sears, & Campbell, 2004). The online setting has its own unique challenges to overcome with fostering transformative learning due to the limitation of the written word. Hanlin-Rowney et al. (2006) found, in a collaborative online inquiry involving a group of graduate students, that overreliance "on predominantly written communication can be misinterpreted without opportunities for face-to-face interaction" (p. 330).

Environmentally one of the most significant contextual issues of transformative learning is temporal constraints. Research suggests that fostering transformative learning is time-consuming, particularly when an effort is being made to provide access to all participants' voices as well as coming to consensus around various group decisions. Furthermore, working with rigid time periods poses additional challenges when engaging intense personal experiences that cannot be resolved by the time class is over. These efforts are further compromised with a traditional classroom setting with short class periods. For example, in a collaborative inquiry project, Kaminsky (1997) found "that inclusiveness in terms of stakeholder membership practically guarantees that groups will have different agendas about what needs to be done, making coming to a consensus an onerous, time-consuming task" (pp. 274–275). The inquiry project involved an intense group experience of lengthy duration, and even under these conditions, teachers and participants felt constrained by the exigency of time. It seems that the very conditions that foster transformative learning—a democratic process, inclusiveness of agendas, striving for consensus, critical reflection, dialogue—create a high demand for time.

Authentic Relationships

A sixth element is the importance of establishing authentic relationships with students. "Fostering transformative learning in the classroom depends to a large extent on establishing meaningful, genuine relationships with students" (Cranton, 2006, p. 5). Previous research found that establishing positive and productive relationships with others is one of the essential factors in a transformative experience (Taylor, 2007). It is through building trusting relationships that learners develop the confidence to deal with learning on an affective level, where transformation at times can be perceived as threatening and an emotionally charged experience. Recent research begins to offer insight into the complex nature of transformative relationships (Carter, 2002; Eisen, 2001; Lyon, 2001). For example, Carter (2002), who explored learning in work-related developmental relationships involving midcareer women, identified four categories of relationships as significant to their learning at work: utilitarian relationships (acquiring skills and knowledge), love relationships (enhance self-image, friendship), memory relationships (of former or deceased individuals), and imaginative relationships (inner dialogue, meditation). Love, memory, and self-dialogue relationships proved significant to transformative learning, with intimate relationships the most significant.

Authentic relationships also allow individuals to have questioning discussions, share information openly, and achieve greater mutual and consensual understanding. Without the medium of relationships, critical reflection is impotent and hollow, lacking the genuine discourse necessary for thoughtful and in-depth reflection (Taylor, 1998, 2006). Through authentic relationships, teachers and learners establish a foundation for transformative learning. The meaning of authenticity in the context of teaching is revealed in a five-facet model: (1) a strong sense of self-awareness, (2) a deep awareness of the needs and interest of learners and how they may differ from the interest of the educator, (3) fostering the ability (of the educator or student, for example) to be genuine and open with others, (4) developing awareness of how context shapes practice, and (5) engaging in critical reflection and critical self-reflection about practice (Cranton & Carusetta, 2004). In essence, by striving for a more authentic practice, the educator is integrating all the core elements of fostering transformative learning.

CONCLUSION

These core elements seem fairly complete, except for one concept: learner-centered teaching. This is an approach to teaching where the teacher is seen as facilitator who strives to balance power with learners through shared decision making, evaluation, and other learning responsibilities in the classroom (Weimer, 2002). As a construct, it is discussed in the conceptual literature (Cranton, 2006; Mezirow & Associates, 2000) as central to fostering transformative learning; however, it has often been overlooked in the research literature. Although it is apparent that many studies have engaged a learner-centered teaching approach, few, if any, have explored in-depth what it looks like in practice, how it is managed, its related challenges, and the implications it has for fostering transformative learning.

Complicating the idea of learner-centered teaching as a core element is the question of whether it is a method that is simply employed like any other teaching technique or is a construct that acts as an umbrella for a whole collection of methods, including many, if not all, of the core elements discussed in this chapter. This means asking whether fostering transformative learning in general and the core elements more specifically rests on the assumption of a learner-centered approach to teaching. Are learner-centered teaching and fostering transformative learning one and the same? A place to begin exploring these questions resides in the theoretical orientation of transformative learning held by the educator. In other words, how do the various orientations conceptualize the role of the teacher in relationship to the purpose of transformative learning? How is learner-centered teaching conceptualized by the different theoretical orientations? These questions and others need to be resolved before learner-centered teaching can be seen as an essential element in fostering transformative learning. I hope that this brief discussion will challenge readers to begin to study this approach more thoroughly and shed greater light on the relationship of learner-centered teaching to fostering transformative learning.

It is clear that much remains unknown about the practice of fostering transformative learning, and so it should not be practiced naively or without forethought or planning. It often requires intentional action, personal risk, a genuine concern for the learners' betterment, and the ability to draw on a variety of methods and techniques that help create a classroom environment that supports personal growth and, for others, social change (Taylor, 2006). Those who venture into this arena will have to trust their teaching instincts, since there are few clear signposts or guidelines, and develop an appreciation for and awareness of their own assumptions and beliefs about the purpose of fostering transformative learning and the impact on practice. Through this awareness and by engaging in a reflective practice, these core elements give meaning to transformative learning.

REFERENCES

Baumgartner, L. M. (2002). Living and learning with HIV/AIDS: Transformational tales continued. *Adult Education Quarterly, 53*, 44–70.

Berger, J. G. (2004). Dancing on the threshold of meaning: Recognizing and understanding the growing edge. *Journal of Transformative Education, 2*, 336–351.

Boyer, N. R., Maher, P. A., & Kirkman, S. (2006). Transformative learning in online settings: The use of self-direction, metacognition, and collaborative learning. *Journal of Transformative Education, 4*, 335–361.

Brown, K. (2006). Leadership and social justice and equity: Evaluating a transformative framework and andragogy. *Educational Administration Quarterly, 42*(5), 700–745.

Burke, A. (2006) Do the write thing. In E. W. Taylor (Ed.), *Teaching for change* (pp. 79–90). New Directions for Adult and Continuing Education, no. 109. San Francisco: Jossey-Bass.

Carter, T. J. (2002). The importance of talk to midcareer women's development: A collaborative inquiry. *Journal of Business Communication, 39*, 55–91.

Chimera, K. D. (2006). The use of reflective journals in the promotion of reflection and learning in post-registration nursing students. *Nurse Education Today, 27*, 192–202.

Christopher, S., Dunnagan, T., Duncan, S. F., & Paul, L. (2001). Education for self-support: Evaluating outcomes using transformative learning theory. *Family Relations, 50*, 134–142.

Cragg, C. E., Plotnikoff, R. C., Hugo, K., & Casey, A. (2001). Perspective transformation in RN-to-BSN distance education. *Journal of Nursing Education, 40*(7), 317–322.

Cranton, P. (2006). *Understanding and promoting transformative learning*. San Francisco: Jossey-Bass.

Cranton, P., & Carusetta, E. (2004). Perspectives on authenticity in teaching. *Adult Education Quarterly, 55*, 5–22.

Davis-Manigualte, J., Yorks, L., & Kasl, E. (2006). Expressive ways of knowing and transformative learning. In E. W. Taylor (Ed.), *Teaching for change* (pp. 27–35). New Directions for Adult and Continuing Education, no. 109. San Francisco: Jossey-Bass.

Dirkx, J. M. (2006). Engaging emotions in adult learning: A Jungian perspective on emotion and transformative learning. In E. W. Taylor (Ed.), *Teaching for change* (pp. 15–26). New Directions for Adult and Continuing Education, no. 109. San Francisco: Jossey-Bass.

Eisen, M. J. (2001). Peer-based professional development viewed through the lens of transformative learning. *Holistic Nursing Practice, 16*, 30–42.

Ettling, D. (2006). Ethical demands of transformative learning. In E. W. Taylor (Ed.), *Teaching for change* (pp. 59–68). New Directions for Adult and Continuing Education, no. 109. San Francisco: Jossey-Bass.

Hanlin-Rowney, A., Kuntzelman, K., Abad Lara, M. E., Quinn, D., Roffman, K., Nichols, T. T., et al. (2006). Collaborative inquiry as a framework for exploring transformative learning online. *Journal of Transformative Education, 4,* 320–334.

Herber, S. (1998). *Perspective transformation of preservice teachers.* Unpublished doctoral dissertation, University of Memphis.

Jarvis, C. (2003). Desirable reading: The relationship between women students' lives and their reading practices. *Adult Education Quarterly, 53*(4), 261–276.

Kaminsky, A. L. (1997). *Individual transformational learning experience as a cross-cultural sojourner: Descriptive models.* Unpublished doctoral dissertation, Fielding Institute.

Kitchenham, A. (2006). Teachers and technology: A transformative journey. *Journal of Transformative Education, 4,* 202–225.

Kreber, C. (2004). An analysis of two models of reflection and their implications for educational development. *International Journal for Academic Development, 9,* 29–49.

Kritskaya, O. V., & Dirkx, J. M. (1999). Symbolic representations as mediators for meaning construction: An exploration of transformative pedagogy within a professional development context. In A. Austin, G. E. Hynes, & R. T. Miller (Eds.), *Proceedings of the Eighteenth Annual Midwest Research-to-Practice Conference in Adult, Continuing and Community Education* (pp. 184–190). St. Louis: University of Missouri.

Lange, E. (2004). Transformative and restorative learning: A vital dialectic for sustainable societies. *Adult Education Quarterly, 54,* 121–139.

Liimatainen, L., Poskiparta, M., Karhila, P., & Sjögren, A. (2001). The development of reflective learning in the context of health counseling and health promotion during nurse education. *Journal of Advanced Nursing, 34*(5), 648–658.

Lyon, C. R. (2001). Hear our stories: Relationships and transformations of women educators who worked overseas. *Studies in the Education of Adults, 33,* 118–126.

MacLeod, R. D., Parkin, C., Pullon, S., & Robertson, G. (2003). Early clinical exposure to people who are dying: Learning to care at the end of life. *Medical Education, 37,* 51–58.

Merriam, S. B. (2004). The role of cognitive development in Mezirow's transformational learning theory. *Adult Education Quarterly, 55,* 60–68.

Mezirow, J. (1991). *Transformative dimensions of adult learning.* San Francisco: Jossey-Bass.

Mezirow, J. (1995). Transformation theory of adult learning. In M. R. Welton (Ed.), *In defense of the lifeworld* (pp. 39–70). New York: SUNY Press.

Mezirow, J., & Associates. (2000). *Learning as transformation.* San Francisco: Jossey-Bass.

Parrott, W. G., & Schulkin, J. (1993). Neuropsychology and cognitive nature of the emotions. *Cognition and Emotions, 7,* 43–59.

Patteson, A. (2002). Amazing grace and powerful medicine: A case study of an elementary teacher and the arts. *Canadian Journal of Education, 27*(2/3), 269–289.

Pierce, G. (1986). *Management education for an emergent paradigm.* Unpublished doctoral dissertation, Teachers College, Columbia University.

Quinnan, T. (1997). *Adult students "at-risk": Culture bias in higher education.* Westport, CT: Bergin and Garvey.

Scribner, J. P., & Donaldson, J. F. (2001). The dynamics of group learning in a cohort: From nonlearning to transformative learning [Electronic version]. *Educational Administration Quarterly, 37*, 605–638.

Taylor, E. W. (1998) *Transformative learning: A critical review.* ERIC Clearinghouse on Adult, Career, and Vocational Education (Information Series No. 374).

Taylor, E. W. (2000). Fostering Mezirow's transformative learning theory in the adult education classroom: A critical review. *Canadian Journal of the Study of Adult Education, 14*, 1–28.

Taylor, E. W. (2003). Attending graduate school in adult education and the impact on teaching beliefs: A longitudinal study. *Journal of Transformative Education, 1*(4), 349–368.

Taylor, E. W. (Ed.). (2006). *Teaching for change.* New Directions for Adult and Continuing Education, no. 109. San Francisco: Jossey-Bass.

Taylor, E. W. (2007). An update of transformative learning theory: A critical review of the empirical research (1999–2005). *International Journal of Lifelong Education, 26*, 173–191.

Taylor, E. W. (2008). Transformative learning theory. In S. B. Merriam (Ed.), *An update of adult learning* (pp. 5–15). New Directions for Adult and Continuing Education, no. 119. San Francisco: Jossey-Bass.

Weimer, M. G. (2002). *Learner-centered teaching: Five key changes to practice.* San Francisco: Jossey-Bass.

Whitelaw, C., Sears, M., & Campbell, K. (2004). Transformative learning in a faculty professional development context. *Journal of Transformative Education, 2*, 9–27.

Yorks, L., & Kasl, E. (2006). I know more than I can say: A taxonomy for using expressive ways of knowing to foster transformative learning. *Journal of Transformative Education, 4*, 43–64.

Ziegler, M. F., Paulus, T. M., & Woodside, M. (2006). "This course is helping us all arrive at new viewpoints, isn't it?" Making meaning through dialogue in a blended environment. *Journal of Transformative Education, 4*, 302–319.

CHAPTER TWO

Transformative Learning Theory

Jack Mezirow

T his book describes and analyzes specific efforts to apply transformative learning in a wide variety of situations. Implicit in this process is an evolving theory and a coherent group of general principles of transformative learning. This chapter elaborates these principles by presenting an overview of transformative learning theory, briefly identifying types of transformative learning, describing its research base, differentiating instrumental and communicative learning, and describing the first doctoral program devoted to transformative learning. The chapter also examines the relationship of transformative learning to psychology and reports this concept's major theoretical issues—cognitive, rational, social, extrarational, and ecological—raised by colleagues and looks at promising directions for the future development of transformative learning.

TRANSFORMATIVE LEARNING: ORIGINS AND DEVELOPMENT

In 1978 I published an article in the journal *Adult Education Quarterly* urging the recognition of a critical dimension of learning in adulthood that enables us to recognize, reassess, and modify the structures of assumptions and expectations that frame our tacit points of view and influence our thinking, beliefs, attitudes, and actions. Thirty years later, this chapter continues my conversation with the field of adult education about transformative learning theory.

Over the past three decades, adult educators have been engaged in professional discourse regarding transformation theory, especially in the context of
the seven international conferences devoted to this subject. Major influences
of my own initial understanding of this concept have included Paulo Freire's
concept of "conscientization," "consciousness raising" in the women's movement, the theory of transformation of psychiatrist Roger Gould, the writings
of Jürgen Habermas and Harvey Siegal, and the transformative experience of
my wife, Edee Mezirow, as an adult returning to complete her undergraduate
degree at Sarah Lawrence College in New York.

The research base for the concept of transformative learning evolved out of
a comprehensive national study in 1978, sponsored by the U.S. Department of
Education, of "consciousness raising" to explain an unprecedented expansion
in the number of women returning to higher education in the United States
(Mezirow, 1978). The study used a grounded theory methodology and conducted intensive field study of students in twelve diverse community college
programs, comprehensive analytical descriptions of an additional twenty-
four programs, and subsequent responses to a mail inquiry by another 314.
Findings identified ten phases of learning that become clarified in the transformative process:

1. A disorienting dilemma

2. Self-examination

3. A critical assessment of assumptions

4. Recognition of a connection between one's discontent and the process of
   transformation

5. Exploration of options for new roles, relationships, and action

6. Planning a course of action

7. Acquiring knowledge and skills for implementing one's plan

8. Provisional trying of new roles

9. Building competence and self-confidence in new roles and relationships

10. A reintegration into one's life on the basis of conditions dictated by one's
    new perspective

Women attending higher education tended to follow this pattern of transformative learning, a pattern that subsequent chapters in this book describe
as varying in other contexts. Another variable dimension of transformative
learning process is the distinction between instrumental and communicative learning.

INSTRUMENTAL AND COMMUNICATIVE LEARNING

Transformation theory, as I have understood it, embraces Habermas's critical distinction between instrumental learning and communicative learning. Instrumental learning involves controlling or managing the environment or other persons, including improving performance. Beliefs are validated by empirically testing—as in science and mathematics—to ascertain whether an assertion is true—that is, it is as it is purported to be. Communicative learning involves understanding what others mean when they communicate with us. We validate or justify contested beliefs pertaining to communicative learning through discourse. Discursive assessment is that type of dialogue in which we participate with others, whom we believe to be informed, objective, and rational, to assess reasons that justify problematic beliefs. "Problematic" beliefs include such abstract concepts as democracy, citizenship, justice, and love. Discourse involves dialectical and critically reflective thinking leading to a best tentative judgment. To freely and fully participate in discourse, participants ideally require, in addition to a reasonable minimum of personal security, health, education, the following:

- More accurate and complete information
- Freedom from coercion and distorting self-deception
- Openness to alternative points of view and empathy and concern about how others think and feel
- The ability to weigh evidence and assess arguments objectively
- Awareness of the context of ideas and taken-for-granted assumptions, including one's own
- Equal opportunity to participate in the various roles of discourse
- A willingness to seek understanding, agreement, and a tentative best judgment as a test of validity until new perspectives, evidence, or arguments are encountered and validated through discourse as yielding a better judgment

These conditions are never fully realized in practice. They reflect democratic ideals such as self-respect, respect for others, acceptance of the common good, and willingness to be open and engage diversity. A key to practicing openness is understanding how humans engage epistemic assumptions.

EPISTEMIC ASSUMPTIONS

Epistemic assumptions are sets of assumptions about what can be known and how certain one can be about knowing (Kitchener & King, 1990). This includes assumptions about the role of evidence, authority, and interpretation in the for-mation of solutions to problems. For example, a reflective thinker understands that there is real uncertainty about how a problem may be solved, yet is able to offer a judgment about the problems that brings some kind of closure to it. This judgment, which John Dewey (1960) refers to as a "grounded" or "warranted" assertion, is based on criteria such as evaluation of evidence, consideration of expert opinion, adequacy of argument, and implications of the proposed solution. Dewey's "grounded or warranted" assertion is more fully developed in Habermas's concept of communicative learning. Habermas argues that to understand scientific theories, we must differentiate empirical-analytical theo-ries from reconstructive theories (like those of Noam Chomsky, Jean Piaget, and Lawrence Kohlberg), which seek to explain universal conditions and rules implicit in linguistic competence, cognitive and moral development, and the nature of human communication. Habermas's theory of communicative action (1991) is another such reconstructive theory.

Transformative learning is also a reconstructive theory. Its focus is on adult learning, and its primary audience is adult educators. As a reconstructive theory, it seeks to establish a general, abstract, and idealized model that explains the generic structure, dimensions, and dynamics of the learning process. Also, it does not undertake a definitive cultural critique, but it attempts to provide the model—constructs, language, categories, and dynamics—to enable others to understand how adults learn in various cultural settings. For example, when epistemic assumptions are being assessed, the following ten questions should be explored:

1. What assumptions support the frame of reference?

2. Where does the knowledge it represents come from?

3. What epistemic assumptions have been taken for granted in defining the problem?

4. How is this knowledge expressed, formulated, and communicated?

5. Has the person defining the problems focused on certain dimensions rather than others to perceive and construe a situation?

6. Has he or she chosen the first useful option that emerged, at the expense of others?

7. Has the object been segregated from its situation or context-related enti-ties or from the observer?

8. Has an earlier framing of the object or situation become obsolete?

9. What was the influence of an authority figure or role model?

10. What and how has this learning been significantly influenced by anxiety, emotion, conation, intuition, bias, habit, or self-concept?

By reflecting on these questions, we are engaging in epistemic cognition, often involving ill-structured problems, with multiple solutions, shedding insight on the limits and certainty of knowledge.

DYNAMICS: THE LEARNING PROCESS

How one categorizes experiences, beliefs, people, events, and the self involves frames of references, which are structures of assumptions and expectations on which our thoughts, feelings, and habits are based. Frames of reference may be rules, criteria, codes, language, schemata, cultural canon, ideology, standards, or paradigms. Frames include personality traits and dispositions, genealogy, power allocation, worldviews, religious doctrine, aesthetic values, social movements, psychological schema or scripts, learning styles, and preference.

Learning may be understood as the process of using a prior interpretation to construe a new or revised interpretation of the meaning of one's experience to guide future action. Transformative learning may be defined as *learning that transforms problematic frames of reference to make them more inclusive, discriminating, reflective, open, and emotionally able to change.* Frames with these characteristics are more likely to generate beliefs and opinions that will prove more true or justified to guide action. A frame of reference is a predisposition with cognitive, affective, and conative (striving) dimensions. Frames filter sense perceptions, selectively shaping and delimiting perceptions, cognition, and feelings by predisposing our intentions, purposes, and expectations. How one categorizes experiences, beliefs, people, events, and the self involves structures of assumptions and expectations on which our thoughts, feelings, and habits are based. We do not normally have conscious access to these nonconscious processes by which our impressions of others are formed, only their results. For instance, falling in love is a result of one such process. Meaning schemes may be transformed by our becoming critically reflective of the assumptions supporting the content or process (or both) of problem solving.

Learning occurs in one of four ways: by elaborating existing meaning schemes, learning new meaning schemes, transforming meaning schemes, and transforming meaning perspectives. The most personally significant transformations involve a critique of premises regarding the world and one's self. A transformative learning experience requires that the learner make an informed and reflective decision to act or not. This decision may result in immediate action or delayed action, caused by situational constraints, or lack of information on how to act, or a reasoned reaffirmation of an existing pattern of action.

Reasoning is defined by Siegal (1988) as "advancing and assessing reasons for making a judgment" (p. 69). More specifically, practical reasoning is reasoning directed toward action: figuring out what to do as contrasted with figuring out how the facts stand. Transformative reasoning involves figuring out how taken-for-granted facts are warranted. This may involve critically examining the epistemic assumptions supporting one's values, beliefs, convictions, and preferences and reassessing reasons that support a problematic frame of reference.

Reasoning involving rational action on the commonsense level is always unquestioned action within an undetermined frame of constructs of taken-for-granted courses of action and personalities. From this frame of constructs, forming their undetermined horizon, particular sets of elements stand out that are clearly and distinctly determinable. The commonsense concept of rationality (Schultz, 1973) refers to these elements.

Transformative learning may be understood as the epistemology of how adults learn to reason for themselves—advance and assess reasons for making a judgment—rather than act on the assimilated beliefs, values, feelings, and judgments of others. Influences may include power and influence, ideology, race, class and gender differences, cosmology, and other interests. However, even these influences may be rationally assessed because rationality is not defined by these factors. The process by which we tacitly construe our beliefs may involve taking-for-granted values, stereotyping, highly selective attention, limited comprehension, projection, rationalization, minimizing, or denial. That is why we need to be able to critically assess and validate the tacit assumptions supporting our own beliefs and expectations, as well as those of others.

Transformations may be epochal (involving dramatic or major changes) or incremental and may involve objective (task oriented) or subjective (self-reflective) reframing. In objective reframing, points of view are changed when we become critically reflective of the content of a problem or of the process of problem solving. A frame of reference is transformed when we become critically reflective of the premise of the problem and redefine it. In subjective reframing, we become coauthors of the cultural narratives with which we have been inscribed.

For example, a teacher who wants to determine who is the best student in the class can focus on content—the comparative quality of her students' written work, participation in discussion, or test results, for example—or on process—by reexamining the comparative quality of student problem solving. If she instead reconsiders and rejects the assumption that she should judge student performance competitively because there are so many socioeconomic and cultural variables differentiating the students, and redefines this premise by adopting the practice of portfolio assessment, in which each student competes with herself and plans what she will learn next with the collaboration of her teachers, the teacher has redefined the premise of the problem. Having described the origins and development of the theory, its assumptions and dynamics, we turn now to one example of its application.

APPLICATION: GRADUATE ADULT EDUCATION

A unique doctoral program in transformative learning, Adult Education Guided Independent Study, was established at Teachers College, Columbia University, over twenty years ago and is still in operation. This highly selective program was designed for professionals with at least five years of experience in adult education.

Classes met one weekend a month and over intensive three-week summer sessions to satisfy course requirements in two years. Students collaborated to deal collectively with most problems with colleagues around tables of six to analyze and practice the process of collaborative inquiry, discourse, and transformative learning. Dialogue included interaction using the Internet. Students commuted from as far away as Saudi Arabia and Alaska.

Applicants were required to write a paper that described an issue in the field, present arguments on both sides, describe their own point of view, and analyze their own assumptions. Faculty members carefully reviewed papers, identifying unrecognized assumptions. Second or third revisions were often required. These exchanges were to assist the students in critically examining their own assumptions and habits of thinking and introduce them to assumption analysis. Grading was limited to pass or incomplete. Academic standards were high: students with three incompletes were required to leave the program.

Courses in the original program included Assumption Analysis, involving a critical review of articles written by adult educators; Life Histories, involving comparative assessment of the turning points in their lives, designed to encourage them to recognize alternative interpretations; and courses in Ideology, Media Analysis, the work of Paulo Freire, and transformations through art and literature. Other courses added over the years have included Program Development, Adult Learning, Research Methods, Adult Literacy, and Organizational Development.

Methods found useful in studying critical reflection of assumptions and discourse include using critical incidents, journal writing, media analysis, repertory grids, metaphor analysis, conceptual mapping, action learning, collaborative learning, and John Peters's "action-reason-thematic technique" (all are described in Mezirow and Associates, 1990).

PSYCHOLOGY AND TRANSFORMATIVE LEARNING

Transformational learning occurs in a wide variety of contexts and under different circumstances. A number of authors have drawn connections between transformative learning theory and Jungian psychology, and others have written about transformative learning in relation to trauma.

Individuation: Jungian Psychology

Jung's theory of psychological type has been interpreted by Cranton (2006) to integrate his concepts with those of transformative learning theory in adult education. Learners' predispositions form one kind of habit of mind, which involves two interrelated processes: becoming more aware and understanding our own nature while at the same time individuating ourselves from the rest of humanity as we learn who we are.

Jung describes a continuum on which one may differentiate two ways of relating to the world and of making judgments: introverted and extraverted. We make judgments either logically or analytically—to assess a problem, weigh alternatives, and make a decision—or rely on deep-seated reactions of acceptance or rejection in which logic plays no part. This differentiation between perception and judgment is close to transformation theory's differentiation between learning outside awareness through intuition and learning within awareness through critical reflection on assumptions. Psychological preferences (thinking and feeling or sensing and intuition) are habits of mind.

John Dirkx (1997) also identifies the goal of Jung's concept of individuation as the development of an individual's personality. This development involves a dialogue between ego consciousness and the content of the unconscious. Transformation involves participating in dialogue with the unconscious aspects of the psyche. This frees one from obsessions, compulsions, and complexes that can shape and distort our frame of reference. The symbolic process of individuation is expressed in the form of images. Through a dialogue between the conscious and unconscious, mediated through symbols and images, learners gain insight into aspects of themselves that are outside conscious awareness but influence their sense of self, as well as their interpretations and actions. These symbols and images express emotions and feelings that arise in the learning process. "Behind every emotion there is an image" (p. 251).

The content or process of formal learning evokes images realized through dialogue. In the course of this interaction, both content and ourselves are potentially transformed. Individuation is an ongoing psychic process. When entered into consciously and imaginatively, it provides a deepening awareness of the self, an expansion of one's consciousness, and an engendering of soul. We become more fully who we are, and we are more fully able to enter into the community of humans. In Jungian terms, this is transformation—the emergence of the self.

Dean Elias (1997) has expanded the definition of *transformative learning* to explicitly include the unconscious: "Transformative learning is the expansion of consciousness through the transformation of basic world views and the specific capacities of the self; transformative learning is facilitated through consciously directed processes such as appreciatively accessing and receiving the symbolic contents of the unconscious and critically analyzing underlying premises" (p. 12). (For additional insight into Jungian interpretations of transformative learning in the context of adult learning, see Boyd, 1991.)

Traumatic Learning

Roger Gould (1978) and Daniel Janik (2005) have both written about the important relationship of transformative learning and trauma. Janik, who holds an M.D. and a Ph.D. in education and linguistics, writes of neurobiological trauma and its applications to education and transformative learning. He describes the potential "that a learner can volitionally transform learning from a traumatic to an alternative, nontraumatic process utilizing curiosity, discovery and mentorship, which utilizes many of the same NL (Neurobiological Learning) processes common to traumatic learning" (Janik, 2005, p. 143). He further states:

> I have repeatedly witnessed individuals embarked on a voyage of curiosity, discovery and transformational learning, with the help of a mentor, "thaw out" and transform even the most frozen of traumatically learned, self destructive, acting-out behaviors. If one understands the neurobiological process involved, one can effectively self-regulate—redefine, or heal, as it were—even that which was taught and learned traumatically. . . .
>
> What I call transformative learning occurs as the result of mentor actions and attitudes that learning discovery is rarely easy. It is at best, discomforting, especially just prior to discovery. When learning feels uncomfortable, TL reinforces learner persistence, until discovery finally pops up or out. Transformative learning, in fact, occurs entirely within the learner, without the assistance of a teacher (teachers are often said by learners to "get in the way" of transformational learning) [pp. 144, 145].

Similarly, psychiatrist Roger Gould's (1978) earlier epigenetic theory of adult development holds that traumatic events in childhood may produce prohibitions that, though submerged from consciousness in adulthood, continue to generate anxiety feelings that inhibit adult action when there is a perceived risk of violating them. This dynamic results in a lost function—the ability to take risks, feel sexual, finish a job—or others that must be regained if one is to become a fully functioning adult. For Gould, transformative learning occurs when one learns to differentiate between the anxiety that is a function of the childhood trauma and the anxiety warranted by his or her immediate adult life situation. Gould has developed a computerized program to permit therapists and counselors to assist learners to think through the choices posed by their situation.

There can be little doubt that transformative learning often occurs as the result of an adult's gaining insight into unresolved traumatic experience occurring in childhood. It also seems apparent that transformative learning may be the result of our gaining insight into other unresolved areas of conflict as well, as in the women's movement, civil rights movement, and in university or adult education programs involving mentoring.

PROMISING DIRECTIONS FOR FUTURE DEVELOPMENT

In her comprehensive review of the development of transformation learning theory, Cranton (2006) elaborates on how colleagues have contributed significant insights in critical areas beyond those I have suggested, including social change and power issues, the cultural context of learning, and personal and imaginative knowing. For example, Dirkx (1998) formulated a four-dimensional approach to characterize directions in which transformative learning has moved, including Freire's perspective, emphasizing liberation from oppression, and my focus on rational thought and critical reflection on assumptions. Daloz (1990) focuses on an intuitive, contextually based, social process, and a fourth orientation by which Dirkx linked transformative learning to spirituality.

Furthermore, Cranton reminds us of the contribution of Belenky, Clinchy, Goldberger, and Tarule (1986), describing women's developmental stages of knowing and differentiating between separate and connected knowers, the latter who attempt to understand another's point of view from their perspective. Connected knowers are more likely to identify with others' transformative learning experience. There has also been considerable innovative interest in relating groups and organizations to transformative learning through action learning and collaborative inquiry. (See Yorks & Marsick, 2000, and Kasl & Elias, 2000, for more information about these concepts.) As a result of the latter research efforts, two areas have been identified that warrant further discussion—imagination, intuition, and emotion; cosmology—as well as some final thoughts on rationality and ideology.

Imagination, Intuition, Emotion

Colleagues have raised several important questions pertaining to transformation theory as I have interpreted it. One view is that I have neglected the role of imagination, intuition, and emotion. This criticism is partially justified. I have noted that the process by which we construe our beliefs may involve taken-for-granted values, stereotyping, selective attention, limited comprehension, projection, rationalization, minimizing, or denial. These considerations are reasons that we need to be able to critically assess and validate assumptions supporting our own beliefs and expectations and those of others. The way we typify persons, things, and events becomes our realities. Expectations may be of events or of beliefs pertaining to one's own involuntary reaction to events. Our expectations powerfully affect how we construe experience; they tend to become self-fulfilling prophecies.

"Imagining how things could be otherwise" (Greene, 1998) is central in the initiation of the transformative process. Because transformation is often a difficult, highly emotional passage, a great deal of additional insight into the role of imagination is needed and overdue. As many transformative experiences occur outside awareness, I have suggested that in these situations, intuition may substitute for critical self-reflection. This is another judgment that needs further conceptual development.

Cosmology

The most comprehensive approach to transformative learning is written by Edmund O'Sullivan and his colleagues (2002) and presented in the book titled *Expanding the Boundaries of Transformative Learning.* The authors include environmental, spiritual, and self-concept issues in what they term "integral transformative learning": a "deep cultural shift in the basic premises of thought, feeling and action...that dramatically and permanently alters our being in the world." O'Sullivan states:

> Such a shift involves our understanding of ourselves and our self-locations; our relationships with other humans and the natural world; our understanding of the relations of power in interlocking structures of class, race and gender; our body awareness, our visions of alternative approaches to living; and our sense of the possibilities for social justice and peace and personal joy [p. xvii].

Colleagues interested in transformative learning, interpreted as the vehicle for arriving at a new cosmology, look forward to further elaboration of this concept's core assumptions—its categories, considering the definition, validity, and relative priority of each of the components designated as essential elements of transformation; the roles of education and adult education; and program priorities and problems involved to effect the broad, multidimensional transformations envisioned.

Rationality and Ideology

Colleagues have criticized the importance I have assigned to the concept of rationality, which they interpret as an ahistorical and universal model leading to a view of learning that fails to adequately recognize the influence of context: ideology, culture, power, and race, class, and gender differences. As an adult educator, I have chosen to follow a Socratic precedent of considering critical self-reflection on assumptions and individual development as essential standards of justice and civic obligation in a democracy, rather than to assume the common understanding that citizenship must emphasize only that which is either cause based, group related, or service oriented (Villa, 2001). In his 1993 book, *The Nature of Rationality,* Robert Nozick observes:

> In recent years, rationality has been an object of particular criticism. The claim has been put forth that rationality is biased because it is a class-based or of male or Western or whatever notion. Yet it is part of rationality to be intent on noticing biases, including its own and controlling and correcting these.... The question is: In what specific ways and by what exact mechanisms, do our particular conceptual schemes and standards distort? Once we are shown this we can begin to make corrections [pp. xii, xiii].

For adult educators, transformative learning theory involves how to think critically about assumptions supporting one's perspectives and to develop critically reflective judgment in discourse regarding one's beliefs, values, feelings, and self-concepts. This process involves thinking rationally. For colleagues assigning priority to "ideology critique" or "critical pedagogy," this is a false assumption.

My response to this view is that transformative rationality may be understood as the process by which we learn to recognize, understand, and challenge or act on taken-for-granted epistemic assumptions supporting our beliefs, values, preferences, and self-concept. Other colleagues have suggested that I have failed to recognize that ideology or social constraints are basic and that rationality is relative to prior ideology or social determinism. Accepting a thesis of ideological or social determinism, or any other thesis, according to Siegal (1988) shows that whether we accept this thesis "depends precisely on what reasons can be advanced in support of the rational force those reasons offer for that claim, thus it is rationality which is basic, not ideology" (pp. 72–73).

If transformative rationality is a function of the human capacity for critical learning, this suggests that when ideological and social circumstances permit, we have a natural capacity to act rationally. In seeking the meaning of our experience, we engage in mindful efforts to learn, accepting others as agents with interpretations of their experiences that may prove true or justified, validating contested beliefs and understandings through reflective discourse, and assessing supporting reasons to arrive at a tentative best judgment—as opposed to resorting to tradition, authority, or force to make a judgment.

We are able to understand the meaning of what is communicated to us by becoming aware of the assumptions (intent, truthfulness, qualifications) of the person communicating and the truth, appropriateness, and authenticity of what is being communicated. We make meaning of our experience through acquired frames of reference—sets of orienting assumptions and expectations with cognitive, affective, and conative dimensions—that shape, delimit, and sometimes distort our understanding. We transform our frames of reference by becoming critically reflective of our assumptions to make them more dependable when the beliefs and understandings they generate become problematic.

This chapter has attempted to elaborate on current thinking regarding the evolving nature of transformative learning and provides a theoretical context that will be helpful in understanding the following chapters describing how transformative learning has been interpreted and successfully applied in a wide variety of contexts.

REFERENCES

Belenky, M., Clinchy, B., Goldberger, N., & Tarule, J. (1986). *Women's ways of knowing: The development of self, voice and mind.* New York: Basic books.

Bennett-Goldman, T. (2001). *Emotional alchemy.* New York: Three Rivers Press.

Boyd, R. (1991). *Personal transformations in small groups: A Jungian perspective.* Princeton, NJ: Princeton University Press.

Cranton, P. (2006). *Understanding and promoting transformative learning: A guide for educators of adults.* San Francisco: Jossey-Bass.

Daloz, L. (2000). Transformative learning for the common good. In J. Mezirow & Associates, *Learning as transformation: Critical perspectives on a theory in progress.* San Francisco: Jossey-Bass.

Dewey, J. (1960). *On experience, nature, and freedom: Representative selections.* Indianapolis: Bobbs-Merrill.

Dirkx, J. M. (1997). Nurturing soul in adult learning. In P. Cranton (Ed.), *Transformative learning in action* (pp. 79–88). New Directions for Adult and Continuing Education, no. 74. San Francisco: Jossey-Bass.

Elias, D. (1997). It's time to change our minds. *ReVision, 26,* 3–12.

Gould, R. L. (1978). *Transformation, growth and change in adult life.* New York: Simon & Schuster.

Greene, M. (1995). *Releasing the imagination.* San Francisco: Jossey-Bass.

Habermas, J. (1991). *The theory of communicative action* (Thomas McCarthy, Trans.). Boston: Beacon Press.

Janik, D. (2005). *Unlock the genius within: Neurobiological trauma, teaching and transformative learning.* Lanham, MD: Rowman & Littlefield.

Kasl, E., & Elias, D. (2000). Creating new habits of mind in small groups. In J. Mezirow & Associates, *Learning as transformation: Critical perspectives on a theory in progress.* San Francisco: Jossey-Bass.

Kitchener, K. S., & King, P. (1990) The reflective judgment model: Transforming assumptions about knowing. In J. Mezirow & Associates, *Fostering critical reflection in adulthood.* San Francisco: Jossey-Bass.

Mezirow, J. (1978). *Education for perspective transformation: Women's reentry programs in community colleges.* New York Center for Adult Education, Teachers College, Columbia University.

Mezirow, J., & Associates. (1990). *Fostering critical reflection in adulthood*. San Francisco: Jossey-Bass.

Nozick, R. (1993). *The nature of rationality*. Princeton, NJ: Princeton University Press.

O'Sullivan, E., Morrell, A., & O'Connor, M. (2002). *Expanding the boundaries of transformative learning*. New York: Palgrave.

Pinar, W. F. (Ed.). (1998). *The passionate mind of Maxine Greene: "I am...not yet."* Bristol, PA: Taylor & Francis.

Schultz, A. (1973). *Collected papers, Vol. 1. The problem of social reality*. The Hague: Martinus Nijhoff.

Siegal, H. (1988). *Educating reason—rationality, critical thinking and education*. New York: Routledge.

Villa, D. (2001). *Socratic citizenship*. Princeton, NJ: Princeton University Press.

Yorks, L., & Marsick, V. J. (2000). Organizational learning and transformation. In J. Mezirow & Associates, *Learning as transformation: Critical perspectives on a theory in progress* (pp. 253–281). San Francisco: Jossey-Bass.

PART TWO

TRANSFORMATIVE LEARNING AS HIGHER EDUCATION

The chapters in Part Two focus on transformative practices found in national and international higher education programs. The programs are quite varied and cover a wide spectrum of academic disciplines and subjects, such as sociology classrooms, a freshman writing seminar, online adult education courses, leadership development, medical education in palliative care, and a faculty development program. Within these diverse settings, a number of transformative practices are explored, such as arts-based approaches to transformative learning, constructive teaching, the role of culture and imagination, dialogic teaching, mentoring, problem-based learning (PBL), and the role of cohorts.

CHAPTER THREE

Creating Alternative Realities

Arts-Based Approaches to Transformative Learning

Shauna Butterwick, Randee Lipson Lawrence

Our stories are narratives of events in our lives. Each of us has multiple stories based on our lived experience and memories, shaped by our positionality and the cultural context where we locate ourselves. The arts are a way to communicate our stories in ways that connect with others.

As educators, we, the authors, have found that incorporating various art forms into our practice can enhance learning and create spaces for transformation to occur. Some examples are drawing visual metaphors to explore the stages of adult development, using cameras to learn about observation techniques in research, creating poems in the analysis of data, and using theater to tell stories. Opportunities for transformative learning can sometimes occur simply by inviting students to write poems, take photos, create weavings or quilts, or engage in other artistic processes to complete class assignments. The outcomes of such engagement are often surprisingly profound; using the arts can help to reveal experiences and insights not readily available in traditional academic texts and discussions.

In these and other activities we have used in our teaching and research, we have found that telling stories through embodied or performative activities, such as popular theater or creating and performing dialogue, can lead to transformative learning—what we define as a kind of shape-shifting or changing the form of ourselves, our emotions, our thoughts, our worldviews, and our relationship to others, toward a more just society. Mezirow (2000) describes transformative learning as a process of changing our taken-for-granted assumptions to make them more inclusive and truthful. O'Sullivan (2002) believes that transformation is an integral process incorporating survival, critical resistance, and creativity. Building on these orientations, we see three key elements of theater (and other arts-based) processes that support transformational learning.

First, theater, as an embodied practice, taps into knowing that is not yet available to us at a conscious level. Second, when we tell stories about our lived and embodied experience, they become public, that is, the story is being shared with others. In that moment of publicity, space can open up for ourselves and others to reconsider the meaning of our experiences. Third, alternative ways of knowing and being become more evident through telling these stories. We can engage in rehearsal for action to change injustice.

As educators, we understand that transformation is a process that occurs over time. It can take place at moments in our teaching contexts and much later, outside those parameters. And although we can set the stage for potential transformation to occur, we cannot always know what the actual impact of the learning experience has been on our learners. In this chapter, we present a brief overview of popular theater and then relate stories about two activities we facilitated that led to the telling of stories that created spaces for transformative learning.

POPULAR THEATER: EXPERIENTIAL AND TRANSFORMATIVE PROCESSES

Popular theater is process that assists individuals and groups to better understand lived experience by putting the experience out in public where it can be examined. In Augusto Boal's *Theater of the Oppressed* (1979), for example, participants share personal stories of struggle and oppression using the medium of spontaneous theater to work out alternative solutions to personal and societal problems, which could then be translated into action. Popular theater is grounded in the principle that audience members are not passive observers. They are actors whose stories become part of the larger performance. Popular theater "deeply involves specific communities in identifying issues of concern, analyzing current conditions and causes of a situation, identifying points of change, and analyzing how change could happen and/or contributing to the actions implied" (Prentki & Selman, 2000, p. 8).

Since theater is a deeply reflexive embodying process, not only can the experience be understood in deeper and new ways, one can also practice alternative ways of responding to a situation, thus creating opportunities for change. The reflexive dimension of popular theater is central to its transformative potential. Significant learning can occur through reflection on one's lived experience as well as through witnessing another's experience enacted.

Reflection can happen through description, oral or written storytelling, or embodied activities. These experiences, which are often painful, may evoke strong feelings that need to be acknowledged and attended to. At times, the words needed to describe the experience may not be available (Lawrence & Butterwick, 2007). As our bodies often hold the knowledge that is not yet present in our conscious minds, theater can be a way of telling our stories and bringing them out in the open, where we can begin to engage in dialogue and eventually create new knowledge and new stories that help us deal with difficult or oppressive situations. Embodying the experience through theater exercises helps us to integrate the experience and then act on this new learning.

To illustrate the embodying experience of theater, we provide two stories of theater workshops we facilitated. Randee's story describes a workshop depicting how these kinds of exercises can be brought into our classrooms. In her story, the issue that emerged was the violence and oppression of homophobia. In Shauna's story, she is both a participant and a facilitator of a process that explored issues of racism and antiracist practice that was developed in a community setting and then performed at a university event. We offer these stories in the spirit of collegiality so that others may adapt these activities to their own practice contexts.

RANDEE'S STORY: IMAGES OF OPPRESSION—LOOKING THROUGH A MIRROR

The following learning incident occurred in a workshop I facilitated for faculty and students based on Boal's *Theater of the Oppressed* (1992) work. The purpose of the workshop, which was clearly articulated prior to and at the beginning of the gathering, was to introduce theater techniques as a way of confronting difficult issues and conflicts and rehearsing alternative strategies for dealing with oppressive situations.

We started with a series of warm-up exercises for people to become comfortable working with their bodies. Most adults are accustomed to learning as a purely cognitive process and need to relearn what they knew as children—that the body is also a source of knowledge. (For examples of warm-up exercises see Boal, 1992, or Spolin, 1963.) To relieve any performance anxiety, I reminded participants that they were not acting; they were exploring an alternative form of learning.

I then asked the participants to recall an incident where they had experienced or witnessed an act of oppression and to create an image to express this oppression using their bodies. One at a time, they "froze" the image while everyone else watched. After a discussion about what it was like to use the body to tell stories of oppression, I asked for a volunteer to create a sculpture of an oppressive situation where he or she was the victim, using the bodies of other group members as the medium in which to depict the oppressors. It is important to emphasize the voluntary nature of this task. Asking someone to expose personal vulnerability in front of a group should never be a requirement.

There is no verbal communication during the sculpting process. As Boal (1992) suggests, it is important that the sculptor work fast, without taking the time to think too much about the situation. Thinking requires translating the image into words. As in moving from one language to another, often some of the content gets lost in the translation.

Carson (a pseudonym), the person who volunteered to create the image, was a gay man. He recalled an incident in which he was attacked by schoolyard bullies for being different from the other boys. He created a sculpture where he was in the middle of a circle hiding his head while others pointed, jeered, and physically beat on him. It was difficult to watch this scene. I felt tears behind my eyes as I imagined what it must be like to be ganged up on by others. At this stage in the exercise, those of us who were observers did not know that the oppression had to do with Carson's sexual orientation since there was no verbalization. We had only the visual image of him being bullied.

In the next phase of the exercise, the oppressed and oppressors in the sculpture, as well as the observers, had an opportunity to talk about their perspectives of the situation. At this point, Carson told us that he had been attacked because he was gay. He talked about what it felt like to be a victim. He felt helpless, as it seemed he could do nothing to change the situation. He could not talk to his parents since he had not yet come out to them. He knew that telling the teachers would only make the situation worse for him. The sculpture that Carson created was not necessarily a literal representation of what occurred; it was more of an embodiment of how Carson was feeling at the time, which is characteristic of this form of theater.

The people who portrayed the oppressors in the sculpture then talked about how they felt in that position. One indicated that she felt empathy for Carson, but at the same time she was afraid of the consequences of not going along with her peers. Another said it felt good to be the oppressor and not the oppressed. Most people disclosed that they felt uncomfortable in the oppressor role. These comments led to a discussion about whether the oppressor/oppressed role was actually a binary dichotomy (Freire, 1970) and the tension created by having to take on one role or the other. We talked about what it meant to give up privilege and if that was really possible. The rest of the group, the observers, then shared their observations about what they saw as outsiders.

In the final phase, the entire group was invited to consider ways in which the scene may be replayed with Carson refusing to accept the victim role. Volunteers were solicited to create new sculptures with different outcomes.

In one scene, the person portraying Carson had his head held high and a confident expression on his face as the oppressors turned away from him. In another, Carson was leaning forward with his finger pointing out as if giving a lecture as the others in the scene listened attentively. A third scenario had two of the former oppressors taking the role of allies to Carson and challenging the other oppressors.

There may be as many alternative scenarios as ideas come forth. This activity was transformative as other ways of being were brought into a public space and rehearsed. Even when it is not possible to go back and change the particular situation (this incident happened in Carson's youth), participants can become empowered to consider similar oppressive situations in the present and future where they would not cast themselves in the role of victim. While people who have been oppressed do not always have control over their situations, they do have some command over their emotional reactions. They can internalize the oppression or choose to see themselves as change agents and explore new ways of responding.

Theater activities like this one can create teachable moments that open doors for difficult conversations to occur. As in any other experiential activity, it is important to allow ample time to process the learning in ways that are respectful and affirming to all.

SHAUNA'S STORY: SPEAKING TRUTH TO POWER

In the fall of 2006, I joined three others in creating a book club to read and discuss ideas that would further our antiracist work. Our group included Parker, an African American man, who had recently moved to Canada from the United States, where he had many years of experience working on issues of race and racism in postsecondary institutions; Indy, an Indo-Canadian woman who had worked for many years at the university level developing student programs and as a student advisor; and Yael, a Canadian Jewish woman who had recently returned to Canada after many years in the United States, where she had been engaged in antiracist work in higher education; she was now developing faculty development programs. My heritage is Anglo-Saxon white, and I am a middle-class university professor of adult education interested in antioppressive pedagogy.

We began by talking about what we wanted to get out of our gatherings, and all shared the desire to have a place to talk, read, discuss, and further our understanding and antiracism work. The first book we read together was *Dancing on Live Embers: Challenging Racism in Organizations* by Tina Lopes and Barb Thomas (2006), which includes many case studies about working with organizations dealing with systemic discrimination. As we worked through this book, our monthly discussions became meaningful and deep. They reminded me of the study circles often talked about in adult education.

In November 2006, Indy suggested that we make a presentation about some of our discussions at Realities of Race (RoR), a week-long event at the University of British Columbia that commemorated March 21, the United Nations International Day for the Elimination of Racial Discrimination. Parker suggested that we use dialogue as the format for our presentations. It reflected the kinds of exchanges we had in our monthly book club meetings, exchanges that had been transformative for me as we talked about very difficult matters such as white privilege, the pain and wounds of racism, and what it meant to be coresponsible for eliminating racism. Our dialogues had involved much patience, trust, and sharing of vulnerability. As Burbules (1993) notes, "Considering dialogue as a kind of relation (with one or more other people) emphasizes the aspects of dialogue that are beyond us, that we discover, that we are changed by" (p. xii).

Parker, who had used this approach before in presentations about racism, helped guide us as we developed our dialogue scripts. It took us three months to create these dialogues, meeting monthly as a larger group and also in pairs. We took turns taking notes of our meetings. We all found that preparing these scripts offered yet another opportunity for deeper reflection on our stories. We decided it was important to tell stories about ourselves, not about others, to avoid abstraction and analysis, to be specific about place, time, who, and what. When developing dialogue and scripts in theater, we also knew that it was crucial to be clear about our objectives and what we wanted to achieve. Playing on the R word, we came up with five key points we wanted to make in our storytelling: (1) to note the difference between race and racism as the two are often conflated, (2) to look at how repetition is part of both racism and antiracist practice, (3) to speak of recognition (how race and racism are often not recognized), (4) to talk about the risk that we unequally shared, because of our different racial positions, as we told stories about race and racism, and (5) to emphasize the matter of responsibility, most particularly the responsibility of Caucasian people in the maintenance of and fight against racism.

First, we wanted to bring attention to the difference between race and racism to indicate that racism, not race, is the problem. This was a strong theme in Parker's story. Second, we wanted to explore the theme of repetition—how racist remarks and actions and systems persist, how people of color experience racism daily and how allies need to understand how what might appear to us as one moment is only the most recent of many that have been accumulating. Yael spoke about this in her dialogue.

Our third objective is closely related to this notion of repetition, that is, the issue of recognition: how racism is seen (or not) within ourselves, our relationships, and our institutions, and how this recognition is often denied within white liberal institutions. A myth in Canada is that the country is truly multicultural, racially integrated, and tolerant. As part of her dialogue, Indy talked about how, as a new immigrant, she learned at a young age that racism was alive and well in Canada. Parker also spoke about how racism is sometimes misrecognized, particularly in Canada, where racism is not as openly discussed as it is in the United States.

We also wanted to emphasize the matter of risk. We discussed how the burden of racism is unequally carried by people of color, and how, when telling stories about racism, the risk is unequally shared. As Lopes and Thomas (2006) noted in their case study of a black executive director, "There's a risk that anti-racism becomes identified as the executive director's personal issue rather than an area important for the organization to pursue" (p. 98). This concern was a key issue in the Parker and Indy's stories.

Finally, we wanted to bring to the forefront the notion of responsibility: that all people need to share the responsibility for eliminating racism, recognizing that Caucasian people, whose privilege is grounded on historic racist beliefs and systems, are implicitly involved in and must participate in the solution of eliminating racism rather than walk away from the struggle. In our stories, both Yael and I spoke about how white people can work as allies with people of color and commit to the long and difficult process.

Another of our objectives was to create a space for listening and discussion that was open—where we would illustrate the relational aspect of learning about race and racism and the trust and vulnerability that such conversations require. At the RoR event, we performed our dialogues at noon, over three days, reading from the scripts we had prepared, which helped us stay focused on the stories we wanted to tell. We requested an hour for each dialogue, planning for fifteen minutes of performance followed by forty-five minutes of discussion. We thought that holding these dialogues at lunch hour would encourage participants to attend. In the first dialogue, Parker and Indy presented; we wanted their stories, explicating the difference between race and racism, to begin our series, but we also recognized the risks they faced in telling these stories about the impact of racism, such as the reprisals that can take place when people of color make such public disclosures.

In the second dialogue, Yael and I focused on our developing awareness of white privilege and our own racism. Unlike the first two dialogues, in which we read from scripts, the third dialogue, among all four of us, used more improvisation. We worked from some basic notes we had developed the evening before. We all agreed that we wanted to talk about the process of developing the dialogues (as outlined earlier), refer specifically to one of the stories told and its impact on us, and also speak to the overall impact of the shared work on ourselves.

We began each of our dialogues with reminders about rules for respectful listening and speaking, and after we finished our scripts, we invited the audience members to take a few moments to note their thoughts and feelings and then, if they wanted, to share their reflections with a neighbor, before we opened it up to large group discussion. We were heartened by the discussion during the first two dialogues, which seemed to create a relatively safe space for people to share their stories. For example, one participant spoke about her mixed-race heritage and the pain of listening to racist comments from those who regarded her as white. Another person wrote in her feedback about her sense of bearing witness, which she felt was quite different from other times when she felt she had been a voyeur listening to stories about racism. Both participants described the dialogue and discussion that followed as transformative. Our positive assessment was tempered with our acknowledgment of the small turnout (eight participants) and the fact that we knew most of the people. Few major university personnel in positions of power attended. We wondered if we were just preaching to the choir.

During the final dialogue, the audience was much larger, about twenty-five people. Present were those who had attended the earlier sessions plus newcomers, including several mainstream institutional personnel. We were no longer preaching to the choir. The discussion following our dialogue was lively, with people telling stories, but also making comments that triggered strong emotional reactions. For example, one Caucasian participant who was a program administrator announced that in relation to hiring practices at the university, "race was irrelevant, just like vegetarianism." Her comments triggered more responses in the large group as participants clarified that for them, the point was that race in a racist society always matters and we are fooling ourselves if we think that racial identity can be ignored. By opening such a space of conversation, we made visible such beliefs and had the opportunity to respond. It was good to have these perspectives spoken and made public so that we might listen and hear other views. In fact, it was hard to hear some of them.

REFLECTIONS

This chapter has highlighted the relationship of arts-based approaches, specifically popular theater activities, to transformative learning through two vignettes, one focusing on an adult education classroom and the other on a public antiracist event. Working with these arts-based processes has illuminated for us the complexity and dynamic nature of transformative learning. The more we engage in these activities, the more we realize that we, as educators, have also experienced transformation. We have become more sensitive and aware of both the power and peril of using artistic processes with our learners. For example, storytelling is getting a lot of attention, but we have noted a tendency toward making "tell me your story" mandatory rather than voluntary. Forcing disclosures can lead to retraumatization. Furthermore, we do not want to suggest that telling stories is somehow inherently emancipatory.

What is sometimes lacking in discussions about storytelling as part of transformative learning is a careful analysis of how power relations are shaping the telling and the hearing of stories. As adult educators working within our formal educational institutions or in less formal community contexts and social movements, we need to take responsibility for creating conditions for respectful listening as integral to storytelling practices. Some days, this feels to us to be an impossibility because in North America, we live in a racist, classist, homophobic, ablest, and Eurocentric society where normative judgments represent the worldviews of those who are Caucasian, English speaking, economically privileged, able-bodied, and heterosexual. That is the location we, as authors, both occupy, so we need to acknowledge that our thinking and acting, even as we write this, are informed (even limited) by our privileged positions. This is the horizon on which a great deal of listening takes place.

Sherene Razack (1993), a critical race and feminist theorist, draws attention to this horizon and how storytelling is central to legal practices and feminist pedagogy. Like Trin Minh-ha (1989), she notes those moments where women who do not occupy powerful locations on hierarchies of privilege and oppression are required to tell their story. These stories are then often interpreted through racist, sexist, classist, ablest, heterosexist frameworks. She points to the inequalities in risk taking in these moments and how storytelling can lead to further oppression rather than empowerment. Speaking truth to power can be risky.

What draws us to popular theater methods for storytelling are the principles that support shared risk taking and processes that are grounded in the recognition of power inequalities. If we are interested in using storytelling and popular theater and other performative or arts-based formats to tell stories, then we must take seriously our responsibilities for creating conditions that support storytelling that are life affirming, not oppressive. How do we support more emancipatory outcomes, and how do we minimize the potential for further oppression? As noted, storytelling should not be imposed or made into a requirement. We need to understand the dangers and inequalities of risk that exist in any group. We need to act with a sense of humility and recognize that we cannot know for certain what those dangers are, what stories might emerge, and what the reactions to the stories might be. Who is speaking and who is listening are key questions that need to be carefully considered before engaging with these kinds of activities.

Stories are not simply told; they are also witnessed. Once the story is performed, it can then be analyzed, and the context or conditions that led to these moments of violence and oppression can become part of the discussion. Abstract conversations about difficult issues like heterosexism, homophobia, and racism often create a distance from the lived experience of these oppressive forces, a distance that maintains the status quo. The two vignettes we shared were based on actual experiences. They demonstrated how, through theater, audience members bear witness to participants' stories and the pain and injustice suffered, and a connection is made through the body and with the heart as well as the mind that can lead to transformative action.

As both stories illustrate, the moment of actively bearing witness is a transformation in the nature of the relationship across difference. Involving audience members as participants can help to disrupt the voyeuristic gaze and create conditions that can lead to relations of solidarity and coresponsibility.

Engaging with arts-based processes to tell stories of oppression that support emancipatory goals requires a commitment in time and energy by all concerned. Time is particularly needed for debriefing—for exploring how actors are feeling, how audience members interpret the stories, and what new stories are being generated in response. As facilitators of these kinds of activities, we need to be ready for the unexpected and be open to feedback from participants. Some of our activities might be troubling for participants, and we need to stay open to hear about these experiences and learn from them. We also need to acknowledge our own power. We are models for our learners. How we ourselves illustrate respectful listening through our bodies and our words is important. We can create an environment where transformational learning can occur; however, without care and attention to the power we have and the work of creating conditions for respectful speaking and listening, we can also contribute to oppression and silencing.

We invite practitioners and facilitators to consider the transformative potential of the arts. Arts-based processes are powerful because they tap into embodied knowing, honor emotions, and create spaces for rehearsal for action. We certainly recognize that transformation in worldviews and structural change are prerequisite to action that corrects injustices. Arts-based processes, we argue, can create spaces for rehearsal and imagining of alternative realities.

REFERENCES

Boal, A. (1979). *Theater of the oppressed*. London: Pluto Press.

Boal, A. (1992). *Games for actors and non-actors*. London: Routledge.

Burbules, N. (1993). *Dialogue in teaching—theory and practice*. New York: Teachers College Press.

Freire, P. (1970). *Pedagogy of the oppressed*. New York: Continuum.

Lawrence, R. L., & Butterwick, S. (2007). Re-imaging oppression: An arts-based embodied approach to transformative learning. In P. Cranton & E. Taylor (Eds.), *Transformative learning: Issues of difference and diversity: Proceedings of the Seventh International Transformative Learning Conference* (pp. 411–416). Albuquerque: University of New Mexico College of Education.

Lopes, T., & Thomas, B. (2006). *Dancing on live embers: Challenging racism in organizations*. Toronto, ON: Between the Lines.

Mezirow, J. (2000). Learning to think like an adult: Core concepts of transformation theory. In J. Mezirow & Associates, *Learning as transformation* (pp. 3–33). San Francisco: Jossey-Bass.

Minh-ha, T. (1989). *Woman native other*. Bloomington: Indiana University Press.

O'Sullivan, E. V. (2002). The project and vision of transformative education. In E. V. O'Sullivan, A. Morrell, & M. A. O'Connor (Eds.), *Expanding the boundaries of transformative learning* (pp. 1–10). New York: Palgrave.

Prentki, T., & Selman, J. (2000). *Popular theater in political culture: Britain and Canada in focus*. Bristol, UK: Intellect.

Razack, S. (1993). The gaze from the other side: Storytelling for social change. In H. Bannerji (Ed.), *Returning the gaze: Essays on racism, feminism and politics* (pp. 36–55). Toronto: Sister Vision Press.

Spolin, V. (1963). *Improvisation for the theater*. Evanston, IL: Northwestern University Press.

CHAPTER FOUR

Constructive Teaching and Learning

Collaboration in a Sociology Classroom

Debra Langan, Ron Sheese, Deborah Davidson

The particular transformation of interest to us as university educators is to have students recognize and challenge the dominant ideological assumptions that are taken for granted in everyday discussions and representations of social (in)equalities. While critical perspectives in sociology address these assumptions, many undergraduate students actively resist critical analyses. For every student who tells us, as one student wrote in her journal, "I hear analyses that are striking a chord with me. Someone is finally speaking my language. I am not alone. It is comforting to know that there is nothing wrong with me because I see things differently from the majority of the people from my culture," there are far more who, when provided with information about structural inequalities, persist in expressing views in individualistic terms. They argue that features of identity (for example, gender, race, social class, ability, age, sexual preference) do not combine to create differing opportunities for individuals. As feminist teachers, we believe that understanding how inequalities are perpetuated and challenged is the first step toward social actions to eliminate societal injustices.

We thank the Social Sciences and Humanities Research Council of Canada, the York University Faculty of Arts, and the York University Faculty Association for their generous support of our research.

46

Over the past nine years, we have studied such resistance and explored classroom strategies for addressing and working with it (Langan, 2001; Langan & Davidson, 2005). Situated in Toronto, Canada's largest city, York University has an enrollment of approximately fifty thousand students. Sixty-eight percent of York's first-year students work for pay at the same time that they are enrolled in courses (Craney, 2007). York's student population reflects the multicultural diversity of Toronto: 43 percent of Toronto's population identify as being part of a visible minority, with the majority of students coming from first-generation immigrant families. York is known as a commuter university: 84 percent of the first-year student population commutes to York from the greater Toronto area (half of those students commute for more than forty minutes), and 64 percent of the first-year student population lives at home. The development of close relationships between York and its students, and among the students themselves, has been a major challenge, partially because of cultural differences and partially because students do not feel a sense of attachment to the school and therefore have little impetus to become involved with it beyond their individual studies. Research on the quality of students' lives at York underscores the notion that a lack of community among students is a serious impediment to achieving student engagement (Alvares, 2007).

In this chapter, we describe how our efforts, in the context of two full-year sociology courses (2004–2005), to achieve the transformative goal were mediated by actions designed to enhance students' engagement with one another. We conceptualized our setting not only as a university course, but also as the site of a feminist, participatory, action-oriented research project in which the students and teaching assistants were collaborators in our efforts to understand, and enhance, the learning environment we created for the courses. The courses were directed by Debra Langan in York University's Department of Sociology, and they involved 325 students (175 in the first-year course, Sociological Perspectives, and 150 in the second-year course, Social Order and Social Organization) who attended one lecture (two hours) and one tutorial (one hour, with 20 to 25 students) meeting each week. Seven graduate student teaching assistants (TAs) also attended lectures (in theater-style lecture halls) and facilitated tutorial meetings (in smaller rooms). Deborah Davidson, a doctoral student, and Ron Sheese a faculty member, joined Langan in working with the TAs in training workshops at the beginning of the course and in a supportive role throughout the year, but they had no direct interaction with the students. Although we describe only the first year of our collaboration, the project continues and has involved 33 TAs and over 1,200 students to date.

THEORETICAL FRAMEWORKS

Like Taylor (1998), we argue that "the practical implications associated with facilitating and encouraging learners to revise their meaning perspectives" (p. 10) have been underemphasized. Central to our mission have been attempts to have students revise their meaning perspectives in a manner that incorporates an awareness of how social inequalities are interpersonally, institutionally, and globally perpetuated and resisted. We see lives as "narratively organized [such that] . . . transformation occurs as a change in how we restory our lives in relation to a particular cultural narrative" (Edwards, 1997, cited in Taylor, 1998, p. 44). Coming into our classes, especially in the first year of university, we greet students who have acquired meaning perspectives "often . . . uncritically in the course of childhood through socialization and acculturation" (Taylor, 1998, p. 13). These perspectives "mirror the way our culture and those individuals responsible for our socialization happen to have defined various situations" (Mezirow, 1991, p. 131). Our goal as educators is to facilitate a perspective transformation by providing both alternative discourses and interaction-based learning opportunities that assist students in developing a more inclusive worldview. Mezirow (1991) defines perspective transformation as

> the process of becoming critically aware of how and why our assumptions have come to constrain the way we perceive, understand, and feel about our world; changing these structures of habitual expectation to make possible a more inclusive, discriminating, and integrating perspective; and finally, making choices or otherwise acting upon these new understandings [p. 167].

The transformative practices of our research have been most significantly influenced by the work of Barbara Thayer-Bacon (1999, 2003), a feminist philosopher of education who argues that theorists need to redescribe critical thinking in a manner that looks beyond logic and that in its account of ways of knowing takes note of such vital qualities as intuition, imagination, and emotional feelings. She adopts the term *constructive thinking* to highlight the creation of knowledge as a "transactive sociopolitical process with others" (p. 48). As seen in the title of her recent book, *Relational "(E)pistemologies,"* she characterizes her epistemological view as relational, and she places particular emphasis on caring as an element of critical and constructive thinking. She describes caring as receptivity to the voice of the other, and she associates it with listening to what others have to say and feeling with them. This conception dovetails well with Sheese's (2000) conception of the ideal teacher-student dialogue in which each participant is alert to the goals of the other. Thayer-Bacon sees caring in constructive thinking as similar to what Belenky, Bond, and Weinstock (1997) describe as playing the "believing game," as contrasted to the "doubting game," which is associated with conventional critical thinking (p. 61). A caring dialogue is her response to the relativism that many associate with epistemologies, such as hers, that favor searching for localized, contextual meanings rather than universal, transcendental truths. It has been important to us that the learning environments we design should support ways of knowing that are consistent with our goal of moving students to understand how truth can be conceptualized as contingent, local, and expressible in narratives of meaning. She emphasizes that knowers must be sensitive to their relation to the known and to other knowers, and she advocates caring and dialogue as pedagogically valuable in acquiring this sensitivity.

TRANSFORMATIVE LEARNING IN A SOCIAL ENVIRONMENT

Simply conceptualizing the course as a learning environment was an initial fruitful step in our design process. The metaphor enabled us to think of our students as moving about cognitively and emotionally in a space that should offer them significant opportunities for development. It made us aware that we could add, remove, or modify components of that space based on their consistency with our goals and on the students' interaction with them. We articulated specific principles characterizing the kinds of learning environments that we had been working to create and on which we wanted to improve. We believed that such principles could be presented explicitly to our TAs and our students as a means of understanding the environment in which they were working, as a guide to how we were approaching the course material and as a framework for how we expected participants in the class to operate. Drawing on Thayer-Bacon's concept of constructive thinking and supported by the earlier phases of our exploratory research (see Langan & Davidson, 2005), we employed the term "constructive teaching and learning" to refer to our approach, which was guided by the following five values:

- *Collaboration* — viewing knowing as social and knowers as in relation with others rather than as isolated individuals
- *Deep learning* — enhancing understanding of course content by promoting connections among its elements
- *Reflection* — encouraging students to connect the course content with their prior knowledge and lived experience
- *Engagement* — discussing and building a point of view by means of feedback and dialogue regarding course activities
- *Caring* — attending and listening to others so as to foster relationships that acknowledge and encourage acceptance of our differences and similarities

Our emphasis was to orchestrate a social environment that would enhance students' engagement in the teaching-learning processes and ultimately facilitate transformations in worldviews. For each principle, we operationalized strategies designed to foster transformative learning. In this chapter, we focus primarily on how we have worked with the principle of collaboration and on challenges to the success of our endeavors that we have identified through our ongoing, reflective analyses.

DOING COLLABORATION

We believe that personal transformations are most likely if an individual is engaged not only with the course material but also with other students in the course. Hence, we have attended to designing classroom activities through which students can learn to work collaboratively and develop mutually enhancing relationships among themselves as well as with the TAs and with us as teachers. Central to our approach has been the use of small group discussions in tutorials and lectures, and this objective has been specified in syllabi by Langan as collaborating "in small groups in the production of knowledge within the classroom." Because we place a high value on the intensive work that TAs do with students in tutorials and during office hours, we hold a series of three-day workshops just prior to the beginning of a course to familiarize them with our constructive teaching and learning approach, model for and with them the kinds of strategies we want them to use in their work with students, and gain their trust in us and each other as collaborators in the teaching and learning environment. At the beginning of the course, the professor (in lecture) and the TAs (in tutorials) randomly assign three to five students to each small group, and these group memberships usually remain the same for at least one term. The small groups formed in lecture and those formed in the tutorials are not the same, in part to increase the variety of others with whom each student collaborates over the term.

Time is devoted to ice-breaker exercises and having students exchange names and contact information as a means of providing peer support when questions about the course arise. The groups always have specific tasks to complete. At times during lectures, student groups may be asked to discuss and prepare a written response to specific questions that relate to the lecture, a film shown during class, a current event, a guest presentation, or the required readings. After the small group work, some groups are called on to present their answers to the larger class. The majority of tutorial time is devoted to small group work (see Langan et al., 2007, for examples of exercises that students and TAs work on in tutorials). During small group work, the professor and the TAs become facilitators, physically moving around, encouraging group participation, and providing assistance to students. While students are expected to work together in this way as part of the course process, most often each student is individually graded for his or her involvement in class and on written tests and assignments. Regular, anonymous, written feedback from each student informs our assessment of how the groups are working and whether changes to group memberships are needed, for example, when problems of absenteeism or marginalization are identified.

One of the most daunting obstacles that we have faced is initial student resistance to group activities. Murphy and Valdéz (2005) note that one reason collaborative models are not readily accepted is that professors and students have received their educations in traditional classroom settings that privilege individual achievement. We have found it essential for the professor to emphasize, in lectures and syllabi, the importance of tutorials as a site for teaching and learning. Furthermore, the professor must explain how the five principles will guide the conduct of tutorials, while still supporting the diverse ways in which TAs work with students on the course material. By allotting a higher-than-usual percentage of the final grade to tutorial involvement (15 percent) and by providing students with a detailed definition of what it means to be "involved" in tutorials (for example, active listening is rewarded, shifting the emphasis away from talking as the sole way to participate), the overarching rules of the game are made explicit for students and TAs. Providing this kind of clarity has enabled us to have students engage in more productive collaborations. Our evaluation data confirm that at the end of the course, the vast majority of students believe that they benefit intellectually and socially from the collaborative small group work.

Deconstructing Democratic Dialogue

Notwithstanding the success of our approach, we have come to critically analyze the notion of democratic dialogue, which underpins the value that we place on collaboration. Like others who advocate collaboration as a teaching-learning strategy, we have "sincere and benevolent desires for a unified and egalitarian classroom" (Jones, 2005, p. 62). Still, our expertise in social psychology and the feminist orientation of our project have attuned us to the unequal power relations that exist among participants. We have been particularly attentive to addressing issues of student and TA marginalization. Inequality in interaction is a central feature of small group dynamics, and given participants' differing social locations (professor, TA, and student) and status characteristics (gender, race, social class, ability, age, sexual orientation) and the power that these confer, the marginalization of participants is an ongoing concern for us. Jones's thinking on this issue coincides with ours: "With a more critical understanding of the complexities and contradictions inherent in apparently benign and progressive desires for dialogue in education, we might reduce our romantic expectations of dialogue, and set about working alongside and with each other in different ways" (p. 66).

One of the strategies that I (Langan) have used to foster an inclusive environment has been to include in the curriculum critical sociological analyses of group dynamics in classroom settings so that students are more informed (hooks, 1994, on social class; Briskin, 1998, on power and silence; and Cannon, 1990, on race, class, and gender). Another way that I work to alter classroom practice is by orchestrating "disruptions . . . the introduction of critical texts that impact student consciousness, that present a meaningful challenge to taken-for-granted understandings of societal relations" (Langan, Oliver, & Atkinson, 2007). Disruptions have included guest lectures by a lesbian mother on lesbian parenting, a transsexual on transsexual identities, a sex worker activist on the legitimacy of sex work, a teaching assistant on gender inequality, and videos on institutional racism, violence against women, and the abuse of older adults. The purpose of such disruptions is to encourage students to bring their views out for examination and reflection, and our research has shown that this approach is extremely effective in fostering deep learning and transformations in worldviews. Disruptions typically turn classrooms into sites of contention, for they lead to complex, confrontational, and emotional responses from students and, subsequently, from us as teachers. Like Boler (2005), we believe that "the obligation of educators is not to guarantee a space that is free from hostility—an impossible and sanitizing task—but rather, to challenge oneself and one's students to critically analyze any statements made in a classroom, especially statements that are rooted in dominant ideological values that subordinate on the basis of race, gender, class, or sexual orientation" (p. 4).

Rather than view the heated emotional discussions and debates as negative, I reflectively deconstruct in lectures with students how the course material is affecting them intellectually and emotionally and why this is the case. When students respond to the disruption, I identify the ideological positionings that are reflected in the discourses that they espouse, and I help them to discern the differences between their opinions and sociological analyses. This approach recognizes the importance of students' contributions (hooks, 1994) and encourages a deeper exploration of the course content and processes and of how individuals relate differently to these. Still, not all students are able to go on record in the larger class discussions and debates (because of class size, feelings of shyness, and so forth), and thus, in addition to identifying for the class as a whole the types of discourses and ideologies being perpetuated during class discussions (and the contradictions embedded in these), I solicit feedback from students at the end-of-class discussions through one-minute papers or brief questionnaires. When possible, I take field notes during heated discussions. I then prepare a critical, reflective quantitative and qualitative analysis of the data generated by students and present this to the students in subsequent class meetings, engendering further discussion and debate.

Appreciating Cultural Differences

Student resistance to our attempts at transformative learning is attributed in part to cultural differences in worldviews. The transformations in consciousness that we seek reflect our cultural positioning, and they do not always sit well with participants in our multicultural classrooms. For example, disruptions like the guest lectures on lesbian parenting and sex work (as legitimate social pursuits) evoked strong, negative responses from students whose religious investments precluded a consideration of these lifestyles. This result has led us to question our use of disruptions since they do offend some class participants. Another concern that relates to cultural diversity is that requiring students to share reflections as part of a course process can be exploitative, as it may coerce students to reveal information about themselves that they wish to keep private. As Jones (2005) argues, "Our education system is based on the western desire for coherence, authorization, and control. This desire fuels the calls for democratic dialogue, or hearing the voices of the marginalized. These are in effect calls for access to the other, and to the knowledge and experiences of the other" (p. 63).

Encountering Structural Obstacles

The lack of institutional support for a collaborative learning environment is one of the biggest challenges in implementing our constructive teaching and learning strategies. As Shor (1996) argues, the architecture of the room and the quality and (immovable) placement of the furniture in classrooms send messages of inferiority and worthlessness to students; most often it is impossible to rearrange furniture so that people are able to sit in small groups on the same level. The norms that persist in university education and the prior years of schooling work against teachers' enacting collaborative dialogue in class (Shor, 1996). The individualistic, competitive models of evaluation that seem to be imperative at the university level also undermine our attempts to create a collaborative environment. Until collaboration is made an explicit objective in the mission statement of the university and attempts to have classrooms become more interactive, engaged spaces will in all likelihood be met with student resistance. Currently these structural obstacles to collaboration make it necessary for instructors to be very explicit about their transformational, interactive, and engaged purposes and strategic in encouraging students to share these purposes.

REFLECTIONS

Of central importance to us has been our realization that as educators, we too are undergoing transformations as learners, and in order for us to develop our learning process, we must also work with one another collaboratively. So what began as a focus on tutorial teaching grew to include attention to how lecture sessions were conducted and to how we collaborated as a teaching team. Our collaborations have led to a strong sense of community among us, and this was an unexpected outcome. At our location, faculty and graduate students often suffer from the same sense of disconnection from one another and from the university, for the reasons outlined earlier. We believe that our sense of community has provided an integral form of support to us as we work to disrupt taken-for-granted ideas of how teaching and learning are typically done in university. Because we have made relationships an object of importance, there is a sense of well-being among us as teachers. The data suggest that students too feel supported by our sense of community. As Langan wrote in her field notes in April 2005, "Putting collaboration and caring on the agenda has changed the way in which I work with students and with TAs. I feel more accountable to act in ways that demonstrate both collaboration and caring, and my assessment is that this has also helped to nurture caring among students and TAs."

Our research has also made us aware that achieving student transformation is dependent on students' overall experience in a course, as much as on their specific investments in understanding the course content. As one student wrote in reference to the collaborative approach, "In the end, it's not what facts you were able to throw onto a test, but instead, it's the experience you got out of it as a whole." Our maneuvering of the environment in our classrooms represents only one part of the students' experience, and we must ask ourselves how to acknowledge and deal with students' emotions, interactions, and personal situations that are happening both in and outside class. Our student body is multicultural and often very distracted because they have limited finances, work long hours at paid employment, and negotiate for family members who do not speak English. These contexts combine for many of our students and make the demands that accompany their courses especially difficult.

Similarly, emotions, interactions, and personal situations in and outside class influence professors' and TAs' experiences in a course. Increasing faculty workloads and abbreviated times to complete graduate degrees make it very difficult for teachers to devote the time and energy to conceptualizing, implementing, and managing collaborative classrooms, especially when the institutional rewards for good teaching are, for many of us, few and far between. While our project is grounded in the belief that the "learning process...is...dependent upon the creation of support, trust, and friendship with others" (Taylor, 1998, p. 43), most of us are not adequately prepared to manage the complexities that arise in learning environments like the ones we try to create. Although research supports the significance of relationships in transformative learning, "The field [of adult education] neither adequately prepares nor supports adult educators to manage the dynamics of helping relationships or the dynamics of transformative learning within the context of these relationships" (p. 43).

Notwithstanding these challenges, we have learned that for transformations to happen, we must attend to how we as teachers can best be engaged in what we are doing in the classroom. Originally we conceptualized our task as one of transforming the students, but we have come to believe that our collaborations as educators fuel our engagement with the course. Through transforming our teaching practices, we will best teach students. No matter how large the class and no matter how resistant the audience, as educators we must find ways to collaborate with our students and develop relationships with them in the classroom. Given the complexity of collaborative relationships and the large number of students in many courses, the task can often seem too great, too energy depleting. Nonetheless, we bolster each other to maintain our commitment to finding out where our students are at, what they need, and how we can work with them more closely in the classroom. Like Shor (1996), we believe that "the primary goal of shared authority is "to restructure education into something done *by* and *with* students rather than *by* the teacher *for* and *over* them" (p. 148).

REFERENCES

Alvares, B. (2007). *Leadership education and academic development program: An assessment and plan for progress*. Toronto: Faculty of Arts Student Caucus, York University.

Belenky, M., Bond, L., & Weinstock, J. (1997). *A tradition that has no name: Nurturing the development of people, families, and communities*. New York: Basic Books.

Boler, M. (2005). *Democratic dialogue in education: Troubling speech, disturbing silence*. New York: Peter Lang.

Briskin, L. (1998). Negotiating power in the classroom: The example of group work. *Canadian Woman Studies*, *17*(4), 23–28.

Cannon, L. W. (1990). Fostering positive race, class, and gender dynamics in the classroom. *Women's Studies Quarterly*, *1–2*, 126–134.

Craney, G. (2007). "National Survey of Student Engagement." Retrieved April 16, 2009, from www.yorku.ca/secretariat/senate/Student%20Survey%20NSSE.ppt.

hooks, b. (1994). *Teaching to transgress*. New York: Routledge.

Jones, A. (2005). *Talking cure: The desire for dialogue.* In M. Boler (Ed.), *Democratic dialogue in education: Troubling speech, disturbing silence* (pp. 57–67). New York: Peter Lang.

Langan, D. (2001). Talking about violence against women: Deconstructing uncontested discourses. In K. Hunt & C. Saulnier (Eds.), *Feminism(s) on the edge of the millennium: Rethinking foundations and future debates* (pp. 87–106). Toronto: Inanna Publications and Education.

Langan, D., Atkinson, L., Mizuguchi, T., Park, J., Raine, L., Teixeira, R., et al. (2007). TA resource handbook. Toronto: Department of Sociology, York University. Retrieved April 16, 2009, from http://www.arts.yorku.ca/soci/dlangan/working_together/index.html.

Langan, D., & Davidson, D. (2005). Critical pedagogy and personal struggles: Feminist scholarship outside women's studies. *Feminist Teacher*, *15*(2), 132–158.

Langan, D., Oliver, M., & Atkinson, L. (2007). The political is personal: TAs on the front lines of the critical consciousness campaign. *Radical Pedagogy*, 9(1). Retrieved April 16, 2009, from http://radicalpedagogy.icaap.org/content/issue9_1/langan.html.

Mezirow, J. (1991). *Transformative dimensions of adult learning.* San Francisco: Jossey-Bass.

Murphy, M., & Valdéz, C. (2005). Ravaging resistance: A model for building rapport in a collaborative learning classroom. *Radical Pedagogy*, 7(1). Retrieved April 16, 2009, from http://radicalpedagogy.icaap.org/content/issue7_1/murphy-valdez.html.

Sheese, R. (2000). Engaging absence with dialogue. Presentation to the annual meeting of the Society for Teaching and Learning in Higher Education, St. Catharines, ON. Retrieved April 16, 2009, from http://www.stthomasu.ca/~hunt/stlhe/sheese.htm.

Shor, I. (1996). *When students have power: Negotiating authority in a critical pedagogy.* Chicago: University of Chicago Press.

Taylor, E. W. (1998). The theory and practice of transformative learning: A critical review. Columbus, OH: ERIC Clearinghouse on Adult, Career, and Vocational Education (Information Series No. 374).

Thayer-Bacon, B. (1999). The thinker versus a quilting bee: Contrasting images. *Educational Foundations*, *13*(4), 47–56.

Thayer-Bacon, B. (2003). *Relational "(e)pistemologies."* New York: Peter Lang.

CHAPTER FIVE

Facilitating Transformative Learning

Engaging Emotions in an Online Context

John M. Dirkx, Regina O. Smith

On the face of it, educational technology in general, and online or e-learning in particular, seems an odd location in which to look for and consider the poetry and mystery of transformative learning. Early machine-like metaphors used in the design, development, and descriptions of e-learning, such as information processing, artificial intelligence, and the mind as computer, left little room for matters of the heart. Emphasis in these earlier versions of e-learning was placed on transmission and mastery of particular bodies of knowledge and skills. Students in these environments often felt as much connected to themselves and to one another as learners in the old correspondence study programs did. Yet within the past ten years, our understanding of e-learning contexts has evolved considerably.

Driven in part by the introduction of interactive, collaborative, and reflective online learning strategies (Roberts, 2003), many practitioners and scholars now view these contexts as relatively complex epistemic, emotional, social, and linguistic environments that represent their own unique challenges to and opportunities for fostering transformative learning. This growing body of literature suggests various ways in which participation in online learning can evoke one's soul. Early approaches to online transformative learning, however, have been largely predicated on notions of meaning making as rational, reflective, and instrumental. In this chapter, we push further into this frontier of transformative learning by focusing on processes associated with the emotional and symbolic realities of e-learning. Such realities are manifest in the expressive dimensions of the online context. Conceptualized as "inner work" or "soul work" (Dirkx, 1997, 2001, 2006a, 2006b, 2008), we explore how transformative learning may be fostered through thoughtful attention to and imaginative engagement with emotion-laden images and relationships evoked through online collaborative work. We emphasize here the emotional and psychodynamic nature of collaborative learning and how online environments provide evocative contexts for these dimensions of adult learning.

OUR CONTEXT

The context for our work is graduate studies in higher and adult education. In this chapter, we focus specifically on our work in one of these courses, a course in adult learning. Among our goals for this course are fostering a deep understanding of the course content and how it may be used to address difficult problems of practice, the students themselves as learners and as group members, and their relationship to the broader social world. We use problem-based learning (PBL) as the primary instructional approach (Barrows, 1994). A given semester-long course may be composed of three to five problem units, varying in length from one to three weeks. The twenty to twenty-five students in a class represent mostly graduate students from a variety of majors. Although the majority are European American, a significant proportion are persons of color and international students. Because the course is online, it is not uncommon to have students participating from across the world: in England, Turkey, China, Japan, and Saudi Arabia, for example.

Students typically participate in this course as members of heterogeneous e-learning teams of about three to four members each. This size provides potentially diverse perspectives but minimizes logistical problems that might arise in online meetings and communications with a larger number. We construct team assignments to purposively maximize diversity within any given team, using such characteristics as learners' interests and degree programs, prior knowledge and experience, learning styles, race, gender, geographical location, and national origin. Because these differences often engender considerable tension and emotionality within collaborative contexts, learning to work within and across these differences represents the primary location for transformative learning in these online environments. Students have opportunities to interact with one another through different venues, such as classwide discussion forums (whole class interaction), group discussion forums, chatrooms (synchronous interaction), e-mail, and telephone.

DESIGN AND PEDAGOGICAL CONSIDERATIONS

In this section, we focus on several key aspects of this course intended to foster self-work and deep learning (Entwistle & McCune, 2004) among participants. Although our sense of transformative learning is informed by Mezirow's (1991, 2000) concept of perspective transformation, we focus primarily on the emotional and symbolic dimensions of students' experiences. For this reason, we rely on a more depth psychology perspective to transformative learning (Boyd & Myers, 1988). From this perspective, human lives reflect both conscious and unconscious dimensions (Singer, 1994). It is, however, the unconscious aspects of our lives that are the most influential in our decision making and actions. To the extent that we remain unaware or unconscious of the factors or issues that influence our decisions and behaviors, we remain susceptible to being buffeted by the emotional forces that may be activated through our interactions with others or our environment.

A goal of transformative learning informed by depth psychology is to develop a dialogical relationship with one's unconscious, so that its dynamic contents may have creative expression within our conscious lives. This relationship is mediated largely through emotion-laden images, relationships, and behaviors (Dirkx, 2008). The interpersonal and social contexts provided by collaborative work often stimulate such emotionality among individuals and groups, and the computer-mediated nature of online learning contributes to both the frequency and intensity of these emotional experiences.

The uncertainty and ambiguity within the interpersonal interactions and social relations that make up online learning also contribute to the perception of the medium as a kind of Rorschach screen on which learners often project deeply held issues that are giving rise to their experiences of emotion within their interpersonal interactions (Turkle, 1995). For example, one student participating in a research project indicated that she got so angry with her teammates that she felt like putting her foot through the computer screen (Dirkx & Smith, 2003). Both the nature of the suggested act and the emotionality associated with it are symbolic of underlying, unconscious issues within the learner that were stimulated by the social context of the online environment.

The lack of nonverbal cues, as well as the ambiguity of printed words, often stimulates fantasies among participants regarding the other's meaning and intent. For example, we commonly observe students perceiving negative emotional content in typed messages from others, only to learn later that the other learner had no intention at all of sending a negative message. It would seem that the former student is projecting into the uncertain and ambiguous nature of online communication his or her own emotional issues without recognizing that this is occurring.

Several design and instructional characteristics of this course contribute to the activation and exploration of emotional issues among learners and provide a means for them to work with and through these issues in a dialogical manner. These characteristics include (1) use of messy, ill-structured practice-based problems as the central pedagogical focus; (2) interactive and collaborative learning; (3) use of consensus group writing teams, (4) individual and team debriefings; (5) reflective activities; and (6) journal writing. We briefly explain each of these strategies and then discuss how they relate to our overall goal of self-work and self-change, illustrating when appropriate with examples from our own practices.

A defining feature of PBL is the use of ill-structured case scenarios that are realistic and grounded in contexts and situation in which learners are likely to encounter in some form within their future practices. This process includes identifying the problem and the various factors in the case that may be contributing to the problem, prescribing actions that are intended to address these factors and the problem, and anticipating potential challenges to implementing their recommended action plans. Within each of these steps, decisions are reached through consensus. To analyze and discuss the case scenarios, students post their thinking to their team discussion forums or chatrooms and respond to how others are thinking about the case.

We also stress the importance of interaction among the students and the development of collaborative relationships. Our use of collaborative learning reflects Bruffee's (1999) understanding of learning as inherently social, non-foundational, and constructive. We expect students to do more than merely master a body of content. Through their collaborative work, we expect them to develop deeper understandings and meanings of the research and theory being studied, particularly as it relates to themselves and their particular practice settings.

This collaborative learning occurs largely within the context of heterogeneous teams. Team members represent different educational and work experiences, different career interests, and different ages, races, gender, and geographical location. They remain together for the duration of the semester, increasing the likelihood that differences among team members will become evident in the various ways in which they think about and approach the assigned problems and the ways in which they relate to each other and the group as a whole.

The instructor is the overall facilitator for the e-learning teams. Although students have ready access to the instructor through e-mail, discussion forums, or the telephone, their learning is largely self-directed and mediated through the work of the team. The teams are responsible for the analysis and disposition of each problem and the development of a team product that states the problem, contributing factors, and what should be done to address the problem. Decisions within each team are guided by a consensus-group approach.

Because learning from the process is a critical dimension of PBL and of our teaching in these courses, we use reflective writing, journaling, and debriefing activities to help direct students back to the concreteness of their lived experiences within the course and their teams. The reflective writing focuses on the student's intellectual understanding and grasp of the material being studied, especially as it relates to prior experiences and current or projected practice contexts. This writing and interaction are conducted almost exclusively within individual learning logs and the team forums. The journaling process, however, is more of an activity of the heart and is informed by the imaginal method used in depth psychology. Students are instructed to use the journaling assignment for explorations of emotions or affect related to particular ideas, relationships, or interactions that have occurred or are occurring within the course. The goal here is for students to take notice of what is within consciousness around particular issues or relationships for which they might feel quite strongly. Logging these contents occurs within the free-writing portion of the process and usually lasts from five to ten minutes. Following the free-write, students are then asked to reflect on the contents of the free-write, noting any aspects that surprise them or feelings associated with reflecting on these contents. They are expected to make at least weekly journal entries. Only the instructor has access to and is able to read or comment on the journal entries of individual students.

Individual and team debriefings, which occur through discussion forums and chatrooms, are also ways in which we direct students back to their experiences within the course. These debriefings are essential to the PBL process and are conducted at the conclusion of each problem unit. In the debriefings, teams are asked to assess the overall quality of their product and the degree to which they have developed a deeper understanding of the theories, concepts, and ideas that comprise a given unit. Related to our focus on self-work and self-change, however, the teams are asked to also review and assess their group process and the various roles assumed by members of the team.

IMPLEMENTATION OF PEDAGOGICAL STRATEGIES TO FOSTER TRANSFORMATIVE LEARNING ONLINE

In this section, we discuss how the strategies are used within this course to foster deep and transformative learning. Because their use is thoroughly integrated within the context of any given problem-based unit, no attempt will be made to systematically discuss each one separately. The PBL approach simulates real-world contexts for confronting and working through similar situations in practice. To foster a connection to the course, we use reflective activities throughout the problem unit, encouraging students to relate what they are studying to their own experiences. For example, a reflective question regarding participation theory and motivation to learn might ask students to describe their own reasons or motivation for pursuing graduate school. They are then asked to relate their responses to the research and theory they have studied on this topic, the ways in which their own experiences are consistent or inconsistent with this theory, and how they might account for any variations they observe.

One student recently reported that she had never thought about her motivation to learn much before studying participation-related theory. After reading and reflecting on her assignments, she realized that as she grew older, she was becoming less concerned about goal-related issues in learning and more interested in learning for learning's sake. For her, this was something of a new awareness about herself as a learner. Further discussion led to an exploration of why and how vocation and passion seem to become more central to us as we grow older.

The case scenarios are challenging, messy, and ill structured, with no clear sense of the problem, what might be causing or contributing to it, or how to address the situation represented in the case scenario. Because they are intentionally ambiguous, the case scenarios invite learners to make use of their own experiences with and knowledge of similar situations, as well as their understandings of the related literature. As a result, team members generate multiple interpretations of what is going on in the case and what to do about it. Working through these differing interpretations and coming to consensus can be evocative of powerful emotional tensions between team members and within the group. These tensions often become visible within postings made to the team forums or chatrooms, or are sometimes expressed more privately to the instructor through e-mail or telephone calls. Such interactions with members of the student teams require careful thought by the instructor about what is consistent with and facilitative of the transformative focus of the course-related activities. Care has to be given to encourage a group-as-a-whole focus, respect and honor all members of the team, and avoid siding with any single member of the team.

Responding to students' discussion forum posts or e-mails regarding difficult emotional relations or interactions represents an important dimension of our online work to foster self-work and transformative learning. Students' initial responses to the emerging presence of emotions within their interpersonal interactions are often directed at reducing their potentially disruptive effect on their relations and the work at hand. This interpretation of the presence of emotions within their learning reflects the broader tendency within our culture to regard emotions as potentially disruptive of rational and reasonable thought and action. A guiding principle we use in our interactions with students around such issues is to encourage them to hold the tensions represented by these differences and embrace their associated emotionalities. A student might share in an e-mail that she is frustrated and angry with one of her team members for not logging on consistently. Rather than responding at first with suggestions as to what to do about this situation, our interventions aim to learn more about the context in which these feelings arise, what seems to evoke them, and to what the student might attribute their manifestation.

In one team, a member approached the instructor with her sense of frustration over the interpersonal conflict involving two other members of the team. She said she had tried everything, and nothing seemed to work; she was at a loss as to how to help out or move her team forward. The instructor empathized with her frustration and asked for elaboration and description of the kinds of interactions that concerned her. She was then asked if she had experienced similar situations in other groups she had been in and, if so, what the group did to address those situations. Through this engagement, she was able to see in what ways her current situation was both similar to and different from previous experiences and also how she may have been implicitly invested emotionally in the conflict over which she was so concerned.

Another strategy that encourages students to work with emotion-laden images, ideas, or relationships is the use of journaling. This process encourages students to identify emotionally powerful aspects of their learning experiences and work with them in a structured activity. In the free-writing portion of the journal, students often generate information or insights that surprise them about the image, idea, or relationship that they are writing about. In the reflective portion of the journal, they are asked to identify the themes that are present within their free-write and elaborate on what these themes might suggest to them with regard to the meaning of the emotion-laden images. They are encouraged to describe some of these images or ideas in more depth, relate them to other aspects of their experience where they may have noticed their occurrence, and, if they are able, relate these experiences to broader trends within the culture or its current stories and myths.

Finally, the team and individual debriefing provide another opportunity for students to reflect on and further probe their experiences with respect to the focus on self-work and transformative learning. In this part of the debriefing, the questions asked focus on what they as a group have learned about group process and development. Teams are asked to post their debriefings to their team forums, so that others in the course can read and learn from their processing and reflections. Individually team members also reflect on their own performance and learning within the unit, identifying what they have learned from the unit's experiences about the process of adult learning and about themselves as adult learners and as group members. They are asked to post their responses to individual reflection logs, which only the instructors read. As instructors, we read these posts, encouraging elaboration on aspects we feel would benefit from further dialogue. We are alert for emotion-laden images, relationships, and interactions that may be evident within the postings of the team or individual member. We reflect back our perception of these emotion-laden images, which often stimulates the student to elaborate on the issue to which we are referring.

REFLECTIONS

The idea of transformative learning is an illusive concept. Although there is little agreement in the literature as to what constitutes transformative learning or how it occurs within practice, it seems even more difficult as a practitioner to perceive and understand this process in action. When one considers transformative learning and its facilitation within the context of online learning, hope of understanding what this concept means and looks like seems to recede even more. Our own experiences, however, as well as reports in the literature, clearly support the potential of this environment to evoke a kind of deep learning that engages learners in a process of self-work, self-change, and transformation. This potential is intimately bound up with the capacity of this environment to evoke powerful emotional experiences. To ensure that such experiences contribute to processes of change and transformation, emotional expressions and behaviors have to be interpreted as a critical imaginative companion to the rational and reasoned processes that have been used to characterize transformative learning in much of the literature.

We have little doubt that group work within the context of online PBL provides such a context for the manifestation of powerful emotional dynamics among and within learners. From the first e-mail message received from an enrolled student before the course even begins to final notes and remarks contained in the course evaluation, the affect evoked among students by this environment is almost palpable. Much of this emotionality seems to revolve around students' perceptions and fears of group work. They bring to this approach their prior experiences with groups that were not often favorable. While some roll up their sleeves and vow to make it work, others psychologically or even physically withdraw. Addressing their issues, feelings, and emotions around group work in a manner that is truly educative is hard and challenging work. When we have a very frustrated student on the line, we can easily discern the savior mentality rising within our consciousness and urging us to rush in and do something to alleviate the anxiety, frustration, and difficulties that the student is experiencing. Often we may also have images of the ratings on our course evaluations dropping with every passing minute. In such situations, it is hard to just listen, whether on the telephone or online, but listening is often what is required. If we are patient, students often provide a rich narrative of their experiences, which tends to help both them and us as facilitators.

Engaging, accepting, and helping students work through these emotional dynamics is perhaps one of the most difficult and challenging dimensions of a kind of teaching that is guided by the concept of transformative learning, and certainly it is infinitely more difficult in the online environment. As we think back over our work as instructors in online environments, however, our concern rests more with creating educative experiences for our students than specifically fostering transformative learning. Everything that we have said in this chapter is fully consistent with designing and implementing learning experiences that are educative in the sense that John Dewey used that term: that they potentially contribute to the growth of the learner. Our belief is that the potential for transformative learning is inherent in the truly educative experience. We do not believe there is anything about transformative learning that sets it apart from a powerful educative experience.

Ultimately whether a learning experience is transformative rests with the learner, not us as instructors or facilitators. Our work is to help learners make the deep connections with the subject matter that we know is possible. Where those connections lead is not under our control, and it may not be in the conscious control of the learner. There is a kind of mystery to the idea of transformative learning, a way of learning that is more an expression of the creative and artistic dimensions of our being rather than the rational, literal, and scientific. Like the unfolding and metamorphosis of the caterpillar into a beautiful, majestic, and soaring butterfly, the process of transformative learning touches on and reminds us of the fundamental mystery that is being human. As educators, we hold for a time the small, delicate creature in the palm of our hands, but perhaps holding is pretty much all we can do. As it turns out, however, that process of holding represents a complex and challenging activity. We have only just begun to understand what it takes in online environments.

REFERENCES

Barrows, H. S. (1994). *Practice-based learning: Problem-based learning applied to medical education*. Springfield: Southern Illinois University of School of Medicine.

Boyd, R. D., & Myers, J. B. (1988). Transformative education. *International Journal of Lifelong Education, 7*, 261–284.

Bruffee, K. A. (1999). *Collaborative learning: Higher education, interdependence, and the authority of knowledge* (2nd ed.). Baltimore, MD: John Hopkins University Press.

Dirkx, J. M. (1997). Nurturing soul in adult learning. In P. Cranton (Ed.), *Transformative learning in action: Insights from practice* (pp. 79–88). San Francisco: Jossey-Bass.

Dirkx, J. M. (2001). The power of feeling: Emotion, imagination, and the construction of meaning in adult learning. In S. B. Merriam (Ed.), *The new update on adult learning theory* (pp. 63–72). San Francisco: Jossey-Bass.

Dirkx, J. M. (2006a). Engaging emotions in adult learning: A Jungian perspective on emotion and transformative learning. In E. Taylor (Ed.), *Teaching for change* (pp. 15–26). New Directions in Adult and Continuing Education, no. 109. San Francisco: Jossey-Bass.

Dirkx, J. M. (2006b). Design as professional development: The inner and outer journeys of learning to develop online learning. In P. Mishra, M. Koehler, & Y. Zhao (Eds.), *Faculty development by design: Integrating technology in higher education* (pp. 147–165). Charlotte, NC: Information Age.

Dirkx, J. M. (2008). Care of the self: Mythopoetic dimensions of professional preparation and development. In T. Leonard & P. Willis (Eds.), *Pedagogies of the imagination: Mythopoetic curriculum in educational practice* (pp. 65–82). New York: Springer.

Dirkx, J. M., & Smith, R. O. (2003). Thinking out of a bowl of spaghetti: Learning to learn in online collaborative groups. In T. S. Roberts (Ed.), *Online collaborative learning: Theory and practice* (pp. 132–159). Hershey, PA: Idea Group Publishing.

Entwistle, N., & McCune, V. (2004). The conceptual basis of study strategy inventories. *Educational Psychology Review, 16*(4), 325–345.

Mezirow, J. (1991). *Transformative dimensions of adult learning.* San Francisco: Jossey-Bass.

Mezirow, J. (2000). Learning to think like an adult: Core concepts of transformation theory. In J. Mezirow & Associates, *Learning as transformation: Critical perspectives on a theory in progress* (pp. 3–33). San Francisco: Jossey-Bass.

Roberts, T. S. (Ed.). (2003). *Online collaborative learning: Theory and practice.* Hershey, PA: Idea Group Publishing.

Singer, J. (1994). *Boundaries of the soul: The practice of Jung's psychology.* New York: Anchor Books.

Turkle, S. (1995). *Life on the screen: Identity in the age of the Internet.* New York: Simon & Schuster.

CHAPTER SIX

Fostering Transformative Learning in Leadership Development

Joe F. Donaldson

For over a decade, the Department of Educational Leadership and Policy Analysis at the University of Missouri-Columbia (MU) has cooperated with four other Missouri public higher education institutions to offer the Statewide Cooperative Ed.D. Program in Educational Leadership. The degree is offered by MU, but partner institutions participate collaboratively in program governance, curriculum design, and instructional delivery. The program is interdisciplinary in that it serves individuals in leadership positions in both the PK-12 arena and a range of postsecondary educational settings. Students are admitted every two years in cohorts and progress through two years of course work together. The majority of students are midcareer educational professionals, who hold midlevel or entry-level leadership positions in their organizations and continue in their leadership positions throughout the program. The program offers no state certification; rather, its purpose is to enhance the knowledge and competencies of educational leaders.

Course work is organized around five major themes: (1) organizational analysis and teamwork, (2) educational leadership, (3) educational policy, (4) the content and context of learning, with particular foci on adult and organizational learning, and (5) inquiry and evaluation. All cohort members attend course work at the MU campus during the first two summers of the program, forming a statewide cohort that has averaged seventy-six students in size. During fall and spring semesters, students take courses at partner institutions, forming site-specific cohorts.

The comprehensive examination, a portfolio-based written and group-based oral assessment of learning and application, is held at the end of course work. For the written portfolio portion of the assessment, students must develop three connection statements, so called because students are to connect what they have learned in the program and identify implications for practice in their institutions and their own professional practice. Students provide evidence of how they have applied their learning within their professional practice by including artifacts of their work in their portfolios and through their connection statements, which describe how these artifacts demonstrate knowledge application. The comprehensive examination is followed by dissertation research. Students' research has ranged from the basic to the applied, although applied research is the focus of this particular degree.

CONCEPTUAL UNDERPINNINGS AND DISCONNECTS

From its inception, the program has been based on several conceptual frameworks drawn from cognitive psychology, adult learning, and education in the professions. For example, the program is developed around the problems of practice (Harris, 1993). Practice-based problems are introduced by using case studies in classes and assigning students actual problems to address—for example, conducting a program evaluation in which issues of power, interests, and negotiation become central concerns (Cervero & Wilson, 2006). Students evaluate a program rather than just learning about program evaluation. Perhaps more important is the program's orientation to praxis, where theory and practice are joined through reflective processes.

Another design principle recognizes that professional knowledge is not just academic knowledge (or syllabus-based knowledge) but also experiential and personal (Eraut, 1994). Thus, instructors draw on students' knowledge of their own organizational contexts but also subject that experiential and personal knowledge to critical reflection using conceptual frameworks introduced in course work. Furthermore, personal and experiential knowledge must be employed in research if the research results have any chance of changing and improving leadership practice and of supporting reform of the educational organizations in which students work. Thus, the program also draws on espoused theories and theories-in-use that students use in their work (Argyris & Schön, 1974), not solely on the syllabus-based knowledge considered in the classroom.

Despite the use of principles to guide program design and delivery, evidence began to accumulate in about the fifth year of the program that instructional practices being employed were not always leading to desired outcomes. For example, in the oral portion of the comprehensive examination, students would espouse the use of transformative leadership principles in their responses to questions. Yet when pressed about their actual leadership practices, they would uncritically describe events in which they continued to use authoritarian, hierarchical approaches to address organizational problems and work with personnel. Furthermore, in a study of the work of one team of students during a summer program, Donaldson and Scribner (2003) found that students used a product- or task-centered orientation to assignments that focused more on task completion than on learning from the task. This orientation was in part a consequence of recipes for action and structures of work appropriated by students from their administrative work settings (Giddens, 1984). These administrative conventions or latent cultural attributes of a cohort (Brim & Wheeler, 1966) served to lead students to concentrate their efforts on efficiently completing assignments at the expense of taking the time to critically reflect on what they were doing and why.

In a related study, Scribner and Donaldson (2001) found that the cohort structure of the program fostered transformative learning in the affective (or person-to-person) domain, noting:

> A critical finding of this study was how students described changes in their beliefs regarding how they should work with and lead groups of teachers, parents, and other education stakeholders. In essence, their experience in the summer cohort illustrated to them the discrepancy between their self-perceptions and espoused values and how their actions may really be perceived by others. We would argue that the intense cohort experience enabled students to gain knowledge and understanding of their own personal strengths and weaknesses as individuals and professionals [p. 627].

However, the same cohort structure, when joined to performance-based assignments under constraints of time, did less well in fostering transformative learning in the cognitive (person-to-content) domain, where students should be using theoretical knowledge as lenses "to interrogate basic assumptions about problem definitions" and their work (Scribner & Donaldson, 2001, p. 631). Rather, students failed to critically assess their assumptions, knowledge, and actions and instead learned course content in instrumental, nonreflective ways.

Finally, although course work has been developed using adult learning principles, the design of the capstone experience has remained somewhat inconsistent with those principles, creating dissonance between the program's instructional approach and overall purpose and how students' dissertation research was being handled. Most dissertation research has been very similar to doctoral research in which students, as organizational outsiders, explore gaps in the literature and other research topics that contribute more to syllabus-based knowledge than to their own and others' leadership practices.

Program faculty have come to recognize that the form, sequence, and order of the capstone work of an advanced degree program designed to advance educational leadership practice and contribute to educational reform must also achieve praxis. For the most part, however, the type of research students have been conducting has provided little or no reinforcement of their own transformative journey to new types of leadership; their research requires little reflection on their leadership practice and style, much less any attention to reform of their organizations—particularly reform that addresses problems of equity and justice in our educational systems. As a result, students are all too able to recite principles of relational and transformational leadership in their comprehensive exams without actually having had the learning experiences needed to achieve genuine change in how they lead.

Thus, the program is in transition conceptually and in practice. Although steps have been taken to facilitate students' transformative learning, program leaders and faculty have recognized that more can be done.

TRANSFORMATIVE PRACTICES

Program faculty members have employed four major transformative strategies to facilitate the development of students as educational leaders: (1) cohort structure with embedded project teams, (2) role-based case studies, (3) reflective assessment portfolios, and (4) participatory action research. The history of the use of each strategy differs, as does the amount of emphasis placed on each. Nevertheless, every strategy contributes to supporting students' transformative learning.

Cohort Structure and Project Teams

Research has demonstrated that the program's cohort structure has contributed to transformative learning in the affective domain (Scribner & Donaldson, 2001). Scribner and Donaldson's research is consistent with the findings of others that cohorts provide a support structure for students and foster strong relationships among students and instructors, contributing to the overall interdependence among participants. Their work also provides detail about the nature of group dynamics in a cohort that leads to shifts in students' meaning structures about how they relate to others and provide leadership within their organizations. An important realization about cohorts is that they are more than an instructional delivery format. They are, in addition, a form of social organization, with all the characteristics, strengths, and weaknesses of any other organization. Thus, cohorts can act to generate and support change or constrain it, and faculty must deal wisely with them to ensure they foster, rather than hinder, transformative learning.

The cohort can become a community of trust and identity for students, a place where they can try new things, experiment with different roles, and provide support to one another. Faculty help develop this sense of community and identity in several ways. We initiate cohort formation during the admission process when applicants who have made the cut in the paper screening phase of the process are invited to the MU campus to interview and complete a writing and problem-setting activity. Applicants meet each other and faculty members during this time and begin to bond by sharing common experiences before being formally admitted to the program. (Most who survive the paper screening are admitted to the program, so the MU phase of the admission process serves primarily to facilitate socialization and cohort formation.)

The first summer's instructional team (faculty) purposely assigns students to project teams on the basis of maximum diversity in campus location, gender, practice arena (PK-12 or postsecondary), and ethnicity. The purposes of these team assignments are to foster networking across the entire statewide cohort and to place students in diverse teams so they can learn to work effectively with individuals different from themselves. The first instructional activity is for students to use paints and other common art supplies to create and then propose a logo for the entire cohort—a logo that captures the meaning of what they want their cohort to become. This activity allows team members to reflect on how their teams work, as well as to generate a symbol to bind cohort members together with a shared identity.

Project teams are used throughout the program, providing students with authentic experiences in working closely with others. Faculty members help students become effective team players and leaders by providing formal instruction on team dynamics and effective teamwork (Lencioni, 2002). In these teams, students are expected to work through conflicts and tensions, address team climate, and reflect carefully and critically on group norms, roles, and work conventions. A requirement of most courses is that students evaluate their own performance on their team as well as the performance of their teammates. These experiences with others create conditions conducive to students' exploring their personal assumptions, skills, and behaviors. Working in teams provides a venue for challenging personal theories of self-as-leader and self–as-follower, helping make assumptions and behaviors explicit so these can become subjects of critical reflection. Furthermore, students at local sites develop their own particular site-specific social structures and identities, providing local sources of support, membership, and solidarity. Students find that the social structures of the statewide and local cohorts and project teams provide not only support for sharing and critical analysis but also laboratories of practice where students can safely examine their strengths and weaknesses and change their thinking and their practice.

The sense of identity and community developed through the cohort and project teams continues to be supported throughout the students' time in the program and after. We publish an electronic newsletter each semester that communicates cohort news, recognizes the achievement of cohort members, and keeps current students and graduates apprised of program developments. In addition, a cohort reunion and award banquet is held each spring to help students maintain contact with their cohort and foster networking among different cohorts, program graduates, and current students. The statewide and local cohorts and the project teams provide students with peer support, a sense of community, and an identity, necessary but not sufficient ingredients for transformative learning. In many respects, the cohort and the project teams in which students work provide the glue and the foundation needed for students' meaning structures to be critically interrogated and changed through more specific and precisely applied instructional strategies.

Role-Based Case Studies

For the first ten years of the program, case studies were a central feature of the first summer of instruction. Faculty used large, complex cases so students could practice using metaphors of organization (Morgan, 2006) or analytical frames (Bolman & Deal, 2003) to analyze difficult organizational problems (Rittel & Webber, 1973). At times, case complexity, coupled with short deadlines required for project completion, increased the stress and anxiety of students, thereby creating psychological impediments to transformative learning. In summer 2007, faculty tried something new. First, faculty members reduced the complexity of cases to be analyzed and shifted the purpose of the assignment from a sole focus on organizational analysis to a more concentrated focus on problem setting. In addition, problem setting was linked to the design of a participatory action research (PAR) project that required the surfacing of personal assumptions, assumptions underlying the conceptual lenses used to set the problem, and research design assumptions. The revised case study approach also incorporated a form of reflexivity that required students to surface and question personal theories and beliefs. But the exercise went beyond these changes: each student team also had to take on the persona of an actor in the case.

In one case, "Changes at Honey Grove High" (Donaldson, Lopez, & Scribner, 2003), a reform-minded high school principal is confronted with changing demographics within his school and district owing to the influx of immigrants to work at a chicken processing plant that had recently opened. Student teams were randomly assigned the roles of the reform-minded principal, a community activist from the underserved Native American community, a representative of the underserved Latino/a community, a recruiter for the chicken processing plant who also was Latino, and representatives from traditionally oriented white power elites within the community and school system. Taking on these personas required students to think outside their own set of assumptions and analyze their own assumptions in light of those of their persona. Even in cases in which students were assigned comfortable roles (or those of power elites like the ones most students play in their own settings), they were forced to confront the assumptions, interests, and power bases of other personas that were being portrayed by other teams, some of which had marginal power and were seen as "other" by power elites in the case.

Faculty found that by moving to role-based case study, students were forced to move beyond an instrumental focus on knowing and applying course content unreflectively to surface and critically explore assumptions they were using in problem setting. Thus, this particular form of case study helped students confront epistemic and sociocultural distortions that frequently interfere with transformative learning (Mezirow, 1990). Meaning structures of self and of others were being challenged within and between project teams, and transformative cognitive learning was being fostered. Although we have only anecdotal evidence of the efficacy of this strategy, instructional team members have been unanimous in their positive assessment of how this particular strategy has helped the program move students' thinking to more critical levels in which issues of justice now play a more central part in their thinking as educational leaders.

Reflective Assessment Portfolios

A central feature of students' comprehensive examination is the reflective portfolio. Students are required to submit in their portfolios statements that integrate the knowledge base of three of the program themes identified at the start of this chapter. They must also share with readers the implications of this knowledge base for leadership in PK-12 or postsecondary settings and address how they have applied (or not applied, since negative examples are allowed) the knowledge base in their practice. The latter requirement is achieved by students' selecting artifacts of their work to illustrate their use of the knowledge base. Students must make explicit in their written statements how an artifact demonstrates program application, and they must also provide explicit reflection about how the artifact relates to their learning and leadership practice.

This particular transformative learning strategy is perhaps the weakest link in the chain of strategies faculty members employ to foster transformative learning. Faculty designed the portfolio experience deliberately to serve as an ongoing experience in which students engage in order to write about and reflect on their learning, in class and out, much like journaling is frequently used for this purpose. Some faculty have been better than others at encouraging students to draft their connection statements as course work proceeds and to select a range of artifacts for possible use in their portfolios. However, for many faculty and students, a focus on the full potential of developing the portfolio over time is lost in the day-to-day pressures of courses, completing assignments, and work. Instead, many students and their advisors do not attend to the portfolio process until after course work is completed and it is time for the comprehensive examination. Despite this weakness in the implementation of this transformative strategy, faculty believe it can be very effective in fostering critical reflection on leadership beliefs and practices. As a consequence, program leaders have targeted this program component for further attention and improvement over the next several years.

Participatory Action Research

Program leadership has become increasingly concerned about the disconnect among the program's purposes, the instructional approaches used in course work, and the form and function of the program's capstone experience or dissertation. As a result, program leadership and faculty have embarked on a change initiative to move to greater use of PAR for the dissertation and toward common use of PAR as a leadership strategy supporting organizational learning and change that disrupts the status quo (Grogan, Donaldson, & Simmons, 2007).

Action research is a form of applied research that links practice with inquiry in the practice contexts in which students work. It is a form of inquiry that is consistent with the program's design principles and course instructional approaches. It has much potential for achieving the level of praxis required in a practice-based degree. PAR also engages others in the organization as coresearcher and actors, thereby moving away from the external expert feature of much doctoral research to research that is collaborative for all co-inquirers, including the leader.

Action research methodologies, unlike conventional approaches to dissertation research, provide no escape from actual conditions; awareness of personal leadership assumptions, beliefs, knowledge, and practices; the tensions of practice; and organizational realities that demand change. Action research requires both critical reflection and action by leaders to change the structures that constrain their own leadership performance and their organization's performance in fostering the learning of others. Action research prepares students to engage in cyclical, integrated processes of action, learning, and change (Coghlan & Brannick, 2005) in their leadership practice during the program and after. Action research is, in short, a form of inquiry that fosters transformative learning.

The movement to use action research in the program is challenging faculty members as well as students, and thereby creating transformative opportunities for both. Faculty are learning how advising differs for action research, are grappling with issues of problem setting within students' own organizations, and are visiting together as an intellectual and practice community to assist each other in addressing a range of other issues about this different form of dissertation research. But faculty and students are also seeing the fruits of this approach. It has permitted faculty to direct questions to students about students' roles as co-inquirers and how that role differs from that of authoritarian leader. PAR has brought to some students an awareness of how hierarchical they are in working with others in their organizations and has also served as a catalyst for others in critically reflecting on their approaches to leadership and research.

The inclusion of PAR in the program has served to tie the transformative dimensions of the program together. PAR's practice is fostered in the safety of a cohort structure: lessons learned about working in teams transfers to working with co-inquirers, and role-based case study provides students practice in setting problems, dealing with justice and equity issues, and seeing problems from other perspectives. Furthermore, the practice-based problems that students address in their organizations and are illustrated in portfolio artifacts have the potential of becoming research problems to be addressed using PAR.

REFLECTIONS

Perhaps the most important thing I have learned in writing this chapter is that transformative learning begets transformative learning. Throughout the program's history, and especially during the past three years, program instructors have been collectively exploring a range of ideas about action research, learning, and instructional strategies that promote critical reflection on personal theories and foster change in leadership practices and reform of educational institutions. Complementing this exploration of new ideas has been a program tradition of openness to evaluative feedback from students and external evaluators in order to continually improve the program. These two factors, along with faculty openness to personal learning and reflection, have led to deepened understanding of the conceptual underpinnings of this professional program and how it differs from the doctorate. It has given faculty the courage to ask hard questions about the program and experiment with program delivery in order to strengthen the program's capacity to foster critical reflection and personal and organizational transformation. Most important, faculty increasingly model transformative learning for students. They are also using their deepened understanding to infuse the program with strategies that promote students' transformative learning.

Arguments are made that much of transformative learning is individual and occurs in the heads and hearts of individuals. But as my examples have richly illustrated, transformative learning occurs with others in social organizations, whether in organizations in which learners work or in those that we educators contrive to support the learning of our students. At least in our program, in which we focus on leadership as a relational social practice, learning is distributed and occurs as action is taken with others in context. I cannot conceive of being able to achieve the transformative results I have witnessed in this program in the absence of the cohort, teamwork, and participation with others as colearners and co-inquirers.

I am also increasingly convinced from scholarly and practice perspectives that PAR holds great promise for a practice-based program aimed at enhancing educational leadership and educational reform. Progress made in PAR in Europe, Australia, New Zealand, and North America over the past decade has built, in rigorous and creative ways, on a number of adult education principles developed by Kurt Lewin, Paulo Freire, Myles Horton, and others to foster collective awareness, critical reflection, and the transformation of adult lives.

REFERENCES

Argyris, C., & Schön, D. A. (1974). *Theory in practice: Increasing professional effectiveness*. San Francisco: Jossey-Bass.

Bolman, L. G., & Deal, T. E. (2003). *Reframing organizations: Artistry, choice, and leadership* (3rd ed.). San Francisco: Jossey-Bass.

Brim, O. G., & Wheeler, S. (1966). *Socialization after childhood*. Hoboken, NJ: Wiley.

Cervero, R. M., & Wilson, A. L. (2006). *Working the planning table: Negotiating democratically for adult, continuing, and workplace education*. San Francisco: Jossey-Bass.

Coghlan, D., & Brannick, T. (2005). *Doing action research in your own organization* (2nd ed.). Thousand Oaks, CA: Sage.

Donaldson, J. F., Lopez, G. R., & Scribner, J. P. (2003). Changes at Honey Grove High. *Journal of Cases in Educational Leadership*, *6*(1), 11–26. Retrieved April 13, 2009, from http://jel.sagepub.com/content/vol6/issue1/.

Donaldson, J. F., & Scribner, J. P. (2003). Instructional cohorts and learning: Ironic uses of a social system. *Journal of School Leadership*, *13*(6), 644–665.

Eraut, M. (1994). *Developing professional knowledge and competence*. London: Falmer.

Giddens, A. (1984). *The constitution of society*. Berkeley: University of California Press.

Grogan, M., Donaldson, J. F., & Simmons, J. (2007). Disrupting the status quo: The action research dissertation as a transformative strategy. In C. A. Mullen, T. Creighton, F. L. Dembowski, & S. Harris (Eds.), *The handbook of doctoral programs in educational leadership: Issues and challenges* (pp. 76–89) Houston, TX: National Council of Professors of Educational Administration Press/Rice University.

Harris, I. B. (1993). New expectations for professional competence. In L. Curry, J. Wergin, & Associates, *Educating professionals: Responding to new expectations for competence and accountability* (pp. 17–52). San Francisco: Jossey-Bass.

Lencioni, P. (2002). *The five dysfunctions of a team: A leadership fable.* San Francisco: Jossey-Bass.

Mezirow, J. (1990). How critical reflection triggers transformative learning. In J. Mezirow & Associates, *Fostering critical reflection in adulthood: A guide to transformative and emancipatory learning* (pp. 1–20). San Francisco: Jossey-Bass.

Morgan, G. (2006). *Images of organization* (updated ed.). Thousand Oaks, CA: Sage.

Rittel, H.W.J., & Webber, M. M. (1973). Dilemmas in a general theory of planning. *Policy Sciences, 4,* 155–169.

Scribner, J. P., & Donaldson, J. F. (2001). The dynamics of group learning in a cohort: From non-learning to transformative learning. *Educational Administration Quarterly, 37*(5), 605–636.

CHAPTER SEVEN

Mentoring

When Learners Make the Learning

Alan Mandell, Lee Herman

*Our educational institutions—those
inspiring, impossible, frustrating,
appealing, appalling systems within
which we usually try simply to find
the space and time to do our work of
teaching and learning.*
—Elizabeth Minnich, *Transforming Knowledge*

By definition, all learning means change. Someone learns, and something is different: a behavior, an attitude, a skill, a rule, a role, or even a way of looking at oneself and the world. For human beings, learned change occurs in every context of life. In this chapter, we focus on learned change occurring among adult students in college. Traditionally, the content and method of learning are prescribed by professors and polices. By contrast, we explore learning that students define for themselves and with their faculty mentors. This kind of independent, collaborative learning transforms the ways institutions operate and the ways in which students and professors think about their roles. When everyone becomes a learner, the institution becomes more democratic or "participatory" (Fischer, 1990, p. 31), study is not divorced from real life, and curricula are no longer fixed. When learners make the learning, learning becomes surprising, inventive, and free.

We are faculty members in a college of a state university system, a college dedicated to practicing student-centered learning. The students are generally working adults, seeking to complete college degrees, usually for practical reasons such as career advancement. Their experience on the job, in communities, and with their families is welcomed as an important source of prior learning and of materials and ideas for new studies. The faculty, who are called "mentors," work individually with their students. Students and mentors collaborate through the creation of topic-specific learning contracts and entire curricula.

These collaborative arrangements offer many opportunities for students to contribute ideas based on their experiences and goals. The mentors help the students shape those ideas into manageable, credit-bearing academic learning.

In this way, mentors become learners, and students become teachers. Mentors need to understand who their students are and what will help them learn. Students need to discover what they want to learn and then help their mentors understand these things. In such a reconfiguration of the traditional educational relationship, there are important role shifts: everyone becomes a teacher and a learner. This mentor-student relationship is, furthermore, grounded in the organization, policies, procedures, and customary practices of the institution. An entire college thus opens opportunities for students to create their own educations. The faculty can share authority with students, who thereby learn academic independence, and the institution itself is flexible enough to accommodate and support these as core academic activities. Mentoring transforms the conventional roles and structures of the academy. We believe, in fact, that there is a strong affinity between transformational learning and mentoring.

At the heart of both transformative learning and mentoring is critical reflection on customary academic roles. The mentor-student relationship could not exist unless teachers remind themselves that their role is not so much to profess as to facilitate, and equally, students understand that their role is not so much to absorb what is professed but to place their ideas and questions at the center of learning. These changes of habit do not occur automatically. They require ongoing attention, thought, and practice. They require reflection on the part of both mentor and student: "Through reflection we *see through* the habitual way that we have interpreted the experience of everyday life in order to reassess rationally the implicit claim of validity made by a previously unquestioned meaning scheme or perspective" (Mezirow, 1991, p. 102). The student taking on this responsibility necessarily is acting more autonomously than someone who is, for the most part, dutifully working to assimilate the learning prescribed in the syllabus. The mentor encourages the student by being a *"facilitator* and *provocateur"* (emphasis in original; Mezirow, 1997, p. 11). Consequently, the mentor is necessarily divesting some measure of traditional authority to the student. The result is that even in a dialogue between a single student and mentor, a small democracy is enacted.

Finally, a transformed institutional context is necessary if this mentor-student relationship is conceived as the main academic activity of a college. Such a college would certainly perform its traditional function of conserving and transmitting the knowledge generally regarded as most worth having. However, as mentor-student learning ripples through the institution, the college learns (through policymaking, hiring practices, faculty development, and student orientation) to become a culture in which the learning it values most can thrive.

In the remainder of this chapter, we explain more thoroughly what mentoring is, especially what it means for students to "make the learning." We do so first by generally describing the principles that define and shape the practice of mentoring. Then we present four cases that demonstrate those principles in action.

The core of mentoring has to do with provisionality and uncertainty. These qualities, we find, open possibilities for sharing authority and inventive intellectual collaboration between student and mentor. However, with this freedom comes incompleteness. Not only is one's learning (whether that of mentor or student) never finished, every opportunity for learning offers any number of reasonable educational responses. Therefore, our case studies do not identify the outcomes we actually achieved or others we might recommend. Instead, we invite readers to consider how they might have responded to these students in a way consistent with mentoring and transformational learning.

THE PRINCIPLES OF MENTORING

Mentoring has many meanings and applications to learning of all kinds. Academic mentoring, as a way that faculty foster student learning, is fundamentally a commitment to entering into dialogue with students, centered on questions and purposes that come from the student. Although academic mentoring cannot be reduced to a recipe, the commitment can be expressed as a set of practical principles that inform and guide behavior in planning and reflection (Herman & Mandell, 2004). The principles of academic mentoring amount to an explication of dialogue.

Genuine dialogue means a surrender of authority to uncertainty. That is, the participants, including the teacher, collaborate with the acknowledgment that because "there are no stupid questions or final answers" (Freire & Faundez, 1989, p. 37), all topics and questions become valuable. As a result, normal professional expertise becomes less valuable. Therefore, the first principle of mentoring is that you act so that what you believe you know is only provisionally true. Education becomes an "experiment" (Kant, 1971).

In order for the teacher to shift from expert to learner and for the student to shift from novice to competent participant, both must respect one another as fully autonomous collaborators (Habermas, 1993; Yorks & Marsick, 2000). This shift can be both cognitively and emotionally "wrenching" (Kegan, 1994, p. 275). We are asking ourselves and our students to "leave the mental homes [we] have furnished and made familiar" (p. 272). By making the occasion of the dialogue something that comes strongly from the students—that is, something they believe is important and are familiar with—they can then bring to the dialogue information, ideas, questions, and purposes that could not, by definition, come from the mentor alone. Rather, the mentor must be a "receptive presence" (Daloz, 1999, p. 246). Moreover, since people learn best what they care about, centering the learning on students motivates and empowers them. In contrast to a conventional set of academic offerings, this principle makes curriculum something that is endlessly shifting and diverse.

And so often curiosity begins in our everyday lives, the lifeworld (Welton, 1995). For those of us who are academics, this likely includes the world of scholarship, but for nearly anyone else, the lifeworld means myriad instances and contexts in which we have to make decisions and accomplish things in order to get along and thrive. Thus, in mentoring, seemingly mundane concerns about family, career, community, beliefs, friendship, and so on can be taken up as inspirations for profound and increasingly learned academic study. Learning from and for ordinary experience makes academic learning meaningful (Mandell & Herman, 2007).

Assessing the learning gained is no longer the simple and apparently complete system of administering tests and measurements entirely driven by the teacher and the institution. Therefore, however strange and "exceedingly difficult after so many years of others evaluating you" (student quoted in Shapiro, 2006, p. 59) this may feel, mentor-student dialogue requires that students become participants in goal setting and evaluation as much as they have been in shaping the study. In the context of formal academic study, this means that while the institution and faculty remain responsible for the final and official assessment, it must be strongly influenced by what students believe they have achieved. Just as student and mentor together need to reflect critically on what they are doing, their assessment of the outcomes is also part of the learning process.

The final principle has to do with the communal importance of this highly individualized approach to academic learning. It rests on the assumption that all things are connected. However seemingly personal or idiosyncratic the starting moment of inquiry might be, eventually the learning will lead by questions and investigations to subjects that human beings generally care about. Honoring one person's curiosity will lead to knowledge most worth having.

These principles represent attitudes by which mentors and students solve educational problems and make cognitive changes. These transformations, large or small, are the principles of mentoring in action. They can occur in any academic encounter and in a variety of ways. Before we present examples, here are the principles of mentoring: provisionality of belief, collaboration of autonomous agents, the indefinite diversity of curriculum, centrality of the student's lifeworld, collaborative evaluation, and the necessary link between individual curiosity and the knowledge most worth having.

FOUR EXAMPLES OF MENTORING

These examples of the principles of mentoring in action (with names and details altered to respect the privacy of the students) illustrate how mentoring can address a typical variety of issues adult college students and their faculty mentors encounter: academic standards, personal life and academic life, academic evaluation of meaningful learning, and curricular tradition and innovation. We have described each case so as to make clear both the problematic issues and the applicability of mentoring principles. However, we have refrained from offering our own solutions to each case because, consistent with the first principle of mentoring, provisionality, and uncertainty, there are many possible solutions, and our readers might imagine some better than our own.

Kathy: Tinkering with the System

Kathy is in the wrong course, an advanced history course on the Reformation, at the worst possible time. This is her final semester of financial aid and support from her employer. She has almost no background in history, she is not doing well, and she cannot transfer to another course. If she does not pass, she will not graduate—and will not be able to for the foreseeable future. She will also lose any chance at the promotion in human resource management she had long been counting on.

When we talk, I see that Kathy is anxious, contentious, and glum: she thinks she will fail, she believes she is not really responsible for her situation, and she has no idea what to do. I think she is about right: her work is poor; she wound up in the study through a combination of chance, an advisor's negligence, and her own inattention; and I am not sure either how to solve the problem.

After we both pause and calm down, I ask Kathy if anything at all stands out for her in this history study, anything that piques her curiosity. She says, "Martin Luther." I ask, "What about him?" It turns out that she is amazed at this insider's audacity. Luther reminds her of some of her own struggles to improve the human resource practices of her corporation. I ask some more about that and learn that in both the advanced management courses she has taken and her management-level work experience, she has dealt with many organizational resistances to change.

I begin to wonder if somehow she could apply what she has learned about the intricate and shifting politics of organizations to understanding the Reformation. If she could, then maybe I could comfortably tinker with the study syllabus to accommodate and reward the learning that was meaningful to her.

Barbara: Integrating Academic Study with Lifeworld Experience

At the start of Barbara's independent study on social class, the mentor knew only that she was a single mother supporting two sons and was thrilled to be completing her degree. Social Class in America began as a rather conventional independent study that the mentor had offered many times.

Barbara's early essays were straightforward—reasonably good summaries of selections by Marx and Weber, Sennett and Cobb's *The Hidden Injury of Class* (1993), and on a book of personal statements about class, *Class Matters* (*New York Times,* 2005). During a telephone conversation about *Class Matters,* I invited Barbara to expand on a point she had made about the vulnerability of those (as she put it) "whose health care was reduced to the emergency room." "How many people are in this position?" I asked. "How unusual is this?" Barbara was quick to respond, but then there was an unusual silence:

BARBARA: Do you mind if I say something personal? I'm not sure it's relevant.

MENTOR: If you'd like.

BARBARA: I don't have any health insurance. It doesn't come with either of my two jobs, with the county or as a waitress. I can't afford it.

MENTOR: Do you mind if I ask you a question?

BARBARA: Shoot.

MENTOR: You've read about "the working poor" and their health care situation and especially their fears about anyone in their family getting sick. Do you worry?

BARBARA: All the time. But my boys are healthy, and I am too, and I'd rather buy them new shirts or take them to dinner a few times a month than pay the medical premium.

Barbara had taken a risk: she had offered her personal world. And as I listened to her, I wanted to reciprocate, to take a risk too: to shift the direction of this tutorial to focus on Barbara's experiences. But what form could this new inquiry take? How could Barbara learn from asking questions about her lifeworld within the context of an academic study?

Bill: Academic Evaluation of the Lifeworld

Just as studies so drained of meaning as to become merely academic are disappointingly trivial, those overfilled with significance can drown students and mentors in bewilderment. The mentor is as uncertain about what and how to evaluate as the student is confused about what and how to learn.

Bill is a middle-aged professional deliberately taking stock of his life. He wants to learn to be happier and believes that he can do so in part by studying great works of literature and intellect that address "the good life." These are works by authors he ignored as much as he prudently could while he devoted his former university studies and subsequently successful career to business and economics. Now he believes that studying these classic texts—he presents me with a long, imposing list—will make his life better. Bill's educational purpose is fascinatingly and eccentrically pragmatic. He is no more interested in retiring a liberal arts requirement than in becoming an academic scholar. But Bill does insist that reading Dickens, Plato, Freud, Shakespeare, and others will help him be a happier human being.

How can we plan such a project? Both of us are very clear this is an academic study. It is not therapy, religious instruction, or spiritual exercise; nor, for that matter, is it simply entertainment for a lively curiosity. But exactly what, then, shall be the learning Bill undertakes? And how would I, could I, presume to evaluate his success? Although I closely know all the works Bill wishes to study, my own learning from them has taught me, if any wisdom at all, to be very uncertain of the goodness of my own life and especially wary of evaluating the quality of another's. What evaluative criteria could we agree to? What would be responsibly academic? And what would address the learning Bill wanted to achieve: a better understanding of happiness?

Carl: Curricular Diversity and the Knowledge Most Worth Having

Carl, who had previously attended three universities and spent ten years on Wall Street, needed a degree. His early interest in technology, mathematics, and the sciences was reflected in the courses that he had taken and had been deepened by significant experience in the professional world of software and database systems. Certainly there would be a way to incorporate Carl's solid math and science foundation, his overall strong academic skills, and his facility with servers, programming, and computer system security into an academic degree. But Carl did not want a curriculum like many others he had found in information technologies.

Carl was fascinated by the myriad connections between Internet technologies and empathy. Instead of new courses in data structures and server applications (areas already part of his professional experience), Carl wanted to learn more about humanistic psychology; about the transformation of technologies and their effects on daily patterns of communication; about "meneplexes," mirror and spindle neurons; about monkey and elephant communities; and about what he described as "the rise in the antiempathy of the purely competitive."

To Carl, these cross-disciplinary problems were quite intelligible, but I was often puzzled by the twists and turns of his vivid curiosity. Indeed, while I carefully listened to Carl's new insights, I was often taken by his enthusiasm. After all, who would not wish for a world that was at once compassionate and sophisticated? I wanted his degree program to work. But I wondered how well anyone else could understand it, how academically prepared Carl was to accomplish it, and even whether one could transform and unify (in an undergraduate degree, no less) a culture of empathy and technology.

REFLECTIONS

These four situations present different academic problems. For Kathy, how can the institution be flexed to help her learn what she must but ostensibly cannot? For Barbara and her mentor, the problem has to do with appropriately balancing the personal and the general within an academic project. In Bill's case, both he and his mentor have to decide how the learning Bill wants can be evaluated without the mentor prescribing and the college authorizing a particular version of individual happiness. Carl, like Barbara, is also dealing with a problem of integration. However, he is trying to integrate within a coherent, legitimate curriculum professional and academic learning from different disciplines and apparently dissonant worldviews.

There is nothing unusual about students' feeling tensions between what they would really like to learn and what the academy offers to them. Conventionally an advisor helps students make curricular selections close to their desires. And as for the remaining distance between desire and what is on the courseware shelf, students assume they have to adapt. But mentoring transforms this situation. Students no longer need practice the ''rueful acquiescence'' (Rorty, 1998, p. 6) of simply taking what is offered. Now the difference between student curiosity and purpose, on the one hand, and what is academically and institutionally given, on the other, becomes the central educational question.

From a mentoring perspective, these tensions and questions are taken as serious academic matters. For example, what the college already has to offer is understood to be incomplete, according to the first principle of mentoring, which points to the provisionality of knowledge claims. Once Kathy, Barbara, Bill, and Carl's questions or problems become starting places of academic inquiry, they and their mentors are pitched into a collaborative, dialogical relationship, the second principle of mentoring. They have to help each other learn what is called for. Roles shift. Everyone, as per the third principle, becomes a learner and a teacher. Moreover, both the points of origin and application of this new learning, whatever it exactly turns out to be, are the lifeworlds of the students (the fourth principle). For example, Kathy will graduate and likely find inspiration in Martin Luther for her own efforts to make human resource practices more equitable. Barbara's experiences with the disadvantages of eking out a living will help her better understand theories of the workings of a class-stratified society. As to the fifth principle, collaborative evaluation, Bill will have to help his mentor devise relevant criteria for assessing the learning he wants. And the mentor will have to be clear with Bill and with himself that he cannot presume to give an academic evaluation of Bill's life.

Finally, it is essential to appreciate how much these students have learned and how important their learning is. Bateson eloquently describes this appreciation as "learning as homecoming" (1994, p. 206). Who would presume to say, contrary to the last principle of mentoring, that a college graduate who uses her history studies in her workplace, that a single parent empowered by a broader understanding of her status, that a successful professional able to take stock of his life, and that a student, like Carl, eager to explore and possibly invent learning that transforms the curriculum, that these students are not seeking knowledge most worth having? This appreciation is not only an acknowledgment of prior learning; it is also part of the core, daily practices of dialogical learning (Herman, 2004).

Mentoring involves large, visible features, such as the organization, policies, and procedures of an academic institution. And it also invests small interactions between students and faculty, such as adjusting course content so that a student can take advantage of her strengths. But whether big or small, these involvements mean changes in the conventional ways most universities have operated. Collectively they amount to a transformation of learning. The heart of this transformation is that in big things and small, the student has an authoritative voice: the learners make the learning.

Indeed, it is important to appreciate that even the most profound transformation is rarely spectacular. Learners make the learning not so much because policy or methodological rules prescribe them, but rather from the character of a relationship and the attitudes of the participants in it. This educational collaboration grows gradually and, but for small moments, is often invisible. As Daloz (1999) observes, "Transformations rarely, if ever, come about abruptly. Rather, they slip into place piece by piece until they become suddenly visible, often to others first and only later to ourselves" (p. 59).

Who can predict what question from a mentor, comment from a student, or period of silence they both spontaneously observe will reverberate? Who can know what opportunities open when a learning community does not prescribe the learning of "the educated person" but rather confidently respects the ability of learners to choose what is next? How could one ever reasonably assume that the agreement a particular mentor and student make between their individual understandings of how best to proceed could not be different and better?

We have sought to embody in our examples the importance of this chronic and collaborative reflective awareness by concluding each one with a question about how the student and mentor might proceed. We did not want to present the actual academic outcome, lest it be thought the only good solution. We have tried to cultivate this collaborative reflective awareness while writing this chapter. We wrote every word together. Moreover, we realized as we reflected about our mentoring that we could write the chapter to echo the first essential principle of mentoring: act so that what you believe you know is only provisionally true. Not presenting our solutions to the cases makes the point that other solutions are possible and could be better. It could also be that the greatest virtue of mentoring is that practitioners not suppose that they know the best way to learn, not suppose that they can predict the consequences and significance of that learning, and not even suppose that they themselves are the important agents of transformation.

REFERENCES

Bateson, M. C. (1994). *Peripheral visions: Learning along the way*. New York: Harper-Collins.

Daloz, L. A. (1999). *Mentor: Guiding the journey of adult learners*. San Francisco: Jossey-Bass.

Fischer, F. (1990). *Technocracy and the politics of expertise*. Thousand Oaks, CA: Sage.

Freire, P., & Faundez, A. (1989). *Learning to question: A pedagogy of liberation*. New York: Continuum.

Habermas, J. (1993). *Moral consciousness and communicative action* (C. Lenhardt & S. W. Nicholsen, Trans.). Cambridge, MA: MIT Press.

Herman, L. (2004). Love talk: Educational planning at Empire State College, the State University of New York. In E. Michelson & A. Mandell (Eds.), *Portfolio development and the assessment of prior learning*. Sterling, VA: Stylus.

Herman, L., & Mandell, A. (2004). *From teaching to mentoring: Principle and practice, dialogue and life in adult education*. New York: Routledge.

Kant, I. (1971). *Education* (A. Churton, Trans.). Ann Arbor: University of Michigan Press.

Kegan, R. (1994). *In over our heads: The mental demands of modern life*. Cambridge, MA: Harvard University Press.

Mandell, A., & Herman, L. (2007). The study and transformation of experience. *Journal of Transformative Learning, 5*(4), 339–353.

Mezirow, J. (1991). *Transformative dimensions of adult learning*. San Francisco: Jossey-Bass.

Mezirow, J. (1997). Transformative learning: Theory to practice. In P. Cranton (Ed.), *Transformative learning in action: Insights from practice* (pp. 5–12). New Directions for Adult and Continuing Education, no. 74. San Francisco: Jossey-Bass.

Minnich, E. K. (2004). *Transforming knowledge* (2nd ed.). Philadelphia: Temple University Press.

New York Times. (2005). *Class matters*. New York: Holt.

Rorty, R. (1998). *Achieving our country*. Cambridge, MA: Harvard University Press.

Shapiro, H. S. (2006). *Losing heart: The moral and spiritual miseducation of America's children*. Mahwah, NJ: Erlbaum.

Sennett, R., & Cobb, J. (1993). *The hidden injuries of class*. New York: Norton.

Welton, M. R. (Ed.). (1995). *In defense of the lifeworld*. New York: SUNY Press.

Yorks, L., & Marsick, V. J. (2000). Organizational learning and transformation. In J. Mezirow & Associates, *Learning as transformation* (pp. 253–281). San Francisco: Jossey-Bass.

CHAPTER EIGHT

Transformative Approaches to Culturally Responsive Teaching

Engaging Cultural Imagination

Elizabeth J. Tisdell, Derise E. Tolliver

The Seventh International Transformative Learning Conference, held in Albuquerque, New Mexico, in 2007, focused on dealing with diversity. In keeping with both the theme of the conference and the local area, a number of sessions drew on Native American and Mexican cultural traditions. The opening plenary was particularly inspiring and featured Cheo Torres and Arturo Ornales on the transformative power of the *curandero,* or healer, in Mexican culture. It ended with a slam poetry performance by Damian Flores. Two poems about his grandparents were particularly powerful—full of rich images behind powerful words, reminiscent of the *mestiza* culture in which he was raised, that came to life in the rhythmic movement of his body, the flash of his eyes, the modulation of his voice, the cadence of his intonation, and the passion of his spirit.

The three presenters at the opening plenary demonstrated a strong engagement with multiple forms of knowing and their own cultural imagination, and in so doing, they invited at least some of the participants to engage with theirs. They moved in their physical bodies, used some Spanish words, expressed a range of emotion, and engaged a passion that connected with the hearts and minds of participants as they told stories of transformation that sprang from their own cultural connectedness. In essence, they engaged the audience in a form of culturally responsive education; they drew directly on their own cultural stories and experience, which caused at least some participants to reflect on not only these speakers' cultural stories but their own as well.

It is our contention that in order to do culturally responsive education, educators must do what Torres, Ornales, and Flores did so well: engage what we refer to here as their own cultural imagination and that of their class participants in the learning process. Both of us have been trying to engage in culturally responsive teaching about diversity and equity issues in higher education for a long time by drawing on multiple ways of knowing and cultural imagination to facilitate transformative learning. This is precisely what culturally responsive education aims to do: find a way to help participants connect to their own cultural roots and that of others. Our purpose in this chapter is to describe what we mean by cultural imagination and then explore how we engage in culturally responsive teaching for transformative learning in our respective higher education settings.

DEFINING CULTURAL IMAGINATION

There has been some discussion in recent years on the importance of attending to imagination in teaching and learning. Educational philosopher Maxine Greene (1995) highlights the important role that imagination plays in knowledge construction processes and suggests that educators should nurture imagination. She argues that drawing on learners' ability to imagine increases their ability to see multiple perspectives and suggests that educators can draw on the arts to release imagination to facilitate dialogue that helps students experience the multiple ways in which they and others (including those from different cultural groups) relate to the world. Dirkx (2006) takes a Jungian perspective on imagination, more from the perspective of how it helps educators know themselves more fully so they can teach out of a greater sense of their own authenticity. He suggests working with images that arise out of emotional experiences and that engagement with such images can serve as a gateway to a deeper understanding of one's self on a soul level that can affect teaching and learning.

We suggest that working with images that arise out of conscious and unconscious memory specifically around aspects of one's culture is a way of engaging cultural imagination that can potentially lead to transformative learning. Culture is never static. We are always in the process of making further meaning of prior experiences, including those specifically related to culture. We reweave new patterns of meaning by combining new threads of cultural experiences with the old threads. Image, symbol, music, art, poetry: they are nearly always related to culture and touch off memory often in unconscious ways. Florio-Roune (2001) describes cultural imagination as the process of people engaging their cultural histories and then reshaping these histories in light of their moment-to-moment engagements and discussion as they weave new threads of meaning about our own and others' cultural lives. Typically in hearing others discuss aspects of their cultural histories, we are flooded with images and memories of our own cultural histories. Working with such images and discussing them in the classroom is engaging cultural imagination.

It is crucial to our work as culturally responsive educators to not just talk about cultural issues but to engage learners in a way that enhances a sense of hope and creative response in trying to create a more equitable society (Huber, Murphy, & Clandinin, 2003; Tisdell, 2007). Engaging and working with cultural imagination in the higher education classroom can lead to transformative learning. It is also potentially a way of responding to Laura Rendón's (2000) call to higher educators in her outgoing speech as president of the Association for the Study of Higher Education that it is time to "blend the scientific mind with the spirit's artistry" (p. 1).

ENGAGING CULTURAL IMAGINATION IN OUR PRACTICE

Each of us teaches classes that deal with diversity and equity issues in higher education settings, and we both draw on cultural imagination in our attempts at culturally responsive education. We each are attempting to help students understand issues of structural power relations and how positionality (race, culture, gender, class, sexual orientation) shapes access to education and classroom dynamics, as well as how these social systems have informed the construction of their own cultural identities. We attempt to build community in the classroom by dealing directly with aspects of our own positionality and drawing on aspects of cultural story, cultural symbol, through narrative, music, art, and poetry. Although we have discussed some of this elsewhere (Tisdell, 2007; Tolliver & Tisdell, 2006), particularly in how this at times can connect to spirituality and transformative learning, our purpose here is to consider how we draw on cultural story and cultural symbol specifically to engage students' cultural imagination as a way to cultivate a greater sense of agency to effect change. Because we are women of different race and cultural identities and teach in different higher education contexts, we now speak in separate voices to consider aspects of cultural imagination in our own personal stories, as well as how we draw on it in our own classes.

Libby Tisdell: Engaging Knowledge "Until It Becomes You"

I am an educator whose life and work have been shaped by my largely white Irish-American-Catholic cultural roots, complete with big families, memories of Catholic grade school, going to Mass every Sunday, and large holiday gatherings with extended family. There is also a peppering of some sprinkled wisdom from my assimilated but Danish-born grandmother who had moved to the United States when she was sixteen and who died when I was nine.

My cultural imagination is sparked through music, poetry, and visual images I see in the media, as well as nighttime dreams, daydreams, and images I create from hearing stories of others or reading novels, though I am rarely conscious specifically of the ways I am engaging my imagination in those processes. I was consciously aware of the sparking of my cultural imagination most recently at the transformative learning conference. Listening to Damian Flores's slam poems about his grandparents and the *mestiza* culture that informed them touched off a long-forgotten image of more than forty years ago of my Danish-born grandmother. I was at her house with one of my brothers; she had just received a letter written in Danish. She was legally blind in her later years and could not see well enough to read the letter herself, so she asked my brother, four years my senior, to read it to her. This was an admittedly difficult task, since he could not have been more than eleven and did not understand Danish. I remember the two of them sitting at her kitchen table; he would try to read it, she would stop him and ask him to spell a word, and then tell him what a Danish word here and there meant.

This image—this spark of my cultural imagination—caused me to reflect on my cultural story in a new way and what I know and do not know about my own cultural roots. I was predominantly socialized around my Irish-American-Catholic cultural ethos. Of my grandparents, I remember only my Danish grandmother, the only one of the four who was an immigrant herself, the others being second or third generation. Why is her cultural background so vague to me, while my Irish-Catholic socialization process is so prominent? Indeed, there was only one Danish woman amid the sea of Irish faces of my many relatives at family gatherings. Yet I wonder if she had to swallow aspects of her own identity to fit into this Irish American enclave that was part of her American world. Did she welcome it, as so many immigrants of her time did who simply wanted to assimilate? Or was there a hint of resentment? Although I will never know these answers, the sparking of my cultural imagination makes me ask these questions as I continue to reweave aspects of my cultural story, this piece being rewoven partly because of a slam poem I heard by a young Latino poet in New Mexico.

I begin with this story because it is an example of how I recently engaged my cultural imagination in my own life and an example of one of the ways I might try to engage cultural imagination with learners in my own teaching. I currently teach classes that deal with diversity and equity issues in an adult education doctoral program. Although there are a few people of color in our program, most of my students are white, middle class, and of European American backgrounds. Many of them at first blush do not have a sense of their own culture; they seem to think that only people of color have a culture that can be articulated. In this class, we do all of the examination of theory that is typical of any doctoral class. But we also draw on multiple ways of knowing that engage heart, mind, body, and imagination. I tell my students that we are doing these various exercises that engage multiple parts of who they are because I do not want them to be able to just spit back elements of critical theory, feminist theory, or critical race theory. Rather, I tell them that I want them to engage this new knowledge in multiple ways, and I say for emphasis, "until it becomes you," a phrase that is equivalent to transformative learning. I believe that for learning to be truly transformative, it must engage one's whole being: new knowledge cannot "become you" simply through engaging rationality. It has to get into our hearts, souls, and bodies and into our interactions with others in the world. Thus, learners not only read and discuss theory and write analytical papers; they bring symbols, sometimes create poems, and do art so the new knowledge can "become them."

The course begins with the students writing aspects of their own cultural stories. I want them to come to new understandings of their cultural backgrounds and to look at messages they received about how they were to behave as people of a particular gender, or race, or class—to examine messages they internalized from their parents, families, schools, and communities about themselves and others of a different race, class, gender, sexual orientation, or religion. This is how they begin to understand the processes of hegemony and the way dominant forces work in the culture and various resistances to it—not just as an intellectual concept but played out in their own lives. I also ask them to bring a significant cultural symbol with them to share with the class, and explain why it is meaningful, as a way of further engaging cultural imagination and drawing on another way of knowing.

This is culturally responsive in that it allows learners to be experts on their own culture and to present it to classmates in a way that they choose as they continue to make further meaning of their cultural experience. I never ask students to do anything that I am unwilling to do myself; thus, I also provide them with a written version of my own cultural story and bring a cultural symbol. I highlight that this process of coming to new understanding of one's cultural story and the social systems that shape that story is an ongoing journey. It is continually reshaped by new experiences that tap our cultural imagination, like how Damian Flores's slam poem heard in New Mexico tapped into my cultural imagination, causing me to examine the processes of assimilation of my Danish grandmother.

Over the course of the semester, in addition to writing the analytical papers typical of doctoral-level courses, sometimes I have them watch and analyze a popular-culture movie for its portrayals of race, gender, class, and sexual orientation. I also engage them in poetry writing exercises aimed at integrating the reading in the course, with their own sense of creativity, so this new knowledge can "become them" in new ways. In small groups, they do a collaborative teaching presentation based on a particular choice of book that deals with some aspect of diversity. They are encouraged not simply to do a review of the book but to engage the class in an activity based on one of the themes of the book that might tap into learners' cultural imagination or ability to create something new. In closing, we often make use of some of what they created throughout the course in a final activity that hints at a ritual through use of song, poetry, dance, art, and ideas from significant readings, while stating our intent of next steps for action. These combined activities tie the theoretical and cognitive world to their affective and experiential world and further anchor it in the symbolic world as it engages cultural imagination. It seems to create a space where they can construct new knowledge and engage in processes, so that this new knowledge "becomes them." Many experience this as transformative learning: they not only critically reflect on assumptions but engage and embody new ways of being.

Although students do have to write an extensive analytical paper toward the end of the course, I encourage them (as opposed to requiring them) to engage their creativity in responding to the texts and ideas we have discussed by trying to create something that arises out of their inner work with the course as well. I do this for two reasons: to increase the way knowledge can become them and because dealing with social issues that examine the state of the world can be depressing. People need to experience their creative power so that they can have a sense of being able to effect change in their own lives and in the world. Engaging one's creative sense is not only integrating; it is also empowering.

Here is an example of a reflection on doing this from one of my students' papers. She created a four- by six-foot mosaic in her garage about her experience of gender and culture as a result of engaging and making new meaning of her cultural story as she recovered from a divorce. The creation of it became a community event that involved her children, Abigail and Emma, and her friends and neighbors who stopped by and watched and made suggestions. In her earlier cultural story, she had written about "Grandma Delores," an Apache woman whom she met and stayed with as young adult in a service-learning experience in the American Southwest. She writes:

> The flowers represent Abigail, Emma and me. This flower imagery took me back to Phoenix, Arizona and the simple explanation our group of college service learners were given before traveling to the Apache Indian Reservation in White River. We were asked to envision ourselves as flower buds opening and then blooming. That blooming flower [representative of Grandma Delores] gave me an appreciation of what culture truly meant. My own Pennsylvania German culture took on new and greater meaning in the face of another way of life.... Social injustice historically and presently glared at me. The red flower dropping petals in the middle of the mural not only represents an unflinching opening of self but also is an iconic

symbol of the dimensions of my historical face and political face. In this metamorphosis the sacred face peeks out [Care, 2006, p. 7].

This engagement of her cultural imagination—experiencing her Pennsylvania German cultural background and her gender in a new way—was
transformative as she created an art piece of the new knowledge that had
become her. It engaged imagination as well as her community in the creation
of it. This example is part of the work of social transformation.

Derise Tolliver: Connecting to *Kuumba*

I am an educator whose life and work have been infused with the soul-stirring
energy of African and African American culture. I have vivid childhood
memories of being awakened by the luscious aroma of bacon, eggs, biscuits,
and grits being prepared for family breakfast (still fondly held in spite of
my now raw vegan life), the smell floating on the reverie of the classical
music of the likes of Sarah Vaughn, Dinah Washington, Wes Montgomery, and
B. B. King. Meals often contained sweet, salt, bitter, and sour tastes, symbolic of
what the world would have to offer a black girl growing up in the United States.
Mealtime was a venue for developing awareness of self through relationship
in my immediate, extended, and community family.

Learning was valued as a lifelong enterprise, understood to be the legacy
of those who had come before me. Schooling was emphasized, but not as the
only learning resource. Family and community stories, written scholarship by
people of African descent, *Pride* magazine in my home town, and *Jet* and *Ebony*
all ignited my imagination of what was and what could be. These filled the
gap often left by mainstream education sources, which at times inadvertently
disregarded or intentionally denigrated the strengths and realities of my cultural
community.

Music helped me to recognize kinesthetic learning and the body as a receiver
of knowledge. Dance and song were not merely entertainment but deep cultural
expressions, reflecting the traditional importance of rhythm in African life. The
richness of the content of music, from spirituals to later works from artists such
as Nina Simone, Odetta, and Gil Scott Heron, informed my early realization of
the obligation for social action (following in the footsteps of ancestors) and the
struggle for social justice and liberation by then contemporary warriors such
as King and Shabazz (Malcolm X). The centrality of spirit and spiritness in my
life was constant, even though my family was not particularly active in many
religious activities.

I learned about myself within family and community and the rest of the
world through multiple ways of knowing: cognitively, affectively, behaviorally,
intuitively, kinesthetically, spiritually. My lived experiences impressed on me
the importance of involving the whole learner, her or his cultural, spiritual,

political, and historical self, in the cocreation of learning spaces that support the remembering, healing, and transformation of self and others.

How then do I, as an educator of adult learners, engage in a transformative practice? I describe one of the exercises I use in an undergraduate course that I designed as an example of my attempt to tap into cultural imagination and ignite "the spirit's artistry" (Rendón, 2000, p. 1), and to help them connect to their own *kuumba* (the Kiswahili term for creativity). I do this in an effort to facilitate learners' intellectual development as well as their capacity to live more fully in the world (hooks, 1994).

Classics from the Africa Diaspora is a ten-week course where the written works of David Walker (*Appeal*) and Carter G. Woodson (*The Mis-Education of the Negro*), and the music of Nina Simone (for example, the songs "Four Women," "Why? (The King of Love Is Dead)," and "Mississippi Goddam") are explored as commentaries on the human experience, with particular emphasis on issues of human development, systems of oppression, and social justice. Although the work of these authors and this artist do not routinely, if ever, appear on lists of conventionally designated classics, which most often reflect knowledge primarily informed by the Western Eurocentric canon and worldview, the inclusion of nontraditional and unconventional texts such as those I use in my course supports a shifting in notions of what is a legitimate academic content and form. This choice of these texts broadens learners' exposure to the cultural experiences and scholarly and creative expressions of people whose voices, experiences, and expressions are too often excluded, disregarded, or misinterpreted in the academy. In a professional field where the written word is privileged, the incorporation of Nina Simone's music as an academic text might be perceived by some as having little scholarly merit. I suggest that its inclusion is liberatory and revolutionary. It acknowledges the reality and recognizes the value of various ways of knowing in the classroom, and it broadens access to learning. The choice of these texts is overtly a political one, in the same way that exclusion of nonconventional educational materials is also a political choice.

In particular, the choice of Nina Simone's music as text illustrates the power of engaging the cultural imagination of adult learners in support of transformative learning. Nina Simone, a musical prodigy who is affectionately referred to as the High Priestess of the Civil Rights Movement, brought a critical creative expression to her work that parallels some of the principles that are supported by hooks's (1994) call for teaching to transgress. Simone experimented with and embraced many forms of music. She performed the blues, jazz, rhythm and blues, pop, and even show tunes, but all in her own styling. She experimented in her work much in the same way that we as educators who are supportive of transformative learning must be ready and willing to experiment with incorporating different approaches in our work.

She defied and resisted outside attempts for easy categorization of herself and her creative expression that might box her in and limit her spirit. She was as comfortable singing about love found, embraced, and lost as she was with calling attention to the injustices of Jim Crowism, discrimination and racism in the United States, and concern about war. She was multidimensional and proudly African American, committed to freedom, liberation, and justice. She fought against systems of oppression even at the risk of threat to her profession livelihood in the United States. Nina Simone presents a model of authenticity and integrity, so in my course, her life also becomes part of our text.

The power of Simone's music is not solely based on her lyrics. In "Four Women," she sings the historical experiences of women of African descent in the United States: hard-working Aunt Sarah, often perceived to be an enslaved African, who is able to live and maintain her strength in spite of the "pain inflicted again and again"; Safronia, the child resulting from the rape of a black woman by a rich white man; the seductive Sweet Thing, who will belong to "anyone with money to buy"; and Peaches, a young woman who is angry at the historical treatment of African people. Learners report being moved by the energy of the music, feeling it "in the bones" in a way that may not be adequately captured by words; it is experienced and known kinesthetically, affectively, and spiritually. They connect with Simone's soulful styling and voice, the haunting melody that reflects the reality of the four women's lives, relating their own personal experiences of enduring and often thriving and prospering in spite of pain and oppression. They find relevant parallels to their own lives.

I play the song and provide the lyrics in class. I ask learners for their initial impressions of what they have heard and read. I may pose specific questions about the song: What does it say about issues of oppression and injustice? What is the impact of these systems on individual development, group, and intergroup relationships, according to the song? They critically analyze the narratives expressed in the lyrics for how they inform an understanding of historical, cultural, and spiritual aspects of the human experience. I then ask them to go into groups and collaboratively develop and present their responses to these questions.

I am always amazed by the variety of presentation styles that emerge during this class. Even more amazing is how learners pull from their own cultural imaginations to present their learning from this exercise. Although some learners protested that this assignment was too difficult because they did not consider themselves to be artists, they all seemed to be moved by Nina Simone's creative energy and expression, which seemed to facilitate their connection to their own *kuumba*, or creativity. Skits, role plays, monologues, and poetry are among the many creative expressions that have emerged, reflective of learners' understandings of the characters' life circumstances, as well as how those circumstances may be mirrored in realities today. The depth, thoughtfulness, and creativity of their meaning making have often been unexpected, surprising, and moving. Learners' engagement with unconventional texts such as the music of Nina Simone, supports transformative learning while revealing the spirit's artistry in action.

I have presented my use of music and song to engage the cultural imagination of learners in the service of transformative learning. However, I have also used the visual arts in my classes as both prompts and activities for this same purpose. Going beyond what is expected and generally accepted as the norm for content and presentation in the conventional classroom can often open the learning space for the voices and participation of those who have been underrepresented in the academy. As Shor (1987) noted, "When the class examines familiar situations in an unfamiliar way, transcendent changes become possible" (p. 93). It is imperative that we as educators of adult learners incorporate what may seem to be unfamiliar ways in order to encourage the continuing learning, healing, and transformation of those with whom we work. Tapping the cultural imagination can be a vehicle toward that end.

REFLECTIONS

Years ago Parker Palmer (1980) suggested that we do not think our way into a new kind of living; rather, we live our way into a new kind of thinking. In dealing with diversity and equity issues in higher education in a culturally responsive way in the hopes of engaging students in transformative learning around social systems, it is not enough to enable them to critically reflect on their assumptions, though this is clearly important. Rather, it is important to provide experiences of living their way into new kinds of thinking. Engaging cultural imagination as well as their whole being is a way to do that until new knowledge "becomes them."

Sometimes this presents its own challenges and can sometimes be more than learners bargain for. Students are used to engaging with rationality in the higher education classroom; seldom are they asked to bring their whole selves into the learning environment and draw on multiple forms of being and knowing in their learning. Sometimes this makes people feel a bit vulnerable; hence, occasionally there can be some initial resistance to some activities that draw on cultural imagination. Thus, we recommend that learners be given choices about different ways of participating in activities that draw on cultural imagination and multiple ways of knowing. For example, rather than seeming to require learners to participate in an activity that engages the body in creating art or movement, learners might also be given the option to participate by observing and actively noting what they see or, as discussed elsewhere

(Tisdell, 2008), by discussing or writing about an image from a movie or a novel that deals with culture around a similar topic and touches off their own cultural imagination. Such an option might allow them to engage in a given activity in a way that is more comfortable for them. In addition, as Cranton (2001) discusses, it is important that teachers and facilitators develop activities that they themselves also participate in to model some sense of engaging completely and authentically in such learning. We find that both providing choices for ways of participating in an activity and modeling the engagement of multiple ways of knowing in keeping with our own personality and cultural backgrounds in our own efforts to be authentic tend to dissipate resistance. It typically also creates a sense of trust in the environment, where learners get excited about engaging their cultural imagination as new knowledge "becomes them." Often it taps into their *kuumba* and helps keep their spirits alive, hopeful, and with the creativity to make change in the world. That is living their way into a new kind of thinking. Indeed, that is transformative learning.

REFERENCES

Care, M. (2006). *The setting place*. Unpublished manuscript, Penn State University-Harrisburg.

Cranton, P. (2001). *Becoming an authentic teacher in higher education*. Malabar, FL: Krieger.

Dirkx, J. (2006). Authenticity and imagination. In P. Cranton (Ed.), *Authenticity in teaching* (pp. 27–39). San Francisco: Jossey-Bass.

Florio-Ruane, S., with DeTar, J. (2001). *Teacher education and the cultural imagination: Autobiography, conversation, and narrative*. Mahwah, NJ: Erlbaum.

Greene, M. (1995). *Releasing the imagination*. San Francisco: Jossey-Bass.

hooks, b. (1994). *Teaching to transgress*. New York: Routledge.

Huber, J., Murphy, M., & Clandinin, D. (2003). Creating communities of cultural imagination: Negotiating a curriculum of diversity. *Curriculum Inquiry, 33*, 343–362.

Palmer, P. (1980). *The promise of paradox*. Notre Dame, IN: Ave Maria Press.

Rendón, L. (2000). Academics of the heart: Reconnecting with the scientific mind with the spirit's artistry. *Review of Higher Education, 24*(1), 1–13.

Shor, I. (1987). *Critical teaching in everyday life*. Chicago: University of Chicago Press.

Tisdell, E. (2007). In the new millennium: The role of spirituality and the cultural imagination in dealing with diversity and equity in the higher education classroom. *Teachers College Record, 109*(3), 531–560.

Tisdell, E. (2008). Critical media literacy and transformative learning: Drawing on pop culture and entertainment media in teaching for diversity in adult higher education. *Journal of Transformative Education, 6*(1), 48–67

Tolliver, D., & Tisdell, E. (2006). Engaging spirituality in the transformative higher education classroom. In E. Taylor (Ed.), *Teaching for change: Fostering transformative learning in the classroom* (pp. 37–48). San Francisco: Jossey-Bass.

CHAPTER NINE

Promoting Dialogic Teaching Among Higher Education Faculty in South Africa

Sarah Gravett, Nadine Petersen

How can educators best be guided in their adaptation and implementation of a teaching approach that diverges considerably from their existing practice? This is the challenge we have been grappling with at the University of Johannesburg in a teaching methodology course that is being presented to two multicultural groups of adult learners. The term *multicultural* as we use it reflects the diversity in terms of both race and home language as a legacy of the segregated history of South Africa, aspects that that remain relevant for teaching and learning. The majority of students have been educated in a segregated, unequally resourced education system, which implies that they have been socialized in different educational histories and practices, which they draw on in this course.

One group of learners consists of approximately fifteen educators within the context of adult and higher education, and the other group consists of approximately 250 nursing students who are preparing to become nursing educators. Both groups enroll for the teaching methodology course as part of a formal qualification in their respective fields. The majority of learners who enroll for the course are used to or implement a predominantly transmission or delivery mode of teaching. Our aim in the course is to guide and assist the learners to adopt a learning-centered, dialogic teaching approach. The conception of teaching as dialogue that we espouse, advocate, and model has been inspired and informed by the views of many scholars, in particular, those of Paulo Freire (1971), Ira Shor (1992, 1996), Nicolas Burbules (1993), and Jane Vella (1994, 2000). We conceptualize dialogic teaching as a reciprocal communicative educational relationship, with participants (educators and learners) exploring, thinking, inquiring, and reasoning together (Gravett, 2005). The communicative educational relationship is respectful, reciprocal, and learning centered and is dominated by neither the educator nor the learners. However, the dialogue is not free-flowing; it is purposefully structured through a series of interconnected learning tasks (Gravett, 2005; Vella, 2000) to enable and foster active intersubjective meaning making related to the topic or learning content under consideration.

The learning tasks involve questioning, responses, comments, reflective observations, redirections, and building of ideas that form a continuous and developmental sequence with a view to breaking through to, articulating, examining, and validating the knowledge that is coconstructed by the educator and learners. Consequently the educator directs the curriculum, but does so democratically with the participation of learners, constantly "balancing the need for structure with the need for openness" (Shor, 1992, p. 16). In doing so, the learning becomes "public and communal" (Shulman, 1999, p. 39). As dialogic teachers, we concur with Shulman that "learning is least useful when it is private and hidden; it is most powerful when it becomes public and communal. Learning flourishes when we take what we think we know and offer it as community property among fellow learners so that it can be tested, examined, challenged, and improved before we internalize it" (p. 39).

Our teaching methodology course is underpinned by the notion that transforming existing ways of thinking and doing requires that learners come to awareness that there is indeed a need for transformation. The process of transformation often further requires the unlearning of outdated information and ways of doing. This means that old views, knowledge, perceptions, and experience need to be examined in the light of either the existing situation or new demands. It can be argued that developmental processes that aim at achieving substantial modification of existing ways of thinking and acting need to focus intentionally on fostering a transformation. This implies that courses or programs aimed at development should not present the new or desired way of thinking and doing as a given, but should involve participants in examining, enhancing, and, if required, converting their current reality. Consequently teaching development processes that focus solely on acquiring or improving techniques or skills usually culminates in superficial and temporary change. Given these considerations, our course was grounded in the notion that an intentional focus on the fostering of transformative learning regarding teaching practice would increase the probability of enduring transformation in teaching. Furthermore, our dialogic teaching approach employs strategies "essential to transformative learning such as promoting critical reflection and establishing trusting and authentic relationships with students" (Taylor, 2000, p. 285–328).

Consequently, the type of teaching and learning that we promote and model sits comfortably within transformative learning theory.

The design and implementation of our course took account of the following aspects and processes that shape a transformative experience (Cranton, 2002; Gravett, 2004; Mezirow, 2000):

- A triggering event (disorienting dilemma) that leads to an awareness of inconsistency among thoughts, feelings, and actions, or a realization that previous views and approaches no longer seem adequate, resulting in the experience of disequilibrium

- Identification of prior interpretations or views (assumptions, perceptions, and presuppositions) that are held largely unconsciously

- A questioning and examining of held views, including the context that shaped them and the consequences of holding them

- An engagement in reflective and constructive dialogue (discourse) in which alternative views are explored and assessed

- A revision of views, and in some cases, broad perspectives, to make them more discriminating and justifiable

- Action arising from revision

- A building of competence and self-confidence in new roles and relationships

In view of these, the course was designed to create a transformative space that would afford the learners ample opportunity to articulate their experience and existing ideas about being educators and to bring these into critical awareness through a dialogic process that induces reflection, challenge, and assessment. In our experience, this critical exploration generally triggers a feeling of disequilibrium that makes learners susceptible to new ideas. We then use this initial exploration as "foundational discourse" (Shor, 1996, p. 41) for introducing new views through a series of carefully sequenced learning tasks.

GUIDING LEARNERS TO ADOPT AND IMPLEMENT DIALOGIC TEACHING

In presenting the teaching methodology course, we have a dual purpose. We implement the content of the course while simultaneously modeling it by way of our pedagogy. In other words, the learners learn the curriculum of the teaching methodology while they participate in its implementation. Learning tasks form the backbone of this course and our version of dialogic teaching. Thus, in the course, we use learning tasks as a teaching-learning method and ask learners to engage with learning tasks themselves in class as well as out of class through a learning portfolio, while they learn how to implement dialogic teaching.

Learning Tasks as Teaching and Learning Devices

A learning task is based on an open question, and it requires that learners respond to or act on the learning content individually or in small learning teams. Some learning tasks invite learners to articulate their existing views, also called inductive tasks or call for summary or analysis of important sections of the learning content, which we refer to as input tasks. Other tasks require critical analysis, reflection, problem identification, problem solving, explanation, application, and synthesis (implementation, summary, and integration tasks; Gravett, 2005; Vella, 2000).

The learning task with which learners must engage is presented to them in writing. For example, an input task could require that learners listen to a short presentation and then, in small learning teams, identify and summarize the main ideas in the presentation, with a time limit for completion. The time allocated to work on the task would vary from two minutes to much longer, depending on the type of task, time available, and level of complexity. After completing the task, teams have an opportunity to respond to the posed question, usually through large group discussions. We then summarize the learners' feedback of their engagement with the task, for example, by exploring similarities and differences among the responses of different teams or by synthesizing the different responses. Further elaboration or explanation follows if necessary. We then move on to the next learning task, ensuring that we maintain the connection between tasks. It is our contention that learning tasks enable reciprocal interaction, exploration, inquiry, and theorizing, which we believe is the type of dialogue referred to in transformative learning terms as reflective and constructive discourse.

Our Teaching Methodology Course

Our teaching methodology course consists of four broad phases. In the discussion of each phase, we explain the underlying purpose, provide examples of learning tasks, and describe how these help to shape transformative learning experiences. In the first phase, we assist learners to describe and examine their existing knowledge, perceptions, experience, and feelings regarding teaching, knowledge, and learning, as well as how they have arrived at these. For example, we start by setting inductive tasks that aim at inviting students to articulate their existing views on learning, teaching, and knowledge. Such tasks are phrased as follows:

Personal Beliefs About Learning

With a learning partner briefly discuss the following for approximately 10 minutes: (1) What is your understanding of the concept "learning" and how would you know when you have learned something? (2) How did you come to this belief about learning? (3) Explain the process you follow when you have to learn something (e.g., new academic material).

Personal Beliefs About Knowledge

With a learning partner discuss the following for approximately 10 minutes: (1) What is your understanding of the concept "knowledge," and what does it mean to be knowledgeable? (2) How did you come to this belief about knowledge?

Personal Beliefs About Teaching

With a learning partner, discuss "My beliefs about teaching" for approximately 10 minutes. Consider such things as: (1) a description of what you think teaching is; (2) how you know whether teaching was successful; (3) how you have come to this belief.

We elicit responses from a few groups and through questioning, contrasting, and hypothesizing, we help learners to analyze their responses carefully. We view this intentional exploration of learners' assumptions, perceptions, presuppositions, and feelings in their own language, prior to the introduction of the academic discourse, as essential. This strategy provides an opportunity for students from different cultural, racial, language, and educational backgrounds to share their views with each other; it thus allows a diversity of voices to be heard. This exposure to a diversity of voices is also valuable for us for future course redesign and planning. The use of inductive tasks, such as the examples provided above, serve as catalysts for critical dialogue between the learners and the educator, a dialogue that is carefully nurtured throughout the course. We hope that the process of critical reflection and discussion that begins here, which learners engage in throughout the course, will enable them to become aware of their beliefs and feelings, open them to revision, and ultimately help them integrate newly appropriated meanings into an informed and conscious theory of practice (Jarvis, 1999).

Learning tasks such as these, and particularly the interactive discussion during the larger group sharing that follows such tasks in this phase, also serve as a triggering event for learners. It is in this process that learners come to a heightened awareness that their previously held ideas and views may no longer be adequate for their practice. Within the first phase, learners are afforded the opportunity to make explicit the assumptions, perceptions, and presuppositions underpinning their existing views about learning, teaching, and knowledge, ideas that are largely unconscious and thus most often unexamined. This is a crucial step in helping learners to start to transform their ideas about teaching and learning in the course.

In the second phase, learners begin to inquire into and assess an approach to teaching that we term *dialogic teaching*. This is accomplished by introducing them to constructivist views of knowledge and learning (Candy, 1991; Phillips; 1995; Garrison & Archer, 2000) that inform dialogic teaching. Learners have the opportunity to examine and explore the newly introduced ideas of learning and teaching, albeit largely on a more abstract level. Learning in this phase is also structured through a sequence of learning tasks, which ask learners to interact with the academic content. In this process, learners are once again prompted to question their deeply held views, examine how they have come to form these views, and reflect on the consequences of holding on to them. They are thus provided with the opportunity to compare their existing ideas about learning and teaching with those that they are being exposed to in the course. As educators, careful sequencing of the learning tasks in this phase allows us to capitalize on the possibilities for extending learners' experience of disequilibrium triggered in the first phase. This provides the ideal space for learners to begin a reflective and constructive dialogue with us in which we can explore together the newly introduced, alternate views. An example of a task used in this phase to structure this dialogue is as follows:

Promoting a Social Constructivist Perspective on Learning for Teaching

1. Listen to a presentation on a social constructivist perspective on learning.
2. Having listened to the presentation, individually write down what you view as the core ideas of this perspective. Share these views with your learning team. We will share some of your responses in the larger group.
3. In your learning teams, describe four ways in which the presentation informs your teaching. We will share some of your responses in the larger group.

In the third phase, the educator and learners investigate the fundamentals of a dialogic approach to teaching, drawing on the content of the previous phase. Here learners, together with the educator, identify and describe the defining features of dialogic teaching and discuss the actions of a dialogic teacher. Learners also have the opportunity to use selected strategies and techniques associated with dialogic teaching. Once again, we use a variety of learning tasks to structure this communication and interaction with students. These learning tasks range from those that ask learners to explain simply the fundamentals of dialogic teaching to those learning tasks that encourage learners to use these in new, creative ways in their own working contexts—for example:

A Graphic Depiction of Dialogic Teaching

Design a graphic representation to illustrate dialogic teaching as you see it in your context. Prepare notes in which you explain the graphic representation. Pay particular attention to the relationship between different concepts encapsulated in the graphic representation.

A Dialogic Learning Event

Think of a theme which you would typically explore with learners in your context. Write the theme as a heading for your learning event. Now design the learning event. Prepare brief notes in which you explain the rationale for your design.

The latter task is helpful for encouraging students to revise their views on teaching and learning because they are required to justify their design choices and decisions. First, in designing a learning event, learners put into practice the dialogic view of teaching they have been exposed to and learn how to apply it in their own teaching contexts. However, it is in the task of providing good reasons for their design that learners' understanding and ability to discern the nuances and subtleties of the new approaches to teaching are tested. This type of task is thus useful for the students because they can judge their ability to differentiate between their old practices and the new approaches and to validate the adoption of new ways of doing.

This process culminates in the fourth phase, designed to facilitate considered action, in that students are invited to pull together and implement all that they have learned. Learning tasks in this phase require that learners design a plan for integrating the various elements of the course within a context of their choice. They are also expected to clarify and discuss the interplay between the various elements of their plan and infuse the theory studied in the course in the explanation of their design. This is followed by practical demonstration of the plan in action, accompanied by feedback from peers and the educator. We have learned from experience that an affirmative response from students to adopting new ways does not necessarily mean that a transformation of teaching practice will ensue. Therefore in this phase, educator and colearner support is crucial to helping learners to start developing the competence and self-confidence in the new roles and relationships they are assuming.

This process is not limited to the classroom. To nurture and sustain the dialogue outside the classroom, we structure a sequence of learning tasks that accompany the in-class activities. Through the duration of the course, learners are called on to respond individually, in writing, to a series of learning tasks on the same themes dealt with in class, thereby compiling a portfolio of their learning. The learning portfolio provides a formal record of students' learning for the benefit of both learners and the educator and therefore serves a dual purpose: it extends the critical dialogue between the educator and the learners outside the classroom and helps to reinforce learning. The out-of-class tasks build on the in-class deliberations but require, in our view, deeper analysis, because students are required to reflect carefully through writing. Used in this way, learning tasks provide learners with "learning experiences that are direct, personally engaging and stimulate reflection upon experience" (Taylor, 2007, p. 182).

REFLECTIONS

What lessons have we learned through offering this course about the fostering of transformative learning in general and enabling change in teaching practice specifically? First, the notion of a learning edge is very important in facilitating transformative learning (Wlodkowski, 1999). Wlodkowski explains that learners are most susceptible to new learning when they are on the edge of their comfort zones, that is, their learning edge. To facilitate transformative learning, educators need to create the conditions under which learners are pushed toward their learning edge, where they are challenged and encouraged toward critical reflection. However, in our experience, educators should be aware that if learners are pushed too far, they can become defensive, resist the new learning, and withdraw in order to keep safe. Our reflections on this course over a number of years have taught us the value of initiating and sustaining a caring and collaborative context characterized by trust and respect in the process of pushing learners to their learning edge. Educators working toward transformative learning therefore need to maintain a careful balance between challenge and comfort in their interactions with learners.

Second, the main focus of this course is to enable revised action, which implies that learners themselves have to implement a new teaching methodology. In our experience of implementing this course, we have found that some learners initially resist both the course content and the pedagogy. We address this resistance by negotiating with learners to persevere while simultaneously modeling explicitly what is expected from them when they have to enact the teaching methodology in their own teaching settings. Coupled with this is the importance of creating space for learners to reflect on the theoretical underpinning of the course, what they see being modeled to them about implementing dialogic teaching, and their experiences as learners in a course using a dialogic teaching approach. We have found that this multilayered reflection is crucial for helping learners move from espousing the new methodology toward implementing it in a reflective manner. Learners have repeatedly indicated that the interaction of theory, modeling (practice), and reflection that they experience in the course serves as a powerful resource on which to draw when implementing the dialogic teaching.

Third, because transformative learning experiences are often unsettling and threatening for learners, we have found that learners require us to create a sense of safety. In our view, structure (of the course and the methods we use) provides a sense of psychological safety for learners. However, transformative learning also requires the opportunity for learners to freely explore and express ideas and views. We have used learning tasks most effectively in designing and implementing transformative learning experiences, as they allow us to maintain an optimum balance between structure and flexibility. Each task, which is based on an open question, requires a thoughtful and original response of learners, conducted in the safety of a small group, thereby enabling their free participation in the ensuing transformative dialogue. Yet the tasks are purposefully designed and sequenced to encapsulate the core ideas of the course, so the dialogue remains structured.

Fourth, the learning portfolio helps to maintain the discipline required for learners to work consistently throughout the course. This is important for fostering transformation because the learning tasks that learners respond to in the portfolio are sequenced to build understanding incrementally while simultaneously helping learners to develop a reflective stance, which is viewed as essential in transformative learning. We concur with the research reported by Taylor (2007) that "the written format potentially strengthens the analytic capability of transformative learning" (p. 182). In addition, as educators, we use the learning portfolio partway through the course to inform our understanding of the learners' levels of reflection, their developing understanding of the new methodology, and possible gaps in their understanding that require addressing. By the end of the course, the learning portfolios provide learners and us, as educators, with a map of the milestones and turning points of learners' engagement with the new teaching methodology. Learners indicate that the learning portfolio serves as a rich resource from which they can draw throughout the course.

Finally, although we are convinced that employing learning tasks to foster transformative learning is beneficial for student learning, we continually grapple with how to design learning tasks that will enable fruitful and appropriate engagement and reflection for all learners and how to arrange the tasks to enable a continual and developmental sequence. Despite the fact that learners frequently tell us that the course indeed has an impact on their thinking and doing about teaching significantly, we nevertheless revisit the design and implementation of the course regularly. The course demands that we function continually on our own learning edge. The result is that the course changes each year based on our own reflections, feedback from learners, and what we learn from the learners' responses in the learning portfolios. Thus, offering this course affords us the opportunity to engage with transformative learning in a dynamic and intentional manner. It is dynamic because we constantly change and adjust it to meet the arising challenges and intentional because our goal is to apply what we have learned to the betterment of the course, student learning, and our own learning as course teachers.

REFERENCES

Burbules, N. C. (1993). *Dialogue in teaching: Theory and practice*. New York: Teachers College Press.

Candy, P. C. (1991). *Self-direction for lifelong learning: A comprehensive guide to theory and practice*. San Francisco: Jossey-Bass.

Cranton, P. (2002). Teaching for transformation. In J. M. Ross-Gordon (Ed.), *Contemporary viewpoints on teaching adults effectively* (pp. 63–92). New Directions for Adult and Continuing Education, no. 93. San Francisco: Jossey-Bass.

Freire, P. (1971). *Pedagogy of the oppressed*. New York: Herder & Herder.

Garrison, D. R., & Archer, W. (2000). *A transactional perspective on teaching and learning. A framework for adult and higher education*. New York: Elsevier Science.

Gravett, S. (2004). Action research and transformative learning in teaching development, *Educational Action Research*, *12*(2), 259–272.

Gravett, S. (2005). *Adult learning: Designing and implementing learning events. A dialogic approach* (2nd ed.). Pretoria: Van Schaik

Gravett, S., & Petersen, N. (2002). Structuring dialogue with students via learning tasks, *Innovative Higher Education*, *26*(4), 281–291.

Jarvis, P. (1999). *The practitioner-researcher*. San Francisco: Jossey-Bass.

Mezirow, J. (2000). Learning to think like an adult. Core concepts of transformation theory. In J. Mezirow & Associates, *Learning as transformation: Critical perspectives on a theory in progress* (pp. 3–33). San Francisco: Jossey-Bass.

Phillips, D. C. (1995). The good, the bad and the ugly: The many faces of constructivism. *Educational Researcher*, *24*(7), 5–12.

Shor, I. (1992). *Empowering education: Critical teaching for social change*. Chicago: University of Chicago Press.

Shor, I. (1996). *When students have power: Negotiating authority in a critical pedagogy*. Chicago: University of Chicago Press.

Shulman, L. S. (1999). Taking learning seriously. *Change*, *31*(4), 10–17.

Taylor, K. (2000). Teaching with developmental intention. In J. Mezirow & Associates, *Learning as transformation: Critical perspectives on a theory in progress* (pp. 285–328). San Francisco: Jossey-Bass.

Taylor, E. W. (2007). An update of transformative learning theory: A critical review of the empirical research (1999–2005). *International Journal of Lifelong Education*, *26*(2), 173–191.

Vella, J. (1994). *Learning to listen, learning to teach: The power of dialogue in educating adults*. San Francisco: Jossey-Bass.

Vella, J. (2000). *Taking learning to task: Creative strategies for teaching adults*. San Francisco: Jossey-Bass.

Wlodkowski, R. J. (1999). *Enhancing adult motivation to learning: A comprehensive guide for teaching of all adults*. San Francisco: Jossey-Bass.

CHAPTER TEN

Transformative Palliative Care Education

Rod MacLeod, Tony Egan

Caring for people near the end of life can be a daunting and frightening task even for experienced clinicians. For many medical students, who have had minimal education about care at the end of life, it can be still more worrying. Finding the right time and the right way to introduce concepts of such care has proved difficult for medical educators. Providing opportunities for students to learn about end-of-life care at any stage of their undergraduate career can be difficult given that they will all need to deal with people who are facing life-threatening illness, one of the most challenging of life's experiences.

In compiling a report on caring for the dying, the American Board of Internal Medicine (1996) put together a persuasive collection of personal narratives by physicians, many of which tell memorable stories of how inadequately they were prepared to encounter both people who were dying and their families. Many of these narratives also provide support for the notion that doctors often learn about the art (as distinct from the science) of medicine from such patients (MacLeod, 2001). Fraser, Kutner, and Pfeifer (2001) similarly report that a large percentage of U.S. senior medical students do not possess the basic competencies identified by the Working Group on the Preclinical Years of the National Consensus Conference on Medical Education for Care Near the End of Life (Fraser et al., 2001).

The ability of doctors to care is influenced by the socialization process they undergo in their training (MacLeod, 2001), perhaps one of the more powerful transformative learning experiences in medical education. The suppression of empathy and humane aspects of care in such education, outlined by many over the past forty years, may inhibit the development of appropriate attitudes to people who are dying and may limit or even erode existing moral values (Feudtner, Christakis, & Christakis, 1994). We therefore need to ensure that this is countered by more appropriate alternative forms of transformative medical education. By *transformation* in this context, we mean the creation of opportunities to stimulate diverse, alternative, and multiple perspectives on events through reflection, that is, by changing specific beliefs, attitudes, and emotional reactions through such reflection either individually or in groups, and in the classroom or in practice. By *reflection* we mean the postevent intentional inspection of experiences that have caught the attention or made some lasting impression on the student. The process is essentially personal and internal in the first instance and centers on the meaning, particularly connotative, of the experience for that subject. Reflections in this sense are frequently prompted by emotionally loaded experiences and tend to be reflections-on-action as distinct from reflection-in-action (Schön, 1987). We do not exclude the latter from our consideration; rather we associate it with higher-level performances of connoisseurs. Most of our work involves students who are struggling with the development of professional identity and are typically constricted to reflection-on-action.

PALLIATIVE CARE

Palliative care has been recognized as a discrete form of clinical practice for over forty years. It is an approach that improves the quality of life of patients and their families facing the problems associated with life-threatening illness through the prevention and relief of suffering by means of early identification and impeccable assessment and treatment of pain and other physical, psychosocial, and spiritual problems (Sepúlveda, Marlin, Yoshida, & Ullrich, 2002). As a discipline, it is founded on a multidisciplinary, patient-centered model of care delivered by medical, nursing, allied health professionals, and volunteers in three settings: home, hospice, and hospital. The variety of settings for the delivery of palliative care poses challenges for educators and students who seek to contextualize professional knowledge and its application, and a number of approaches have been reported (Lloyd-Williams & MacLeod, 2004). However, given the personal nature of the knowledge on which practice is based, there is a case for the argument that the issue in palliative care education is not one of learning about palliative care or of learning in palliative care; rather it is one of learning through palliative care (James & MacLeod, 1993).

Many students' perceptions and observations in learning to care for people near the end of life are influenced by their lived experiences, which have had an important bearing on their development as caring health professionals. Some have difficulty adjusting to their own emotional responses, as well as to the more detached stance typical of more traditional biomedicine. Their adaptation is not only influenced by the culture of the medical profession but also by each school's culture, methods of teaching, and the peer groups to which each student belongs. The diagnostic technology now available encourages a focus in medicine more on the physical features of disease, often lending an impersonal dimension to patient care, unresponsive to the patient narrative, and creating increasing distance between doctors and patients. Providing transformative learning opportunities by working with people who are dying may help to address the disparity between the personal lifeworld of students and that of their profession. The socialization of laypeople into the medical profession leads them to expect certain actions and reactions to various events. All that the students previously know of death and dying is of their own experience; providing exposure to dying patients and their families gives them opportunities to become familiar with the experiences of others. Such a mode of learning helps students focus on and examine their previously held assumptions about the way that people die, their personal belief systems and ways of coping, and how professionals respond in practice.

DESCRIPTION OF TRANSFORMATIVE PRACTICES

The Mary Potter Hospice and the Department of General Practice, Wellington School of Medicine and Health Sciences, in New Zealand developed a palliative care module that would enable students to visit, over time, a family where someone was dying (MacLeod, Parkin, Pullon, & Robertson, 2003). This module is located within a context of a community practice experience during which students are involved in a number of aspects of medical care in the community. It comes early in their undergraduate career, when they have limited exposure to end-of-life care in any setting. The predominant aim of the attachment was to create an environment that might enable students to have early opportunities for understanding what the care of people who are dying means in both a personal and a professional way.

The objectives of the attachment are to (1) spend time with a patient and, where possible, family members in their home, hearing their story, and exploring issues of importance to them; (2) gain an understanding of the community-based network of resources used by the patient and family living with terminal illness, including the place of the general practitioner and other health professionals within that network; (3) identify and reflect on the feelings and anxieties experienced in talking with someone who is dying; and (4) respond appropriately to relevant ethical considerations.

All students are expected to participate in the module. In preparation for the home visits, they spend a day at the hospice learning about the palliative care service. The realities of caring for a person who is dying and his or her family are explored using experiential techniques (MacLeod & Robertson, 1999). These techniques include a "sculpting" exercise that focuses on the dynamics of a family in which a member is dying (Baldo & Softas-Nall, 1998; Satir Centre of Australia, 2005). Sculpting is a tool for making an external picture or sculpture of an individual's perception of a situation. The "sculptor" positions people in varying positions in order to demonstrate their perceptions of relationships, patterns of communication, power, closeness, and so on. Asking the other group members to assume a specific body position helps show how the sculptor perceives a given family situation. Then the individual can remove himself or herself from the picture to gain a more objective view, which opens the possibility for new insights. This can also be witnessed by those not involved in the sculpting. This is a less confrontational exercise than role play in that the participants need not speak if they do not wish to. Students take the roles of family members and health professionals and adopt the role of the dying person if they feel comfortable doing so. In addition to this exercise, personal experiences, such as identifying personal losses in a confidential way, and contemporary theories of loss and grief are revisited, and occupational stress management is discussed. These activities provide students an opportunity to discuss their own experiences if they feel able to in a supportive environment.

Students in pairs make their community visits to a family where someone is dying. We ask that they visit a number of times (a minimum of two) in order to become familiar with the family and the situations they find themselves in. Each student compiles a portfolio containing the patient's story, observations about the nature of care and the way it is delivered, and reflections on his or her feelings about the experience. At the end of the attachment, each student makes an oral presentation that includes the patient's history, the effect of the illness on the patient and family, the perspectives of the health professionals involved, and personal insights into the effects the visit may have had on him or her. After the presentation, the staff and students have an opportunity to discuss different aspects of the presentation, including not only practical aspects of providing care but also feelings aroused or experienced by patient, family, health professionals, or themselves. Successful completion of the portfolio is a requirement for this module.

In order to better understand the effects of such learning, we evaluated the process and outcomes. We asked the students to comment on how they viewed the process in an informal discussion at the end of the module. As part of that evaluation, we reviewed their writings to identify the essence of their personal reflections and comments. Essentially this was a commentary on what they had experienced over the module and how, if at all, it had affected them.

VALUE AND RESULTS OF EVALUATING THE EXPERIENCE

Five key themes were identified: (1) a different experience from what they had anticipated, (2) the emotional element of the experience, (3) spiritual and religious elements, (4) personal reflections, and (5) future caring approaches.

The conventional and clichéd image of someone near the end of life lying suffering, helpless, and in pain had colored the expectations of some students. Although they had some experience of clinical medicine, they had only limited exposure to sick and dying people. They reported varying degrees of uncertainty about the visits. These uncertainties related to both their own feelings of discomfort and anxiety and perhaps the novelty of meeting someone approaching death in their capacity as a medical professional rather than as a layperson.

Emotional involvement poses challenges for medical students, as it does for physicians, because the content of emotions is not objective; rather, emotional thoughts and ideas reflect individual perspectives. Many of the accounts indicated a sense of intimacy with the patients that led to feelings of sadness, helplessness, vulnerability, or admiration. We hoped the encounters would encourage students to review their own spiritual frameworks and previously held beliefs in a way that other clinical experiences had not. By incorporating an element in the assignment that encouraged them to think about their own views rather than encouraging them to "think like a doctor," the hope was that it would help them to reflect both in and on their practice, thus creating new ways of managing the situation and incorporating personal knowledge and understanding into this aspect of practice (Schön, 1987).

Some medical students recognized the varying needs of each person who was dying and presented, in compelling language, what they had learned about death and dying from those who were dying. Two-thirds of the students were able to identify ways in which their future caring practices could be developed based on the experience they had gained from these encounters. This was achieved by reflection on their own values and beliefs and incorporating them into their activities through attention, sensitivity, and exploration.

Many of the students eloquently described the emotional impact of meeting and talking with people near the end of life. Sadness, sympathy, vulnerability, and helplessness featured in their reports. Many described an empathic response that they had not anticipated or previously identified. There were, of course, varying degrees of responses, ranging from laughter to sadness, and even tears at times. We had previously warned the students that such work can evoke strong emotions and had talked of the consequences for us as individuals of displaying such emotions. Part of the setting of ground rules for such work incorporates guidelines for staff and students alike for such occurrences. Being in a small group also provided opportunities for staff to disclose some of their own feelings, fears, and anxieties about such encounters, thereby giving permission to others to do so if they wished. We also made sure that the students were aware of the support mechanisms available from the teachers, the hospice counseling staff, and the more formal university student support systems.

OTHER REFLECTIVE APPROACHES

In 1999, as part of curriculum development influenced by local and global factors, the clinical schools in the Faculty of Medicine at the University of Otago introduced expanded professional development programs for undergraduate students. These included reflective exercises such as the palliative care module at Wellington School of Medicine. At the Dunedin School of Medicine, students were asked to participate in an ambitious process involving journaling of significant experiences and discussions in peer groups of three prior to meeting, as a group, with a mentor. At the time, it was suggested that the experiences recorded in their personal journals might serve as subjects of discussion in the peer groups or in meetings with the mentor (Wilson, Egan, & Friend, 2003).

There was some student resistance to this innovation. A number of the group members felt they were being forced to disclose in their journals to their peers and to their mentors. Although this was not the case, denials by staff did not reassure these students. Staff were accused of social engineering and being authoritarian. While faculty saw themselves as creating opportunities that could be taken or ignored, some students felt that they were being manipulated into inappropriate forms of self analysis. Although as many students supported and valued the journaling–peer review–mentor process as were critical of it, it was clearly unsustainable and, for some at least, running counter to faculty objectives. As a result, a number of changes were made to the process. Journaling was dropped altogether, and in its place, students now complete thought-provoking episode reports. These are reports of student experiences in which students identify a particular incident that they have found themselves talking about or that has stayed in their mind for some time (such as student-patient boundaries, managing personal emotions and beliefs, reconciling clinical ideals with practice) and then write a detailed story of the event, including their thoughts and feelings at the time. This is followed by an analysis and review of the story aimed at identifying significant issues, evaluating how they were handled at the time, and drawing conclusions or identifying lessons learned, Later they can discuss these issues with their group or their mentor. Experiences of dying patients are consistently among the more frequently reported episodes. This more focused exercise appears to be less demanding or threatening than an open-ended journal.

Similar examples of self-reflection have been described. For example, Brady, Corbie-Smith, and Branch (2002) used narratives to track a group of house staff through three years of training to give the authors an understanding of the "interplay among residents' interactions with patients, their own personal issues and their struggles during several discrete stages of their professional development" (p. 220). One goal of the exercise was to encourage the trainees to become self-reflective. The authors felt that residents progressed through a period of "expressing ideal images of themselves as physicians through a bleak, discouraging stage of development and finally entered a stage where they could feel confirmed as professionals by their relationships with patients" (p. 222). By adopting this method, the teachers encouraged deeper and clearer thinking about the young doctors' roles and, in so doing, helped them to realize that things they learn about themselves can and will influence their practice as physicians in much the same way as the students in Wellington and Dunedin suggest they will.

Relf and Heath (2006) argue that effective teaching in palliative care needs to translate knowledge into behaviors that make a "positive difference to the people we work with, namely our colleagues, patients and all those who care for them" (p. 157). They identify a number of experiential techniques, as others have done, to provide opportunities for reflection and support, raising awareness of what influences attitudes, assumptions, and the way we respond, and for experimentations. They also suggest the use of role play with reflection and sculpting as useful educational methods to stimulate reflection and self-awareness.

Weissman, Branch, Gracey, Haidet, and Frankel (2006) used role modeling by clinicians to demonstrate humanistic care to learners who observed the desired behaviors directly. They suggest that role modeling practices developed by individual faculty physicians through iterative self-reflection are an effective method of teaching the human dimensions of care.

The reflective journals and thought-provoking episodes reported by the students in Wellington and Dunedin confirm the significance of role models in that students often write about their own experiences of watching and experiencing physician behaviors over time, revealing the students as astute observers of not only clinical practice but also of human behaviors. Providing the opportunity to reflect on their observations of clinical practice allows at least some students to evaluate the many dimensions of practice away from the heat of the action. Professional development of competent practitioners must encompass ethical and moral development, as well as the more clinical aspects of medical practice, and this is facilitated by these processes. We believe that there must be a reflective component to all our work. Such an approach is essential for the practice of palliative care. In order to provide effective care for people near the end of life, we must be aware of our own moral, spiritual, and ethical standpoints in order to understand all aspects of those for whom we care. In order to help someone who is dying, one needs to be attentive and empathetic and to be able to stick with them no matter how uncomfortable it may feel for the practitioner. Working with people near the end of life can help students understand those aspects of themselves they may not have examined too closely in the past. Participation in a hospice community and listening to people who are dying can help them develop differing ways of seeing the world through the eyes of someone who is living until he or she dies.

REFLECTIONS

Educational methods such as those described help students focus on and examine the assumptions that underlie their beliefs, feelings, and actions with particular regard to people who are dying. They also aid in the assessment of the consequences of these assumptions and enable learners to identify and explore alternative sets of assumptions and forms of action.

By encouraging new forms of practice and perhaps even new ways of being, the learners test the validity of their assumptions through effective participation in reflective dialogue. Such a dialogue can be undertaken with others and eventually, with practice, themselves. In this way, practitioners become more reflective and critical, more open to the perspectives of others, less defensive, and more accepting of new ideas.

There are some warnings, though. Transformative (reflective) learning opportunities are challenging in this context because they (1) involve attitudinal and emotional domains as well as the cognitive; (2) run counter to clinical detachment (which has been deemed appropriate in much of medical practice); (3) run counter to student expectations by introducing the subjective alongside the objective; (4) draw on the lifeworld at a time of transition from layperson to professional; and (5) require personal disclosure and are predicated on trust.

We have found that this method of learning by necessity engages emotions that some students find uncomfortable. This is illustrated in the workshops by varying degrees of discomfort. At times, we are challenged as this is a different way of learning that is unfamiliar to some, and so the possibility of disruptive behavior by students is always a possibility. This is anticipated, and the ground rules are set beforehand. We are, however, prepared to deal with a varying degree of emotion and have strategies to deal with laughter, sadness, and anything in between. Much of medical teaching suggests that students should not get involved, so developing an intimacy with people who are sick runs counter to what most students have experienced previously. Modeling behaviors and self-disclosure by teachers can mitigate any discomfort or uncertainty the students may feel. We work to develop a feeling of trust and respect for difference in the classroom; we state this and work at it. We encourage participants to say what they feel and to know that confidentiality is one of the stated ground rules. It can be uncomfortable at times for staff dealing with such issues, but no more so than dealing with emotions in our clinical work.

Clearly this transformative process may well take time (and may not occur for all students); hence, the need to embrace the concepts of palliative care from an early stage in medical education. Adopting reflective practices in preclinical work will facilitate a more effective way of learning. Using strategies such as those described by Samuels and Betts (2007), it is possible to learn to reflect on intentions as well as actions, thoughts, and feelings, and we encourage this in our own work. Their small-scale study involved learners using a self-assessment schedule to assess the process of their written reflections against the stages in Kolb's (1984) learning cycle. This sort of process of reflection could well be incorporated into the curriculum, in particular in palliative care learning, to help facilitate the transition from student to doctor and, in doing so, equip students more fully to deal with issues relating to dying and death.

While retaining our enthusiasm for the use of reflective processes in facilitating transformational learning, we must be mindful of students who feel threatened, uncomfortable, or alienated by the process. Our students in 1999 had mixed reactions to our innovations, and the institutional context in which they took place was not unambiguously supportive of reflective practice. Resistance was evident not only among the students but also some staff. At the time, our colleague Rose Friend coined the phrase "honor the resistance" as a reminder for us to temper our enthusiasm. Transformational learning, whether it is of the knowledge base or the person more generally, is challenging stuff, particularly when it challenges traditions such as clinical detachment in a profession as hierarchical as medicine.

In conclusion, in order to provide effective care for people who are dying, some degree of personal or social transformation is needed, and we, as medical educators, must be able to create the conditions where this may take place. Caring for people near the end of life is not easy, and any education that can alleviate the burden of such care is to be encouraged. Meeting and working with people who are dying is a privilege, and often it is a turning point in learning to care. For many, such experiences are clearly a significant event in that they challenge their previously held beliefs about such people. They encourage reflection on personal meaning as it relates to living and to dying and the identification of ways in which care may be improved. As medical educators, we must ensure that students are supported appropriately through this time of their learning and also strive to encourage those learners to reflect in and on their practice and learn about life through such potentially transforming experiences.

REFERENCES

American Board of Internal Medicine. (1996). *Caring for the dying: Identification and promotion of physician competency*. Philadelphia: American Board of Internal Medicine.

Baldo, T. D., & Softas-Nall, B. C. (1998). Family sculpting in supervision of family therapy. *Family Journal, 6*(3), 231–234.

Brady, D. W., Corbie-Smith, G., & Branch, W. T. (2002). "What's important to you?" The use of narratives to promote self-reflection and to understand the experiences of medical residents. *Annals of Internal Medicine, 137*, 220–223.

Feudtner, C., Christakis, D. A., & Christakis, N. A. (1994). Do clinical clerks suffer ethical erosion? Students' perceptions of their ethical environment and personal development. *Academic Medicine, 69*, 670–679.

Fraser, H. C., Kutner, J. S., & Pfeifer, M. P. (2001). Senior medical students' perceptions of the adequacy of education on end-of-life issues. *Journal of Palliative Medicine, 4*(3), 337–343.

James, C., & MacLeod, R. D. (1993). The problematic nature of palliative care education. *Journal of Palliative Care, 9*(4), 5–10.

Kolb, D. A. (1984). *Experiential learning*. Upper Saddle River, NJ: Prentice Hall

Lloyd-Williams, M., & MacLeod, R. D. (2004). A systematic review of teaching and learning in palliative care within the medical undergraduate curriculum. *Medical Teacher, 26*(8), 683–690.

MacLeod, R. D. (2001). On reflection: Doctors' learning to care for people who are dying. *Social Science and Medicine, 52*, 1719–1727.

MacLeod, R. D., Parkin, C., Pullon, S., & Robertson, G. (2003). Early clinical exposure to people who are dying: Learning to care at the end of life. *Medical Education, 37*(1), 51–58.

MacLeod, R. D., & Robertson, G. (1999). Teaching about living and dying: Medical undergraduate palliative care education in Wellington, New Zealand. *Education for Health, 12*, 185–192.

Relf, M., & Heath, B. (2006). Experiential workshops. In B. Wee & N. Hughes (Eds.), *Education in palliative care: Building a culture of learning* (pp. 157–169). New York: Oxford University Press.

Samuels, M., & Betts, J. (2007). Crossing the threshold from description to deconstruction and reconstruction: Using self-assessment to deepen reflection. *Reflective Practice, 8*(2), 269–283.

Satir Centre of Australia. (2005). *Group therapy methods (Virginia Satir's Sculpting Methods)*. Retrieved April 19, 2009, from http://www.satiraustralia.com/groups.asp.

Schön, D. A. (1987). *Educating the reflective practitioner*. San Francisco: Jossey-Bass.

Sepúlveda, C., Marlin, A., Yoshida, T., & Ullrich, A. (2002). Palliative care: The World Health Organization's global perspective. *Journal of Pain and Symptom Management*, *24*(2), 91–96.

Weissman, P. F., Branch, W. T., Gracey, C. F., Haidet, P., & Frankel, R. M. (2006). Role modelling humanistic behavior: Learning bedside manner from the experts. *Academic Medicine*, *81*(7), 661–667.

Wilson, H. J., Egan, A. G., & Friend, R. (2003). Teaching professional development in undergraduate medical education. *Medical Education*, *37*, 482–483.

Wilson, H. J., Dixon, G., Egan, A. G., MacLeod, R., Anderson, L., Clark-Grill, M., et al. (2007). ["Not knowing how to respond." Vulnerability in the transformation of medical student to health professional]. Unpublished data.

TRANSFORMATIVE LEARNING AS WORKPLACE EDUCATION

The chapters in Part Three focus on transformative learning in relationship to workplace education. Chapter Eleven, by Stephen Brookfield, brings to life the difficult process of engaging trainers, consultants, and managers in critical reflection who work within corporate America. Next, Chapter Twelve on storytelling, by Jo Tyler, offers insight into overcoming barriers to critical discourse through storytelling—"a narration of personal experiences." Beth Fisher-Yoshida introduces in Chapter Thirteen the concept of executive coaching and the role it plays in fostering transformative learning among managers. Victoria Marsick and Terrence Maltbia discuss in Chapter Fourteen the role of conversations grounded in action learning, where people use their work involving projects or problems as a way to learn. Kathleen King and Barbara Heuer discuss in Chapter Fifteen the fostering of transformative learning in adult basic education and workplace learning in three settings: a suburban adult literacy center, an urban school system, and a nursing home. Patricia Cranton closes Part Three in Chapter Sixteen by describing an educational program for tradespeople who are being schooled in the practice of teaching.

CHAPTER ELEVEN

Engaging Critical Reflection in Corporate America

Stephen Brookfield

In terms of the core propositions in Mezirow's transformational theory, critical reflection is integral to transformative learning. Mezirow believes that adult learning occurs in four ways—elaborating existing frames of reference, learning frames of references, transforming points of view, and transforming habits of mind—and names critical reflection as a component of all of these. We transform frames of reference through critical reflection on assumptions supporting the content or process of problem solving. We transform our habits of mind by becoming critically reflective of the premises defining the problem. Mezirow (2000) contends that the two central elements of transformative learning, objective and subjective reframing, involve either critical reflection on the assumptions of others (objective reframing) or on one's own assumptions (subjective reframing). He further argues that the overall trajectory of adult development is to realize one's agency through increasingly expanding awareness and critical reflection. In this trajectory, the function of adult educators becomes to assist this development by helping learners reflect critically on their own and others' assumptions. So in terms of Mezirow's transformational theory, it is clear that transformative learning cannot happen unless critical reflection is involved at every stage.

This chapter explores the difficult process of educating managers, trainers, and organizational development consultants to engage in critical reflection within corporate America. I define *critical reflection* as the deliberate attempt to uncover, and then investigate, the paradigmatic, prescriptive, and causal assumptions that inform how we practice (Brookfield, 1995). Paradigmatic assumptions are the structuring, framing assumptions that permeate our outlook on life and are central elements in our worldviews. They are close to what Mezirow calls *meaning perspectives*. Prescriptive assumptions are assumptions we hold about what best practice should look like, how we should behave, and so on. Causal assumptions refer to cause-and-effect links—if I do A, then B will happen—that we focus on in the day-to-day particularities of practice. They are central to what Mezirow (2000) calls *meaning schemes.*

But critical reflection is not just the examination of paradigmatic, prescriptive, and causal assumptions in any sphere of activity. It has as its specific purpose a focus on two human processes: power and hegemony. Critical reflection calls into question the power relationships that allow, or promote, one set of practices considered to be technically effective. It assumes that the minutiae of practice have embedded within them the struggles between unequal interests and groups that exist in the wider world. It also views classrooms not as limpid, tranquil, reflective eddies cut off from the river of social, cultural, and political life but as contested arenas—whirlpools containing the contradictory crosscurrents of the struggles for material superiority and ideological legitimacy that exist in the world outside. For reflection to be considered critical, then, it must have as its explicit focus uncovering, and challenging, the power dynamics that frame practice. Critical reflection also focuses on uncovering and challenging hegemonic assumptions, those assumptions we embrace as being in our best interests when in fact they are working against us. It endeavors to make people aware of how practices that are viewed as natural, common sense, and desirable (such as assuming we show our commitment to students by being available to them 24/7) are in fact constructed and transmitted by powerful minority interests to protect the status quo that serves these interests so well. After all, if you knock yourself out by being always available to supervisors or customers and are always ready to take on more work to demonstrate corporate loyalty and effective team membership, this means employers can reduce staff and increase profits. This, of course, is a perfect illustration of Marx's theory of surplus value (Marx, 1967). In any workday, people reach a point when what they have produced will cover the costs of their labor (their wages); once they work beyond that point, they are producing surplus value (profit).

The idea of criticality at the heart of critical reflection is grounded in a particular intellectual tradition: that of critical theory. Critical theory views thinking critically as being able to identify, and then to challenge and change, the process by which a grossly iniquitous society uses dominant ideology to convince people this is a normal state of affairs. As a body of work, critical theory is grounded in three core assumptions regarding the way the world is organized: (1) that apparently open, Western democracies are actually highly unequal societies in which economic inequity, racism, and class discrimination are empirical realities; (2) that the way this state of affairs is reproduced as seeming to be normal, natural, and inevitable (thereby heading off potential challenges to the system) is through the dissemination of dominant ideology; and (3) that critical theory attempts to understand this state of affairs as a prelude to changing it (Brookfield, 2005).

When viewed from a critical theory perspective, critical reflection focuses not on how to work more effectively or productively within an existing system, but on calling the foundations and imperatives of the system itself into question, assessing their morality, and considering alternatives. Since critical theory regards the mainstream majority as being ideologically manipulated to conform, critical reflection also entails the experience of taking a perspective on social and political structures, or on personal and collective actions that is strongly alternative to that held by a majority. Its focus is always on analyzing commonly held ideas and practices for the extent to which they perpetuate economic inequity, deny compassion, foster a culture of silence, and prevent people from realizing a sense of common connectedness. Understood in this way, critical reflection is a reflexive habit, a stance toward the world in which the deconstruction of ideas and professional practices for the interests they serve becomes second nature.

On the face of it, encouraging the practice of critical reflection seems at best highly problematic, at worst doomed to failure, if critical reflection is defined the way I regard it: as the process by which people learn to challenge dominant ideologies of capitalism, white supremacy, homophobia, and patriarchy and to recognize how hegemony encourages workers to collude in their own oppression. Few working as educators or process consultants are hired to root out hegemony and challenge capitalism, since such projects are directly in opposition to the interests of boards of directors and shareholders. And I have never seen a contract that specifies the trainer is charged with helping workers see how their labor is commodified and individualized in such a way as to prevent the emergence of collective forms of resistance, such as union chapters. Nonetheless, there are many working in capitalist America who stand for these purposes and are trying to negotiate the delicate task of encouraging critical reflection while holding down a job.

The context for the analysis in this chapter is my work as a workshop leader running workshops on critical thinking and critical theory at Teachers College in New York. Although "critical reflection" is not part of the workshop title, its practice is threaded through all workshop activities. Since 1987, I have taught these workshops to thousands of students, the vast majority of whom come from graduate programs in organizational psychology and who are preparing for, or currently work within, jobs in corporate America. Each workshop runs for two consecutive days, and I am usually the only faculty member in the teaching role. The workshops are run as professional development institutes, but those who wish to take them for one credit can register for this, though I grade only on a pass or fail basis.

CRITICAL REFLECTION, CRITICAL THEORY, AND CAPITALISM

My students work in corporate America, the apogee of capitalism. They live in a country where capitalism is propounded as dominant ideology, as obviously a good thing that supports admired values of freedom, liberty, and individuality. Capitalism is lauded for the prosperity it brings, the technological advances it stimulates, and the way it disseminates the innovative spirit of entrepreneurship among the population. For those working at the heart of capitalism to hear a sustained critique of its workings, and a documentation of its injuries, is highly threatening.

This is why it is important early on to get students to distinguish between capitalism's ideology and functioning and their own role in the system. There are many who work in corporate America who believe strongly in the need for workplaces to be locations for the exercise of human creativity, as well as many who think they are working to humanize an inhuman system. When students in my courses read Fromm on alienated labor (1961), they find it expresses many of their own misgivings about their own workplaces. They would not use Marx's language to describe their reality, but they recognize the spiritual and creative diminution signified by the relentless devotion to the bottom line of corporate profits.

One of the first things I do when teaching critical theory as the foundation for critical reflection is position it as a response to Marx. I do this as a matter of scholarly honesty. Since I believe Marx's work to be the foundation and fulcrum of critical theory, that is, its theoretical starting point, it would be disingenuous not to make this clear. Hearing this is difficult for some students, who ask, "Does this mean I have to be a Marxist to study critical theory?" The rampant Marxophobia in the United States means that any body of work connecting to Marx's ideas, no matter how critically these ideas are examined, is immediately suspect. Students with a strong commitment to values of individuality, liberation, and creativity—the same values emphasized in Marx's manuscript on alienated labor—see reading Marx almost as an unpatriotic act. It is as if by opening the pages of any work by Marx, they are rejecting democracy, free speech, even America itself.

It is important to say that it is not only third- or fourth-generation American students who have this difficulty. Students from former communist regimes who have fought in wars, suffered the loss of family members, seen the disappearance of livelihoods, and been forced into exile by those regimes also have an understandable visceral reaction to Marx's association with critical theory. It does not seem to matter how many times I point out that critical theorists unequivocally condemn the automaton conformity, surveillance, and one-dimensional thought they see in totalitarian communism or how many times these theorists assert the primacy of true democracy. Once Marx is mentioned, unless it is to denounce anything associated with him, you have immediately created a problem in several students' minds.

So how do I respond to this situation? One thing I try to do early in any course is emphasize the self-critical nature of critical theory itself and how this critical perspective is applied to Marx's work as well as to capitalist ideology. I also construct an early assignment around a critical appraisal of Marx. This assignment asks students to identify omissions, ethical blind spots, and inconsistencies in Marx's work, as well as to consider points of connection or resonance between their experiences or practices and his ideas. It is important to stress, however, that Marx should not be introduced so circumspectly as to rob his ideas of any force or power. There is a thin line between encouraging a healthy skepticism of Marx, or of any other theorist, and predisposing people to dismiss him. The point is not to set him up for easy demolition, but to demonstrate that a serious reading of Marx can happen without students feeling they somehow have to convert to Marxism.

So at the same time as affirming students' right to disagree with and condemn Marx, I also affirm my right as a teacher to insist they engage him before they ritualistically dismiss him. Furthermore, if students' engagement does lead to their dismissing his work, it is not enough for them to dismiss him out of hand. I invite, even require, students to be critical of Marx, but I ask that these criticisms be specific. Students are expected to provide page citations and direct quotes that indicate those aspects of his work they most take exception to. It is not acceptable to make only general criticisms, such as that Marx is antidemocratic, misunderstands the natural competitiveness of human beings, or has no awareness of the complexities of cyberspace or the postindustrial workplace. If these criticisms are leveled, I ask that each of them be illustrated by at least three specific references to his work. These should be either quoted in the paper or their location in his work indicated clearly enough for me to be able to find the relevant passages.

When I am working with students wholly unfamiliar with critical theory, I usually begin a class with some introductory exposition. My assumption is that those who have read little or nothing in the area, and who may be resistant to it for the reasons outlined in this chapter, need me to build a case early on for the relevance of this material. As I summarize the contours of big ideas like ideology, hegemony, alienation, or power, I try to talk about their meaning in my own life by giving examples. I show how dominant ideology shapes my decisions as a teacher, how my practice is commodified, how I engage in self-surveillance, how repressive tolerance manifests itself in my attempts to broaden the curriculum, or how automaton conformity (the pressure one feels to conform to some imagined norm of common sense opinion) frames my response to new practices or ideas. I also present critical theory as grounded in three understandable core assumptions regarding the way the world is organized: (1) that apparently open, Western democracies are actually highly unequal societies in which economic inequity, racism, and class discrimination are empirical realities; (2) that the way this state of affairs is reproduced as seeming to be normal, natural, and inevitable (thereby heading off potential challenges to the system) is through the dissemination of dominant ideology (defined as the system of ideas, values, beliefs, and practices accepted as common sense truth); and (3) that critical theory attempts to understand this state of affairs as a prelude to changing it.

After this introductory exposition, I often ask students to spend some time reading extracts from critical theory literature. They do this individually and privately during classroom time. The extracts themselves are not long—a few paragraphs here, a page or two there—since I prefer students to read a few pivotal sections carefully than to try to become familiar too early on with the range of broad debates and interpretations surrounding an idea. When this period of private reading is finished, students work in small groups to discuss their reactions to the reading. Following are examples of some of the questions I suggest they consider in these groups:

> After you have read (privately and individually) the materials on ideology, please form into groups of 4–6 and discuss your reactions to the readings. Some suggested questions:

Ideology

1. What aspects of the writings on ideology were most resonant or discrepant for you?
2. What are elements of the dominant ideology in the USA today?
3. What hegemonic beliefs and practices have you, or those you know, embraced?
4. To what degree is your learning at this university commodified, and to what degree have you commodified learning for others in your own practice as an educator?
5. How do you see this university, or your employing agency, working as an Ideological State Apparatus (ISA)?

Alienation

1. What aspects of the writing on alienation were most resonant or discrepant for you?
2. How do you see your own labor—or other aspects of your life—as characterized by alienation?

3. What pressures do you feel towards automaton conformity in your life, your learning, or your practice of education?

4. How does the marketing orientation manifest itself in your life, learning, and practice?

5. How did you find the language: Congenial? Intimidating? Puzzling? Illuminating?

Power

1. What aspects of the writing on power were most resonant and most discrepant for you?

2. What regimes of truth do you see in your learning, life, work, or educational practice?

3. In what ways do you feel under anonymous surveillance?

4. How does your experience of power match or contradict Foucault's idea of power as a chain, flow, or web—both oppressive and emancipatory simultaneously?

5. How have you managed to subvert dominant power?

6. How did you find the language: Congenial? Intimidating? Puzzling? Illuminating?

Try and bring back one or two questions or issues you'd like addressed in the large group.

One of the most interesting features of this process is students' favorable reactions to periods of private reading being inserted into the workshop. In any half-day analysis of a major critical concept such as ideology, alienation, or power, students have the chance to spend forty-five minutes or so individually reading the materials I have provided. They roam around the college and find quiet spaces for their individual struggles with what are often difficult materials. To my surprise, students socialized into large-class learning often mention the periods of individual reading as one of the most productive activities in the workshop.

MODELING: THE BEGINNING OF TEACHING FOR CRITICAL REFLECTION

In setting up these two-day workshops on critical reflection, the importance of modeling is always at the forefront of my mind. It has long been a tenet of my teaching that before I ask any student to do something, I first show how I am trying to do it. So early on in workshops, I try to ensure that I model critical reflection through specific actions. I use a great deal of autobiographical illustration to describe how the process plays itself out in my own life. Much of this is anecdotal and (I hope) fairly humorous, such as the way I naively have believed that I could stay within a room in which I had positional power as a fly on the wall but, through my silence, blend in with the wallpaper so no one would notice me. However, as the workshop proceeds, I may use my own experiences fighting clinical depression as an example of how the dominant ideology of patriarchy caused me to believe for many years that I should be able to look depression squarely in the eye and defeat it by applying inner fortitude and mental strength to snap out of it (a waste of time as those in this state will know). This assumption that I could think and reason my way out of depression meant I also assumed that using drugs to treat depression was a sign of weakness, an example that I was not a "real man."

Second, my use of the critical incident questionnaire (CIQ) is a deliberate attempt to model critical reflection in front of students. My workshops are spread over two consecutive full days, and at the end of the first day, all participants fill out the CIQ. This is a one-page form, anonymously completed, containing five open-ended yet specifically worded questions about the most engaging and most distancing moments in the class, most helpful and most puzzling actions anyone took in the class, and whatever surprised participants the most about the first day's activities. It takes about five minutes to complete, and as they leave the room, students place the completed form by the door, face down. That evening I read through the comments and prepare a report summarizing the main themes that appear on the form. In doing this, I use a basic frequency analysis: if something is mentioned by at least 10 percent of the group's members, then it makes it into the report. I also reserve the right to report single comments that are particularly provocative or interesting.

At the beginning of the next day's workshop, I give the report, usually trying to summarize the results visually on a screen, board, or newsprint. I state that the CIQ data have helped me check the assumptions that informed how I set up the first day's activities and tell participants which of my initial assumptions were confirmed and which were challenged. I then proceed to discuss how the CIQ data have influenced how I plan to set up the second day's activities, by either confirming my plans or causing me to make alterations. Throughout this process, I stress what I am doing in critical thinking in action: using the lens of participants' perceptions as an important data source to help me check my assumptions as workshop leader. To me, this is an important step in modeling my own involvement in critical reflection.

In any attempt to help people become more critically reflective, I believe it is important for me to earn the right to ask them to undertake certain risky activities only if I first model my own engagement in these in front of them. As well as using frequent autobiographical examples, I try to model how I use the techniques I am asking students to try. For example, in the critical conversation exercise, which typically happens halfway through the second day of the workshop, students are asked to pose questions to each other, provide guidance on assumptions each other holds and different ways of interpreting experience, and offer advice in nonjudgmental, descriptive ways. Before asking them to do these things in small groups, I provide a teaching demonstration of what they look like for the whole workshop.

PEER LEARNING: THE CRUCIBLE FOR CRITICAL REFLECTION

I regard critical reflection as a social learning process involving a great deal of peer learning. By that I mean that people come to a better understanding of their own assumptions and develop the ability to judge their accuracy and validity only if they involve peers as critically reflective mirrors who provide them with images of how their practice looks to others. Becoming aware of our assumptions is a puzzling and contradictory task. Very few of us can get far doing this on our own. No matter how much we may think we have an accurate sense of ourselves, we are stymied by the fact that we are using our own interpretive filters to become aware of our own interpretive filters. This is the cognitive equivalent of a dog trying to catch its tail or of trying to see the back of your head while looking in the bathroom mirror. To some extent, we are all prisoners trapped within the perceptual frameworks that determine how we view our experiences. A self-confirming cycle often develops whereby our uncritically accepted assumptions shape actions that then serve only to confirm the truth of those assumptions. We find it very difficult to stand outside ourselves and see how some of our most deeply held values and beliefs lead us into distorted and constrained ways of being. To become critically reflective, we need to find some lenses that reflect back to us a stark and differently highlighted picture of who we are and what we do. Our most influential assumptions are too close to us to be seen clearly by an act of self-will.

Hence, early in any workshop, I try to introduce some exercises that stress to students the importance of listening closely and intently to each other's comments. The circle of voices is one such beginning exercise. Here students discuss a theme or question in small groups (five is a typical group size) with two ground rules in place. First, every student takes a turn to have the floor for up to a minute and during that time speaks about whatever is on his or her mind about the topic. Once every student has had a period of uninterrupted airtime, general conversation ensues, governed by a second ground rule: whatever a participant says can only be about what someone else has already said in the opening round of voices. These ground rules are designed to ensure that careful listening is seen as the most crucial contributing behavior to good discussion and to prevent egomaniacs' grandstanding and co-opting the conversation to further their own self-esteem or agenda.

Another workshop exercise I use is the circular response method, a somewhat more demanding exercise than the circle of voices, though superficially it seems quite similar. As with the circle of voices, this is a small group conversation (it works best with a group of about eight) that starts with each person in turn taking up to a minute to talk, without being interrupted, about an issue or question the group has agreed to discuss. In contrast to the circle of voices exercise, however, speakers are not free to say anything they want. They must incorporate into their remarks some reference to the preceding speaker's message and then use this as a springboard for their own comments. This does not have to be an agreement; it can be an expression of dissent from the previous opinion. The important thing is that the previous person's comments are the prompt for whatever is being said in circular response. If the new speaker can find no point of connection to the previous speaker's comments, then she or he can talk about the source of the confusion about those comments, such as the confusing language the speaker has used or the very different interpretation the new speaker has of shared experiences.

REFLECTIONS

Critical reflection as conceived in this chapter is never a content-free process, never just a deep probing of assumptions. Rather, because it is grounded in critical theory, critical reflection's purpose is always to uncover power and hegemony, to critique the dominant ideologies of capitalism, white supremacy, homophobia, patriarchy, and so on. As such, encouraging this while staying employed in corporate America is always a risky business. But my experience has been that learners quickly recognize the validity of critical ideas if they are introduced incrementally, supported by modeling, and embedded in structured but collegial conversations.

In writing up my own approach to getting learners to engage with critical reflection, I am struck by two potential potholes in the road to practice. The first concerns the predictable resistance to the process exhibited by those well schooled in dominant ideology. Whoever is charged with getting people to question assumptions they have previously been happy embracing is likely to be resented, at least initially. This has repercussions for employment and advancement in organizations like many universities. If students rate you poorly because you ask them to question capitalism and white supremacy, this means your career is compromised. The second is the degree to which practitioners are wholly transparent about their practice. I have believed that as a general rule, it is easier, and fairer, to be as transparent as possible about one's motives, agenda, and directions. But I am struck by how this can be counterproductive and how one is probably well advised to reveal the more contentious and difficult aspects of critical reflection only after some initial trust has been built. But what of the potential destruction of the trust that has been built that happens as one starts to push students to reflect on how they perpetuate hegemony? Clearly, working in capitalist America means working at a perpetual point of contradiction.

REFERENCES

Brookfield, S. D. (1995). *Becoming a critically reflective teacher*. San Francisco: Jossey-Bass.

Brookfield, S. D. (2005). *The power of critical theory: Liberating adult learning and teaching*. San Francisco: Jossey-Bass.

Fromm, E. (1961). *Marx's concept of man*. New York: Frederick Ungar.

Marx, K. (1967). *Capital, Vol. 1* (S. Moore & E. Aveling, Trans.). New York: International Publishers. (Originally published in 1867)

Mezirow, J. (2000). Learning to think like an adult: Core concepts of transformation theory. In J. Mezirow & Associates, *Learning as transformation: Critical perspectives on a theory in progress* (pp. 3–34). San Francisco: Jossey-Bass.

CHAPTER TWELVE

Charting the Course

How Storytelling Can Foster Communicative Learning in the Workplace

Jo A. Tyler

W hen I suggest to students—adult practitioners in our program who are working in various aspects of human resource development (HRD)—that it is possible to foster Mezirow's ideal conditions for communicative learning and rational discourse (Mezirow, 1991) in their corporations, government agencies, and nonprofit organizations, they politely but vigorously protest. Their workplaces, they tell me, are better suited for fostering what Mezirow discusses as the barriers that inhibit critical discourse in groups. I do not argue whether this is the case (for I believe it might be), rather that there are ways to overcome those barriers, that storytelling is one of those ways, and that overcoming them is a goal worthy of pursuit.

Organizations fundamentally depend on communicative learning for, among other things, the creation of novelty, conflict resolution, and growth. Individual and organizational capacity for critical reflection and dialogue underpins many forms of success in organizations, since the focus of these activities "is not establishing cause-effect relationships but increasing insight and attaining common ground through symbolic interaction" (Mezirow, 1991, p. 80). Stories are a natural approach to communicative learning based as they are in language, which renders them highly symbolic. Their rich texture of images, moreover, moves listeners to see beyond a skeletal structure of problem (or crisis) and dénouement, of cause and effect, to see the points at which the personal experiences of tellers and listeners intersect, diverge, and overlap. These points hold rich potential, but they require exploration, travel through the choppy waters of unexamined assumptions, and the undertow of defensive routines.

There is little question that the ideal conditions for rational discourse suggested by Mezirow as necessary for communicative learning can be challenging to achieve. This is especially the case in organizational milieus, such as conference rooms and classrooms, where efforts to create them often bump up against quite resistant social, political, and environmental constraints. Still, I exhort my students to rise up as practitioners to meet the challenge rather than shirk it out of frustration or despair. Facilitated storytelling, I tell them, is an effective approach to fostering the sort of discourse that helps employees understand what others mean and to make their own meaning clear, to communicate in ways that will advance the goals of the organization. The focus of this chapter is to help practitioners apply storytelling as a starting point for opening up critical discourse among and between client groups.

Storytelling here is not meant as a trick or tool in the practitioner's toolbox. It is not meant as an entertaining diversion or a touchy-feely exercise for group bonding. Here, I mean to consider storytelling as a legitimate organizational process with both strategic and tactical implications that can cut across the whole organization, affecting large-scale changes to key processes and shifting the workplace practices and assumptions of individual contributors. It is not an automated process or a fast one. It requires attention and slowing down. Thoughtful practitioners will find that the attention and the investment of time will yield high and often surprising returns. One way of ensuring that returns outstrip the investment of care and appropriate pacing is to consider the ideal conditions as underpinning norms for the process. At the same time that practitioners are working to foster the ideal conditions that will support storytelling and subsequent discourse, the storytelling process is working recursively to build the very scaffolding that supports the conditions. Done earnestly, it can produce profound results, but it is no process for the faint of heart. At the least, this sort of facilitated storytelling demands that both practitioners and their colleagues adopt a willingness to experiment and take risks. From practitioners, it requires brave and unhurried facilitation of the reflection and dialogue generated by the storytelling. Undertaken in this way, the process can deepen the experience of engaged tellers and listeners and produce outcomes that matter.

STORYTELLING: AN OPERATIONAL DEFINITION

Storytelling has been enjoying a revival in America since the late 1970s (Sobol, 1999), and since the late 1990s that revival has been actively dancing in and around the edges of business. Publications on the link between storytelling and leadership (Gardner, 1995), constructs that identify stories as both an element and a product of communities of practice (Wenger, 1998), and research that positions storytelling as the very fabric of organizations (Boje, 2001) have helped to reclaim stories from the domains of children's bedsides and lakeside campfires. A growing body of literature on stories and storytelling in organizational contexts describes what they are and are not. Since they are in fact many things, it will be helpful to establish a reasonably narrow and straightforward operational definition for our purposes here. In the context of this chapter, I use the term *story* to refer to a narration of personal experience. I will not, for example, consider myths, fables, or folklore, even as they pertain to entrenched stories of the organization, its history or its brands. Rather, we will consider the stories that emerge from the direct experiences of organizational members (employees as well as, potentially, customers, suppliers, and other stakeholders) as they interact in the process of undertaking the work of the organization. These may be stories of success in the organization, of transcending obstacles on the way to individual or collective "wins," or they may be stories of marginalization, silenced voices, or oppression within the organization that stymied innovation or compromised values.

The telling of these stories of experience is an act, a process, a dynamic, that occurs in organizations every day. It is a natural part of the organization's work, and on an informal basis, stories are told regardless of whether they feel positive and helpful, challenging and difficult, or simply benign. So here, the term *storytelling* will focus on personal experiences that are conveyed orally and directly, face-to-face by a teller to listeners in a facilitated forum. This storytelling in small groups of employees telling their own stories, often prompted by the stories of others, is distinct from the performed storytelling of product launches, conferences, shareholder gatherings, and all-hands meetings. This latter storytelling typically conveys more sculpted and practiced stories. While it can usefully serve the organization (Tyler, 2007), this sort of storytelling often focuses on stories that have been tidied up to align with and support the dominant narrative of the organization and that may be told with persuasive or manipulative intentions that will shut down, rather than open up, the sort of discourse that is our goal here.

Telling stories of personal experience in small groups is not an entirely rational process. The stories may be told from the heart rather than from the head. They may emerge as messy and as nonlinear as some of the events that they convey. They may be filled with sudden remembrances that prompt the teller to go back and fill the listeners in on an important detail. They may not start at the beginning, and they may not have the neat endings we have come to expect from performed stories, because the experiences of the tellers are not neat and are ongoing.

Exchanges where one story spontaneously sparks another, unexpectedly leading tellers and listeners into previously unexplored territory, can at times feel quite irrational. I have come to see it as a process that operates quite outside the domain of rationality, but in ways that catalyze rational discourse. The fact that this type of storytelling erupts effortlessly at a bar, in ladies' rooms, and in locker rooms can make it seem easy enough to implement in more organized settings, but it is not enough to simply bring people together in a conference room with coffees and snacks and expect it to simply happen. In an organizational context, creating opportunities for authentic storytelling requires considered planning on the front end, trust and candor on the part of the tellers and listeners, and thoughtful facilitation of the reflective dialogue and relationships it is capable of generating. Moreover, it requires elbow room for tellers and listeners to take action on the learning that emerges from the exchange.

One beauty of this authentic storytelling that has its genesis in the teller's interpretation of his experience lies exactly in its potential for fostering learning, shifting meaning perspectives, and establishing shared understanding or even values at the same time that it contributes practically to the organization, generating new ideas, developing novel approaches to work, or supporting organizational transitions. The shift from reflection to action is rational, so our next step is to consider the conditions Mezirow (1991) outlines for rational discourse.

MEZIROW'S SEVEN CONDITIONS AND THEIR STORYTELLING CONNECTIONS

Mezirow (1991) offers a set of ideal conditions for participation in critical discourse and adult learning as "essential components in the validating process of rational discourse through which we move toward meaning perspectives that are more developmentally advanced, that is, more inclusive, discriminating, permeable and integrative of experience" (p. 198). These conditions connect significantly to the construction of storytelling and, perhaps more significant, "story listening" spaces that are both liberating and generative.

The first of these is that participants will "have accurate and complete information" (Mezirow, 1991, p. 77). Implicit in this process is that tellers relate their own stories. This means that they have access to their complete experience as they recall it and have the ability to fully address clarifying questions and points of curiosity their story arouses in their listeners.

A second condition is that participants will "be free from coercion and distorting self-deception" (Mezirow, 1991, p. 77). It is useful to consider these two elements separately. While people are getting accustomed to the idea of storytelling, it may be useful to level the power dynamic to the greatest extent possible. Early sessions that do not include high-risk relationships such as manager-employee combinations, or integrate internal employees with outsiders such as customers and suppliers, will help participants grow accustomed to candidly sharing their stories without fear of reprisal or other unsavory outcomes. Composing early groups in ways that palpably lower the risk for the participants will allow them to experience the potency of the process. This can foster willingness or even an organically emergent desire to experiment with alternative group formations that include greater risk alongside the promise of more compelling insights and outcomes.

The second element, self-deception, may be present in the way a story is initially experienced and consequently narrated, but the full storytelling and listening process we are after here provides for subsequent reflection and dialogue, for an engagement between tellers and listeners in which they can poke and prod at the assumptions of both parties, turning them over, and holding them up to the light. This same process of posing questions to the teller that clarify and deepen understanding or prompt the teller to examine his interpretation of his own experience supports a third condition of rational discourse: the ability "to weigh evidence and assess arguments objectively" (Mezirow, 1991, p. 77).

A fourth condition, the capacity to "be open to alternative perspectives" (Mezirow, 1991, p. 77), sits neatly at the heart of the storytelling process. Listeners will naturally hear stories through a filter of their own experiences, thereby yielding an alternative point of view, often about how they, were they the protagonist, might have proceeded. These alternative renditions can be the starting point for dialogue that follows the telling. In addition, even others who took part in the events conveyed by the story are not likely to have experienced it in the same way as the teller, so with respect to the first condition discussed, no one teller's perspective can represent any event completely. Alternative perspectives can be brought into the telling and listening space for examination by including the people who hold them and asking them to both tell and listen.

The ability "to become critically reflective upon presuppositions and their consequences" (Mezirow, 1991, p. 78) is linked directly to storytelling as a social phenomenon that involves listeners whose interpretations of and questions about the story can prompt the teller's exploration of his or her own assumptions. A collaborative exploration of assumptions with members of the group may reveal deeper or stronger assumptions that are held mutually among those present and may be operating across the organization at large. Stories provide a unique opportunity to explore consequences by allowing listeners to undertake a form of mental rehearsal (Bandura, 1986). In a form of restorying (Rosile & Boje, 2002), tellers and listeners can safely play with pivotal elements of the story, incorporating what-if scenarios based on alternative assumptions to generate and try on alternative endings to the story, the best of which can be moved into practice.

A sixth condition, the "equal opportunity to participate, including the chance to challenge, question, refute, and reflect and to hear others do the same" (Mezirow, 1991, p. 78), can depend largely on the proficiency of the practitioner who is implementing the storytelling process. One key here is to ensure that while the opportunities are equal, no individual is coerced into telling his or her story or responding to one told by a colleague. The second critical point, also contingent on the practitioner, is that sufficient time is provided for all participants to reflect on the story or a reaction to it, process it, and respond. This is a condition that cannot be rushed. It requires slowing down, taking a physical and metaphorical breath.

The final condition Mezirow (1991) specified is the ability "to accept an informed, objective, and rational consensus as a legitimate test of validity" (p. 78). An advantage of live telling is the power inherent in groups of listeners gathering together to situate themselves in the experience of the teller as they are conveyed in the story and to begin to understand it through a process of collaborative exploration. With sufficient time for questions, the telling of related stories from the listeners' experience, and the development of alternative scenarios, dialogue that includes critical reflection and ideology critique can build to an informed, objective consensus. The stories supply the raw materials for consensus, as does the exploration of universality and critical outliers in the tales of the listeners-turned-tellers, but it is not like magic. This notion of consensus, which seems necessary for practical action and sustainable outcomes, benefits from the aid of a thoughtful and unobtrusive facilitator able to direct participants' gaze toward their own learning processes and thwart attempts to manipulate conclusions and decisions to the point where they cease to be consensual or valid.

With these connections between the ideal conditions and facilitated storytelling in mind, we can turn to the practicalities of implementing the process in an organizational context.

IMPLEMENTING STORYTELLING

The decision to create spaces for facilitated storytelling and listening in organizations is not cavalier. Stories are deeply personal and vulnerable to the alchemical mix of forces within the environment where their telling is negotiated. Important practitioner considerations linked to the ideal conditions include the context in which stories will be told, creation of psychosocial spaces that invite authentic stories and deep listening, and the sensing of approaches that will invite stories and foster reflective dialogue grounded in the experience of tellers and listeners.

Identifying the Context

Practitioners setting out to work with stories have choices to make. I recommend that they consider beginning their work with storytelling by integrating storytelling sessions into training classes, prompting storytelling, reflection, and dialogue that are relevant to the course content. This is an excellent way for a practitioner to begin in a domain where she may retain considerable control over the agenda before experimenting with the second type of venue: specially designed sessions that dedicate space for facilitated storytelling and listening. Specially designed sessions may focus, for example, on particular topics critical to the vitality of the business and the employees, such as innovation, employee retention, or fostering diversity. The basic tenets of these storytelling sessions relative to their ability to foster communicative learning are the same as storytelling sessions incorporated into training contexts or into similar, naturally occurring events in the business. These dedicated sessions, however, are typically associated with a high level of commitment and awareness, as well as high levels of tenacity and low levels of risk aversion, among senior management. Without these, it is nearly impossible to implement specially designed storytelling sessions in ways that reflect the ideal conditions. The increased visibility of storytelling as a legitimate business and leadership practice in the Fortune 500 has helped to distance the concept somewhat from the traditional associations with children. Using benchmarking visits or even scholarly and trade articles and books to demonstrate that other respected organizations are already experiencing success with storytelling can effectively jump-start discussions about storytelling with senior management, but the best way to pique their interest remains, in my experience, to get them telling some stories and listening to those of others, so that they connect with the power of the process firsthand.

Whether the storytelling is embedded within a naturally occurring event or is the focal point of a special event, practitioners can develop a sort of sixth sense for emergent opportunities to depart from a prepared agenda or specific activity and spontaneously dig into salient topics where there is a disparity of experiences that lead to differences in closely held and often unexamined assumptions. In the context of facilitating, stories can help to reveal the sources of the variety of opinions or approaches participants bring to an idea or problem. Often when I sense divergence in the views of the group members, I suggest some storytelling as a sort of "stop-reflect" that can make the group more fully aware of the reasons behind what might otherwise escalate into debate rather than dialogue or an impasse rather than action. The stories slow the process and provide a backdrop for facilitated sharing of and inquiry into experience that makes it difficult to later dismiss out of hand.

Creating Spaces for Storytelling and Story Listening

Storytelling happens everywhere: at the coffee station, the fitness center, the parking lot. However, the power dynamics that are assumed, if not inherent, in any forum sponsored by management or the organization can effectively shut storytelling down. Whenever employees are brought together in the context of a facilitated event, it is the job of the practitioner to rekindle the natural desire of people in groups to tell their stories.

An important element of this process of reinspiring the stories, giving them breath, is to model the sort of storytelling in which the practitioner desires the group to engage. If the practitioner is hoping the session will elicit stories of authentic experience, regardless of the extent to which they may run contrary to the espoused story of the organization, she must tell a story of her own authentic experience. The process of storytelling is one of reflective unmasking that involves choosing what will be left in the story and what will be left out. These choices are imbued with risk and possibility, positively correlated. That is, the greater the willingness to risk telling authentic stories from the heart, the greater the possibilities are for stories to spark other stories, authentic dialogue, an exchange that can open new perspectives, make sense, and create new meaning. The extent to which the practitioner hopes participants will take off their corporate masks, revealing their true experiences and their authentic interpretation of them, is the extent to which the practitioner must demonstrate this unmasking.

Practitioners are well served by their own risk taking. The participants will use the practitioner's story as a gauge. The extent to which they perceive the story they have heard as an authentic countercultural story is their perception of where the boundary of acceptable (safe) versus unacceptable (unsafe) storytelling lies. If a practitioner tells a namby-pamby story of dancing along the edge of the organization, participants are likely to stop far short of sharing their stories of experience embedded in the margins of the organization. In addition, participants will take from the practitioner's story cues regarding other attributes that are deemed appropriate, such as length and whether the stories should be told as personal experience in the first person or from the safer distance and relative anonymity of third-person telling.

This process of unmasking relates directly to the participant's perception that this is a safe space free from coercion. It is not enough to set up norms of "what we say here stays here," though these may be worthy of articulation at the opening of any such session. The practitioner's willingness to stand in authentic relationship to a difficult story of her own is what helps to assure participants that there will be no effort to recast their stories with a glossier version more neatly aligned with the organization's preferred, espoused story. This frees the participants to tell their stories more completely, to flesh out the important message they hope the story will convey with images that are particular, vivid, and real. They will not need to figure out how to tell the story without the key piece of information that could land them in the most "trouble" with management. It is one thing to raise an unpopular opinion, and another to share a richly detailed story of experience that may be connected with aspects of your fundamental self—your identity, self-image, or personal values—or that may reveal mistakes or regrets.

Prompting Stories

There are at least three essentials to getting storytelling started. The first concern is with the prompts that participants receive to support the selection of their story. The second is the provision of sufficient time for participants to reflect on the incident that lies at the heart of the story they wish to tell. The third is to begin by working in small groups.

The story that the practitioner models is only one of the influences on the stories participants tell. The second is the prompts that are posed to the group. These may be totally open-ended, as in, "What is the most compelling/disconcerting/surprising/rewarding... event that happened to you at work this week/month/in recent memory?" Sessions that start this way can open up unexpected discursive windows that would otherwise escape the practitioner's notice. Or the prompts a practitioner uses to begin a session may be more focused on a particular topic that is the context for the session. In this case, it is helpful to first explicate as briefly as possible (reducing the possibilities for coercion) the purpose of the session, the topic of interest, and why it matters to the organization. This can be followed by a series of subprompts. For example, a session focused on innovation might begin with the practitioner stating that innovation is, for example, the topic, that it matters to the organization because it has struggled with innovation for some period of time, and that the key to reigniting the inventive spark in the organization lies in the stories of the very people who have innovated in the past, who are now wrestling with innovations that seem somehow just out of reach. The practitioner might then say, "Think of a time in the past year when something compelling around your research occurred. It might be a time when you were excited, disturbed, optimistic, or confused. Or something else all together. Choose the first event that comes to mind that you are willing to share in this group. Get that story in your mind now." Providing a balance of positive and difficult options, as well as the caveat that anything connected to innovation is fair game, renders these prompts fully electable by the participants. The goal is to open up the greatest number of possibilities for the participants and keep the prompts general and free from restrictive criteria.

The second essential is to slow the group down before they pair up to tell, giving them time to reflect on and shape the story. This is most easily done by saying something like, "When you think of the story you want to tell, cast your mind back to the incident that lies at the heart of that story. Recall how it felt to be part of the incident at the time, what your role was, and who else was involved. Take a minute to get the story in your head." Then actually do it: give the group a minute of silence in which to remember the story. Help participants structure their story by suggesting that they identify the primary message they intend the story to convey. Give them a minute to clarify this in their own mind. Finally, let the participants know how long they have to tell their story (two to four minutes is optimal at the start) and suggest that on the basis of the time frame, they take a minute to locate the images that will be essential to communicating that message to their listeners. These three minutes of individual reflection will pay dividends in the tellers' ease with the story and the listeners' ability to make sense of it.

Equipped now with a tellable story, the participants can move into pairs (or trios if time permits), choosing one person to tell and changing roles after the allotted time is complete. It is also helpful to carve out a few minutes following each story for listener inquiry, so that they can ask clarifying questions, clearing up points of misunderstanding or addressing points of curiosity.

Starting in small groups (and keeping the stories short) reduces the perceived risk and saves the stories from being "performed" as theater or presentations. As the conversation in the large group after the story is told evolves through skillful facilitation, the group will coalesce around certain topics, becoming more open to telling new stories related to emergent ideas. As the capacity for working with stories in groups and in the organization matures, practitioners should follow their instincts, experimenting with alternative storytelling formats, instructions, and group configurations, including asking participants how they would like to proceed.

Facilitating Dialogue After the Storytelling

The best facilitators are not afraid of silence. They let stories sink in, giving listeners the freedom to come to the conversation in their own time. Once listeners have had a chance to ask any lingering questions about the story and sit with it for a minute, you can fold the small groups back into a larger discussion prompted with simple questions, such as, "How did it feel to tell your story?" "What was your experience as a listener?" "What surprised you?" or "What did you notice?" As participants begin to fill in the silence—and they will—they will do so in the interest of sending the conversation deeper, striking and following rich, energetic veins of insight and curiosity.

One form of success is when participants no longer look to the practitioner-facilitator for the next prompt but begin to speak spontaneously, responsively, and directly with one another. This leaves the practitioner free to notice patterns and divergent outliers that may be useful thresholds as the dialogue evolves. At this point, a critical skill is the ability to stay open to negative or difficult stories and commentary from listeners that runs contrary to the dominant stories in the organization. Create a clearing for this turn in the conversation just as you would for observations and ideas that are upbeat and optimistic. Graciously welcome the serious, sad, or scary, and invite the group to explore what others bring. It sounds trite to admonish you to trust the process and relax into it, even though it may feel messy and emotional. In this case, it is the stories you can trust. The stories will help you guide the conversation to its most meaningful levels. When the dialogue feels out of control, ignore any compulsion to shut it down. Instead, focus sparse interventions on eliciting stories that will enhance the group's ability to deepen its exploration and widen the lens through which you view the organization.

REFLECTIONS

What bubbled up as I wrote this chapter is how deeply embedded storytelling is in relationships. It both depends on them and creates them. Relationships are the reason that storytelling is so powerful, and they are the source of its fragility. While I have tried to provide some simple steps to begin, there is no formula that practitioners can reliably adopt. The stories are energetic forces, as unique and unpredictable as the people who tell them. Prescriptions can never anticipate their complexity and depth when they are well told in safe surroundings, or their ability to skim across the surface when it feels as though there is too much at risk. I see now that I have come to rely on stories' capacity to foster the principles Mezirow advocates, fooling myself into thinking that I had techniques for manufacturing them and that I could relate what they were. In fact, what I see here is that it is fundamentally my ability to fully trust the stories, to cede control to them, that has made my work in this area so richly rewarding for individuals, including me, and so productive with regard to organizations at large.

Stories have provided me with the insights and relationships that have fostered my success as an insider in organization development in multinationals around the world for a quarter of a century. Now storytelling and story listening are the core of my approach when consulting with organizations on learning, innovation, change, and strategy. They are the heart that keeps my teaching alive, and they are the muscle of my research. Because I have become as unwilling to coerce stories as I am to coerce the employees who come together to tell and to listen, some organizations decline to work with me, turning to more conventional processes that can be more predictably navigated. But because I have watched stories grab the rudder and steer through roiling waters, for me there is no other way to sail.

I hope that the practical ideas in this chapter are sufficient to inspire practitioners to let go of the ship's wheel and become crew. If so, they will soon be convinced, as I have been, to chart a fearless course toward a horizon that holds a whole new story filled with mystery and promise.

REFERENCES

Bandura, A. (1986). *Social foundations of thought and action.* Upper Saddle River, NJ: Prentice Hall.

Boje, D. M. (2001). *Narrative methods for organizational and communications research.* Thousand Oaks, CA: Sage.

Gardner, H. (1995). *Leading minds: An anatomy of leadership.* New York: Basic Books.

Mezirow, J. (1991). *Transformative dimensions of adult learning.* San Francisco: Jossey-Bass.

Rosile, G., & Boje, D. M. (2002). Restorying and postmodern organization theatre: Consultation to the storytelling organization. In R. R. Sims (Ed.), *Changing the way we manage change* (pp. 270–289). Westport, CT: Quorum Books.

Sobol, J. D. (1999). *The storytellers' journey.* Chicago: University of Illinois Press.

Tyler, J. A. (2007). Incorporating storytelling into practice: How HRD practitioners foster strategic storytelling. *Human Resources Development Quarterly, 18*(4), 559–587.

Wenger, E. (1998). *Communities of practice: Learning, meaning and identity.* Cambridge: Cambridge University Press.

CHAPTER THIRTEEN

Coaching to Transform Perspective

Beth Fisher-Yoshida

O rganizations are often faced with the dilemma of what to do when they have a highly talented manager, who is technically a star performer but does not have adequate managerial or interpersonal skills. Does the organization fire the manager, warn the manager, look away, or develop the manager so he or she can be a well-rounded contributor to the organization? Organizations that value the manager's input to the bottom line and care about the emotional well-being of their employees and the overall productivity of the unit look for ways to develop their managers so that they have a positive impact on the financial health of the organization, while developing and supporting their staff members to become positively contributing employees.

One way to develop these managers is to offer them the right balance of challenge and support for growth by providing executive coaching (Harvard Business School, 2005): a valued member in an organization is recognized for his or her potential and receives individualized feedback in one-on-one situations with a coach. There is generally not enough performance feedback given or solicited, and in essence, many people work within a vacuum, unsure of how others perceive them and the impact of their work. When they do receive feedback that differs from their own perceptions and assumptions about their performance, the noted difference can be a disorienting dilemma (Mezirow & Associates, 1990), and this is where transformative learning may take place. These disorienting dilemmas can transform their perspectives and how they make meaning from their encounters in the workplace.

A CASE OF COACHING

I explore one coaching case in this chapter in which I was an external consultant to a global financial institution and was asked to work with a high-potential candidate in a coaching engagement. The office and the candidate were from the United States. Corinne was a very smart person who grasped concepts quickly and was a high-achieving performer. She had worked in this institution for six years and has been in the financial industry for fifteen years. She was being considered for a promotion and transfer to one of the business's offices in Europe. The office had gone through major changes recently and was in need of someone to get it back on track by raising its revenues and developing new staff members.

Corinne reported to two bosses in this matrix organization. Her geographical boss, who recommended her for the position in Europe, fully supported her and noted that he often consulted her as she was strategically brilliant. He knew she could be tough, and he often fielded many complaints about her, but he assumed that this was partly attributed to her being a woman in a tough male-dominated business. Realizing that her behavior got in her way, he initiated coaching for Corinne. Her functional boss, the global sales manager, was based in Asia and was new to the organization, and he did not know Corinne's capabilities firsthand. What he knew about her was that she could be curt on the telephone, and there were many complaints from his staff in Singapore about her abusive nature. He was less sure about her qualifications and was concerned about the type of work environment she would create in the European office.

I was briefed on the situation and looked forward to meeting Corinne. I was intrigued by her dynamism and directness. She did not mince her words, and I could see this getting her into trouble. She was playful and had a sparkle in her eye, and her self-deprecating humor caused her to confess that she was a mess—referring to her interpersonal skills, not her technical expertise for which she had been consistently rewarded. Corinne had been receiving mixed messages about her performance. She was constantly being praised and promoted and given hefty bonuses for exceeding expectations for the amount of revenue she generated. At the same time, she was reprimanded for being aggressive, uncaring, and unsupportive of those she needed to manage and work with as colleagues.

Corinne was set to be transferred in about six months, and we set up a coaching schedule that included a needs assessment and a series of coaching sessions spaced about ten days apart. Corinne was expected to work on her own between sessions to reinforce the learning that took place and instill a reflective practice in her day-to-day work life. She rarely, if ever, stopped to reflect on her interactions with others. To incorporate the viewpoints of those with whom she worked, we conducted a 360-degree feedback assessment, a multirater tool that allowed Corinne to receive anonymous feedback from her bosses, colleagues, and direct reports, to complement her own comments about the work situation and the dynamics of her relationships.

WHY TRANSFORMATIVE LEARNING?

The main purpose for the coaching intervention was to develop Corinne's interpersonal skills, so that when she transferred to this European office, she could start off by building constructive new relationships. As a leader in a global organization, she needed to develop her cultural sensitivity so she could better moderate her behavior in working across difference. This would prove to be one of her biggest challenges. The demand for immediate information and action due to intense time constraints caused her to make demands without considering the other person. In the majority of situations, Corinne found fault with her colleagues and considered them to be incompetent, lazy, and rude. She did not see her role in her relationships in terms of the impact she had on others (Fisher-Yoshida, 2000). Her expectations were that everyone working for the same organization should know what is expected and should just carry out the requests.

I thought transformative learning principles and approaches would be suitable to this coaching scenario for several reasons. The first was the importance of Corinne's being able to transform her perspective from a right and wrong dichotomy to a palette of possibilities as a result of many existing influences, cultural diversity being one of them. Corinne could do this by developing more self-awareness in understanding her own behaviors and the impact she had on others (Fisher-Yoshida, 2003). She had to see that her behavior was created as a result of the assumptions she unknowingly carried and that they influenced all of her actions and reactions to others (Brookfield, 1987). The surfacing of assumptions was critical to Corinne's development as a leader (Geller, 2005).

Incorporating transformative learning could help Corinne develop an awareness of her operational assumptions, how they were not working well for her and may have even been working against her (Brookfield, 1987). Corinne saw the world through her own perspective and did not have the conscious awareness that there may be equally valid alternative perspectives (Mezirow & Associates, 1990, 2000). She had her worldview, and others had their own way of seeing and interpreting the world through their own governing variables (Argyris, 1993), frames of reference (Mezirow & Associates, 1990, 2000), or mental models (Senge, 1990). In addition, this organization operated globally, which meant differing customs as to the meaning of work, various protocols as to the functions and responsibilities of colleagues, along with a variety of communication styles that incorporated many unspoken rules of conduct (Tisdell, 2003). Corinne needed to become more in touch with her own physical, mental, emotional, and spiritual reactions to these situations (Nagata, 2002).

In engaging with new clients, I need to consider the existing state of self-awareness the client has as compared with the desired state of where the client wants to be and the breadth and depth of that difference. There are different amounts of transformation that can occur, and the level of self-awareness of the person being coached is critical in determining the level of readiness to transform. While perspective transformation may or may not occur in response to the coaching, I believe it is important to aspire to that level of change even if it is not achievable at this stage. We begin the process of change in thinking and awareness that may manifest itself in transformation at some future time and place.

GETTING READY TO BEGIN

We saw that in eliciting feedback from others, on some points there was unanimity in opinion about Corinne and in other places a divergence of opinion. We related this information to Corinne's current and recent past experiences in the organization and in her past working environments to see if we could detect patterns in her interpersonal relationships.

In the needs assessment and in conversations, I was impressed by how open Corinne was to sharing her perspective about her experiences. The challenge was that she firmly presented her own point of view as though it was the only one. An important next step for Corinne was to pay conscious attention to how she made meaning of her interactions and to try to understand how her colleagues made meaning of the same interactions, and that these meanings may not be the same. This I supposed would help Corinne broaden and deepen her understanding and those of her colleagues around the globe (Pearce, 2004). It was important for Corinne's development that she work on these other less developed areas to enable her to become more balanced in her interpersonal interactions.

THE COACHING SESSIONS COMMENCE

We laid the groundwork for how the sessions would be conducted and for our roles in the coaching relationship. I took the responsibility to model the desired behaviors in how I acted and responded to her. As a coach, I believed I was in a different type of relationship with Corinne than her peers or bosses, and to act on this by offering her constructive and supportive feedback would enable her to see her role in her interpersonal relationships from as nondefensive and nonthreatening a position as possible (Marsick, Sauquet, & Yorks, 2006). She was adept at challenging what she felt were inconsistencies, and so for me to be credible, I needed to walk the talk. It also provided a concrete example of what the behavior looked like rather than a conceptual description subject to interpretation that may not achieve the desired results.

One of the main purposes of the coaching sessions was for Corinne to make more explicit the ways in which she knew what she knew. This has also been referred to as *ways of knowing* in the literature. Specifically, I refer to the three levels of knowing as *instrumental, socializing,* and *self-authoring* (Kegan et al., 2001). In the instrumental way of knowing, we pay attention to concrete and observable data that we understand from only our own perspective. We set up the world as dichotomies of right and wrong, black and white. In the socializing way of knowing, we involve more internalized processes, consider our values and purpose, and our interactions with others are more complex based on our relationships. In the self-authoring way of knowing, there is a much stronger sense of ownership in determining how we will structure our framing for understanding and making meaning of the world around us. Corinne operated most of the time at the instrumental level of knowing, and I wanted her to develop the skills to become more reflective so she could also function at the socializing and self-authoring levels of knowing.

TOOLS IN THE COACHING

Using tools would enable Corinne to entertain different perspectives in a structured manner, which could shift her perspectives and way of knowing from instrumental to socializing level. I introduced some of the heuristics of coordinated management of meaning (CMM) to Corinne, which required her to draw on information she did not typically consider in her interpersonal encounters (Pearce & Pearce, 2000). The three basic principles of CMM are *coherence*, in which we try to make meaning and develop understanding of our experiences; *coordination,* as in a dance we are trying to be in rhythm with those around us to develop understanding and mutuality in our relationships; and *mystery,* learning that the world is a complex place, and since we are not able to have all the information in any particular situation, we enter into it with curiosity while developing comfort with ambiguity (Pearce, 2004).

In one of the heuristics, the daisy model (see Figure 13.1), a tool that depicts the multiple conversations taking place about one event at any given time (Pearce, 2004), Corinne was asked to place a particular exchange in the

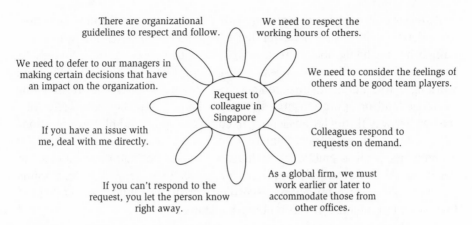

There are organizational guidelines to respect and follow.

We need to respect the working hours of others.

We need to defer to our managers in making certain decisions that have an impact on the organization.

We need to consider the feelings of others and be good team players.

Request to colleague in Singapore

If you have an issue with me, deal with me directly.

Colleagues respond to requests on demand.

If you can't respond to the request, you let the person know right away.

As a global firm, we must work earlier or later to accommodate those from other offices.

Figure 13.1 Daisy Model of an Interaction with a Colleague

center of the daisy. On each petal, Corinne provided her own expectations and assumptions, the internal conversations she had about the event and her counterpart. She stretched her thinking and wrote in the other petals what she supposed her counterpart might have said if she were asked to complete some of the petals.

This activity was a stretch for Corinne because she was so entrenched in her own point of view. When she did begin to become less rigid about her perspective, she viewed her counterpart's perspective with strong judgment. After many discussions about what it means to be a team player and that not everyone acts on it in the same way, Corinne was able to open up and consider that her counterpart in an Asian office also values being a team player. After accepting that, with much judgment, she stated that the way the colleague is a team player is wrong. This latter statement seems counter to "considering" her counterpart. Corinne acknowledged her assumptions about being a good team player, but she could not let go of the evaluative component. For her, there was a lack of consistency between what she viewed as the espoused approach of her colleagues and the approach they actually took (Argyris & Schön, 1994). This inconsistency caused Corinne to be judgmental. Since her colleagues were doing the same in return, there were conflicts between them (Fisher-Yoshida, 2005).

Corinne's communication style was blunt, direct, and emotionally expressive. She processed her reactions aloud and did not progress past voicing that differing points of view were wrong. This elicited a defensive response from her colleagues, and the emotional antagonism between them escalated. Corinne did not realize she influenced the direction her interactions took toward having constructive or destructive outcomes (Deutsch, 2006). We created scenarios to explore the possible alternative outcomes of these interactions.

After several months of working with these scenarios, Corinne was able to understand how one behavior led to another. I believe she was really baffled by not being able to read situations with people more accurately as she was able to do in a business transaction. Although Corinne had been working in this global organization successfully for six years, she was not able to understand or appreciate the diverse backgrounds of her colleagues. She pushed her way through transactions to completion and had physical reactions while relaying these stories. She could also describe the physical symptoms accompanying these emotional exchanges, yet did not use them as clues to become more self-aware of what was taking place (Nagata, 2002). But Corinne and her colleagues were getting exceedingly frustrated with one another, so this pattern of interaction was no longer sustainable.

PREPARING FOR THE TRANSFER

As a next step, it made sense to support Corinne in clarifying what she actually knew, what she thought she knew, and what she needed to know as part of her preparation. This was an important next step in framing (Coleman, 2004; Gray & Putnam, 2003) the situation, so that she did not operate from preconceived notions and assumptions of what to expect. For this, I introduced Corinne to another CMM heuristic, the LUUUUTT model or storytelling model (Pearce, 2004). LUUUUTT is an acronym (stories Lived, Unheard stories, Untold stories, Unknown stories, Untellable stories, stories Told, and storytelling). In this model, a framework is offered for structuring the stories surrounding a particular event or situation. Corinne had many stories to consider.

An increasing amount of pressure was being placed on her to go to the European office and clean up the employment mess. The organization professed that it wanted her to succeed and develop her people skills, yet they were sending her to the new office with a hatchet and the authority to fire staff. Therefore, it was especially critical that as Corinne began establishing relationships in this multicultural European office, she set the tone of being firm yet fair.

Corinne's rapid-fire decision-making behavior, interpreted as command and control, needed to be softer and less intimidating. In order for Corinne to establish good working relationships with her colleagues and direct reports, she had to be approachable and demonstrate respect for cultural differences (Fisher-Yoshida & Geller, 2008). Although she relied on information collected by others, in the end, she would have to make her own summations of the individuals and group as a whole. Corinne used the LUUUUTT model to map out the information she had to confirm and identify the critical missing information (Figure 13.2).

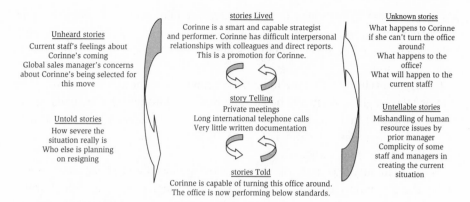

stories Lived
Corinne is a smart and capable strategist and performer. Corinne has difficult interpersonal relationships with colleagues and direct reports. This is a promotion for Corinne.

Unheard stories
Current staff's feelings about Corinne's coming
Global sales manager's concerns about Corinne's being selected for this move

Unknown stories
What happens to Corinne if she can't turn the office around?
What happens to the office?
What will happen to the current staff?

story Telling
Private meetings
Long international telephone calls
Very little written documentation

Untold stories
How severe the situation really is
Who else is planning on resigning

Untellable stories
Mishandling of human resource issues by prior manager
Complicity of some staff and managers in creating the current situation

stories Told
Corinne is capable of turning this office around.
The office is now performing below standards.

Figure 13.2 Stories About the European Office

Corinne found the LUUUUTT model useful because I posed many questions to her as she was completing the chart to challenge her assumptions about how she staked her claim of knowing. It was evident in the earlier stages that Corinne was operating predominantly at the instrumental level of knowing as she took verbatim the comments she had been hearing (Kegan et al., 2001). Corinne had moments of a socializing level of knowing because she understood from experience the dynamics of the workplace and how people behave with questionable ethics when they need to accomplish a particular task quickly. It was critical for her to accept that the comments she heard and her initial assessment were only the foundation of understanding and that they raised many more questions than answers. The storytelling part of the LUUUUTT model helped her realize there were reasons that some of this was not being documented in writing.

The advantage of posing questions to Corinne is that it provided her the opportunity to reflect on her own assumptions and question certain comments she had previously accepted as absolutes (Brookfield, 1987). Corinne began to deepen and broaden her self-awareness and how it related to others around her. She began to develop a deeper understanding of her colleagues as she started to see the diversity and complexity in their thinking. She recognized shades of gray.

REACTION TO PERSPECTIVE SHIFTS

The process was not always smooth. Corinne held a deep commitment to her belief system, which was continuously reinforced with her professional success. She understood in a superficial way that her interpersonal skills were not strong, yet the message she received in the workplace was that she was a star performer. There was little incentive for her to want to improve her interpersonal relationships, but her achievements came at a cost. Corinne still believed she would be successful in this new endeavor because she had always been successful.

It was unnerving for Corinne to be told that what she thought was absolutely true or false might not always be so. She believed strongly in her assessment of the world and that misunderstanding was a part of it. While she was quick to identify difference, she did it from a position of judging right or wrong according to her own standards.

The immediate pressure of the demands being placed on her caused Corinne to be more committed to the coaching. She struggled as she shifted from seeing the world as black and white to grasping the ambiguity in interpersonal communication. She was willing to accept difficult relationships as the sacrifice for her professional success and did not think she could have both professional success and satisfactory relationships. She saw the same around her and thought this was the way it had to be. The transformations Corinne did have allowed her to engage with others in more meaningful and mutually beneficial ways, and she began to redefine herself from being a difficult colleague to one who could get along with others in the workplace.

REFLECTIONS

One year after our coaching sessions had concluded, I met Corinne for dinner to learn about her experience in settling in to this new environment. We discussed her success in moving forward with the changes for which she was charged. She fired and hired staff and created a new social dynamic in the office. While she acknowledged having fits and starts, overall she felt as though the transition had been successful. She still used humor to criticize the habits of those different from her and mentioned she was working on accepting those differences, but she was not sure she would be able to accept them completely.

Corinne said that in all our time together, I never told her how I felt about her, and she wanted to know my personal opinion. I asked why that mattered, as the coaching was about her, not about what I thought. Although I did not think it appropriate to divulge all that I thought, I did consider her need to hear my comments. Since we were no longer in a coaching relationship, I felt comfortable telling her that I thoroughly enjoyed her and that while her self-deprecating humor can be amusing, it can get in her way. I told her how brave I felt she was in addressing these challenges and that it is not an easy thing to manage.

After further reflection, I wish I had been firmer and more demanding of Corinne midway through the coaching sessions. Initially I thought it was important to establish trust and build rapport, which I still support having done. Then I think Corinne could have responded with greater growth (deeper self-awareness and a more developed skill set) to being pressed more firmly to work on her assignments outside our coaching sessions and to show that she viewed these efforts at helping her become a better manager as important and something she sought. Perhaps she needed to be more honest with herself about how important success in managing others was to her and whether these development efforts were worth the investment. If she did not think so, we could have ended them earlier. Corinne probably felt pressure from those around her to continue, and that may have been a way to appease them.

There are challenges in the coaching situation. One is to clearly define the client. Is it the person calling me in, or the person I am coaching? This is critical because of confidentiality concerns and developing trust. If the client is the person who hired me, then I have an obligation to reveal information that would not allow me to honor my confidentiality agreement with the person being coached. Commitment is a second concern. The person being coached must want to engage in the change process, or it will not be effective. As a coach, my purpose is to act as a guide to provide opportunities that will foster transformative learning. Typically this involves the other person's being able to see more broadly than her own point of view and to understand that her opinions are formed by her experiences and that they are loaded with assumptions and expectations that may not be shared.

The process of transformative learning and disorienting dilemmas may cause emotional distress in clients, and this may create resistance and blockages to learning and change. It is disconcerting for them to find that the beliefs they carried for so many years are being challenged and reformed. The ambiguity usually brings clients to a state of discomfort.

Each coaching session causes me to reflect on my own interactions and whether I am modeling the skills. I usually go through a process of checking my own assumptions about what I know about the client, what I expect from this client and from myself, and challenge myself for what else I can do to provide opportunities for discovery and transformation.

REFERENCES

Argyris, C. (1993). *Knowledge for action: A guide to overcoming barriers to organizational change*. San Francisco: Jossey-Bass.

Argyris, C., & Schön, D. A. (1994). *Theory in practice: Increasing professional effectiveness*. San Francisco: Jossey-Bass.

Brookfield, S. D. (1987). *Developing critical thinkers: Challenging adults to explore alternative ways of thinking and acting*. San Francisco: Jossey-Bass.

Coleman, P. T. (2004). Paradigmatic framing of protracted, intractable conflict: Towards the development of a meta-framework–II. *Peace and Conflict: Journal of Peace Psychology, 10*(3), 197–235.

Deutsch, M. (2006). Cooperation and competition. In M. Deutsch, P. T. Coleman, & E. Marcus (Eds.), *The handbook of conflict resolution: Theory and practice* (2nd ed., pp. 23–42). San Francisco: Jossey-Bass.

Fisher-Yoshida, B. (2000). *Altering awareness of self, relationship and context in conflict resolution: Impact, feedback and reflection.* Dissertation Abstracts International, 61/03, 1694B. (UMI No. 9966201)

Fisher-Yoshida, B. (2003). Self-awareness and the co-construction of conflict. *Human Systems: The Journal of Systemic Consultation and Management, 141*(1–4), 169–182.

Fisher-Yoshida, B. (2005). Reframing conflict: Intercultural conflict as potential transformation. *Journal of Intercultural Communication, 8,* 1–16.

Fisher-Yoshida, B., & Geller, K. (2008). Developing transnational leaders: Five paradoxes for success. *Journal of Industrial and Commercial Training, 40*(1), 42–50.

Geller, K. D. (2005). *A model of relational leadership development for multinational corporations in the 21st century.* Unpublished doctoral dissertation, Fielding Graduate Institute. Retrieved January 2006 from ProQuest Digital Dissertations database. (Publication No. AAT 3158283)

Gray, B., & Putnam, L. L. (2003). Means to what end: Conflict handling frames. *Environmental Practice, 5*(3), 239–246.

Harvard Business School. (2005). What an executive coach can do for you. *Harvard Management Update, 9*(12), 1–2.

Kegan, R., Broderick, M., Drago-Severson, E., Helsing, D., Popp, N., & Portnow, K. (2001). *Toward a new pluralism in ABE/ESOL classrooms: Teaching to multiple "cultures of mind."* Cambridge, MA: Harvard University Graduate School of Education.

Marsick, V., Sauquet, A., & Yorks, L. (2006). Learning through reflection. In M. Deutsch, P. T. Coleman, & E. Marcus (Eds.), *The handbook of conflict resolution: Theory and practice* (2nd ed., pp. 486–506). San Francisco: Jossey-Bass.

Mezirow, J., & Associates. (1990). *Fostering critical reflection in adulthood: A guide to transformative and emancipatory learning.* San Francisco: Jossey-Bass.

Mezirow, J., & Associates. (2000). Learning to think like an adult: Core concepts of transformation theory. In J. Mezirow & Associates, *Learning as transformation: Critical perspectives on a theory in progress* (pp. 3–33). San Francisco: Jossey-Bass.

Nagata, A. L. (2002). *Somatic mindfulness and energetic presence in intercultural communication: A phenomenological/hermeneutic exploration of bodymindset and emotional resonance.* Unpublished doctoral dissertation, Fielding Graduate Institute. Retrieved June 2002 from ProQuest Digital Dissertations database. (Publication No. AAT 3037968)

Pearce, K. A., & Pearce, W. B. (2000). Extending the theory of the coordinated management of meaning (CMM) through a community dialogue process. *Communication Theory, 10,* 405–423.

Pearce, W. B. (2004). The coordinated management of meaning. In W. Gudykunst (Ed.), *Theorizing communication and culture* (pp. 35–54). Thousand Oaks, CA: Sage.

Senge, P. M. (1990). *The fifth discipline: The art and practice of the learning organization.* New York: Doubleday.

Tisdell, E. J. (2003). *Exploring spirituality and culture in adult and higher education.* San Francisco: Jossey-Bass.

CHAPTER FOURTEEN

The Transformative Potential of Action Learning Conversations

Developing Critically Reflective Practice Skills

Victoria J. Marsick, Terrence E. Maltbia

I n this chapter, we describe a structured protocol, action learning conversations (ALCs), that we have developed and used in both its pure form as a learning activity and as a heuristic to guide coach development. At the heart of ALCs and the coaching practice we describe is critically reflective practice that we think supports transformative learning. We discuss the roots of ALCs and describe how we use these as a stand-alone learning activity and as a heuristic. We conclude the chapter with reflections on what we have learned and realized through the process of writing this chapter.

ACTION LEARNING CONVERSATIONS

Judy O'Neil began developing ALCs for use within action learning (AL) programs by drawing on her own experience and protocols used in England (O'Neil & Marsick, 2007). We have used ALCs with principals, superintendents, and teachers in schools; faculty and students in higher education; leaders in businesses, government, and nonprofit organizations; and coaches who work with leaders in many settings.

What Is Action Learning?

ALCs are shaped by the principles of action learning, which we define as "an approach to working with and developing people that uses work on an actual project or problem as the way to learn. Participants work in small groups to take action to solve their problem and learn how to learn from that action. Often a learning coach works with the group in order to help the members learn how to balance their work with the learning from that work" (Yorks, O'Neil, & Marsick, 1999, p. 3). Although AL takes a number of forms (O'Neil & Marsick, 2007), many agree on the criticality of alternating cycles of action and reflection, driven by questions, to generate strategic insight. Increasingly organizations want to invest in strategic forms of learning, defined as "intentional and performance driven learning linked to strategy that clearly defines the knowledge, skills and mindset necessary for current and future organizational success; involves establishing planning and accountabilities systems to ensure that learning is embedded in the actual work and major business processes of the enterprise" (Maltbia & Power, 2008, p. 4).

In the context of AL, strategic learning is enhanced by the capacity to change perceptions based on experience (Revans, 1989), change how one interprets a given situation either by altering one's values or judgments about how things actually work in a particular situation, and change the set of alternatives from which to select future action.

The Role of Reflection in the Transformative Potential of AL and ALCs

Some people enjoy the opportunity for time to review what has or has not been working in order to make informed choices about next steps. Yet others get impatient when asked to use a learning journal to review action—their own or the group's—with the help of peers. We have observed over time, however, that many people come to value reflection once they understand how this practice can improve the quality of their results, especially when it is coupled with probing questions from others. To borrow an analogy from medicine, where time is often of the essence and a mistake can be a matter of life or death, physicians are taught to refrain from coming to a decision until all the objective facts are assembled and all possible hypotheses, interpretations, and assumptions are carefully considered. ALCs support this kind of slowing down in order to support a better outcome.

Critical reflection—that is, reflection that helps identify underlying values, beliefs, and assumptions—is especially powerful in the context of ALCs because it enables people to see how they can change a situation by changing the way they frame it and act on it. We argue that reflective practice skills can help people to transform existing meaning perspectives (both habits of mind and the resulting points of view) to those that are potentially more accurate and complete given the temporal context, less coercive and self-deceptive in nature, and more inclusive, discriminating, and open. As Mezirow (1991) argues, such transformation offers a broader range of options to guide action in ways that are experienced as true or justified.

Structuring Action Learning Conversations

The heart of ALCs is working in peer groups (as small as three people but preferably no larger than a group of six or seven) on a highly meaningful challenge or problem. The process takes the problem holder sequentially through these recurring cycles:

- Framing of the challenge as a question
- Unpacking meaning through sharing information about the context and prior action
- Peer questioning (to which the problem holder does not immediately respond) to unlock mental models that make one blind to other points of view
- Identifying assumptions that underlie current ways of framing the challenge
- Reframing one's understanding of the situation
- Making more informed decisions and taking informed action to address the challenge

Figure 14.1 shows that we have structured our general approach to ALCs in three phases: framing and engaging, advancing, and disengaging. Work is done in groups selected for maximum diversity. A learning coach introduces the process, guides people through it, and holds the space for learning (O'Neil & Marsick, 2007). In its purest form, using the sequential ALC protocol to address

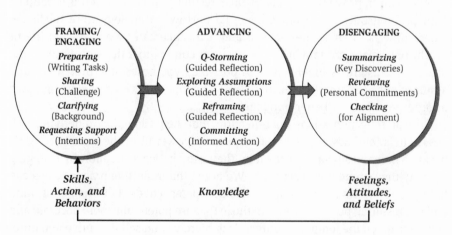

Figure 14.1 Action Learning Conversations

one person's challenge takes about one hour, depending on the nature of the problem, the size and composition of the group, whether people are working on the challenge for the first time or if this is a continuation of prior work, and other contextual factors.

We warn participants that it will feel unnatural to work through the protocol because it artificially channels conversation. Peers are guided to ask questions or offer observations without giving advice about how to address the challenge. The person receiving the consulting help does not respond to questions or observations in the moment but does write down what he or she hears. Each phase offers an opportunity for short, selective responses by the person receiving the consulting help, but remarks are held until that point in the protocol.

Phase 1: Framing and Engaging. In the first step, everyone writes about an important challenge in the form of a question. We use the STAR approach to guide participants in structuring critical incident examples by outlining the following components (Flanagan, 1954; Butterfield, Borgen, Amundson, & Maglio, 2005):

Situations (the what, where, when and who)

Task (or intentions, what was or is to be accomplished)

Actions (what has been done already, planned next steps, associated thoughts and feelings)

Results (the outcomes to date, desired future outcomes)

Writing focuses attention. Members briefly share their challenge questions, after which the group picks a person with whom to begin work. That person takes about ten minutes to provide the background. Peers help by asking what we call "objective" questions to clarify the context and surface essential background information (the facts about the situation, external reality, relatively direct observable data). Phase 1 concludes with the challenge holder stating the support that would help in thinking about the presenting challenge (that is, framing).

Phase 2: Advancing. Phase 2, the heart of the process, is divided into four key steps, each of which takes a minimum of ten minutes. During each step, the person receiving peer support listens and writes but does not respond. At the end of each step, the person can respond selectively to what he or she heard before moving to the next step. Phase 2 begins with more questions. Questions have always been at the heart of AL in that they free people to think in new ways, whereas advice giving can reinforce prior mental models that inhibit fresh solutions.

We use two tools to support questioning: Q (Question)-storming, developed by Marilee Goldberg Adams (2004), and the ORID framework (**O**bjective, **R**eflective, **I**nterpretative, and **D**ecisional Data) introduced by Laura Spencer of the Institute of Cultural Affairs (1989). People first silently think and write down questions related to the challenge holder's question, which are then shared in a round of Q-storming. Often we use a sequential round-robin process whereby each person raises one question at a time until all questions are asked. The challenge holder remains silent throughout, but at the end can choose to comment, provide more information, or remain silent.

We then introduce the ORID framework, a powerful tool for enhancing progressive forms of questioning and listening. Specifically, the framework distinguishes among objective, reflective, interpretative, and decisional questions useful when one is posing questions or a way to determine the nature of a speaker's response when one is listening. Objective questions center on "What is happening?" Reflective questions probe "How am I feeling/reacting?" Interpretative questions seek to answer, "What does it mean?" "What are we learning?" Decisional questions focus on "What do I do?" and "How do I respond?" Objective questions begin to be asked in phase 1 when people share their challenges. In phase 2, although some objective questions can still be asked, we focus learners on reflective and interpretative questions. We recommend refraining from decisional questions early in the process.

Decisional questions become more important as people engage in iterative cycles of ALCs because at that point, they are reviewing action taken on decisions made in earlier ALC cycles. A common pitfall when first engaging in this questioning process is to provide advice disguised as a question. As we discuss later when introducing our coaching example, transforming one's mind-set from advice giving to question asking is a key outcome of the ALC process.

The ORID framework parallels the steps in Kolb's (1984) experiential learning cycle, which we also often use in tandem with ALCs to reinforce a holistic learning process. In Kolb's cycle, people take in information through some mix of concrete experience or abstract conceptualization, and they transform that information through some mix of reflective observation and active experimentation. Combining ORID and Kolb's cycle helps learners work through the following sequence of questioning and sometimes of listening in order to classify questions or comments that may not be adequately grounded in objective data.

Objective questioning focuses on facts and draws on our senses in terms of what we see, hear, say, and do, that is, what is relatively observable—largely externally focused and an important foundation for a common picture of a slice of reality (concrete experience). Reflective questioning focuses on reactions and how we respond to external data, largely internally focused on emotional domains, including how we connect a current experience with prior situations and on images that the situation triggers for us, or the highs and lows (that is, reflective observation). Interpretative questioning focuses on critical thinking related to the external and internal data that make up the context by probing patterns, themes, values, and implications. It is largely meaning focused, geared toward answering, "So what?" (that is, abstract conceptualization). Decisional questioning focuses on outcomes and determines future intentions or actions; it is largely "doing" focused (that is, active experimentation).

The second step in phase 2 is to explore assumptions. People are frequently not aware of underlying assumptions that drive actions. In this next step, members silently write down relevant assumptions they think the person being helped might hold or that they themselves might hold were they in a similar situation. We often introduce the "ladder of inference" (Argyris, Putnam, & McClain-Smith, 1985, p. 59) as a tool for helping groups make explicit their assumptions, evaluations, and attributions. Using the ladder of inference, learners see how they selectively focus on a piece of directly observable data (first rung of the ladder), add their own meanings (second rung of the ladder), and escalate their assumptions (cultural, epistemological, psychological, and so forth) without inquiring into the validity of their views. This process, often called "jumping up the ladder," is unpacked by using the ORID framework. As in the prior step, assumptions can be shared through a round-robin, although we sometimes use a "fly on the wall" process whereby peers talk as if the challenge holder ("fly") were not present. In both cases, the challenge holder listens and writes and then may selectively share reactions.

The third step in phase 2 is to reframe the original question. New information typically leads to fresh thinking. Often the person begins to see how he or she contributes to the gap that can exist between intentions and impact or identifies other views of people in the situation. In this step, members write down ways they might now reframe the challenge and then, in round-robin fashion, share these reframes. At the end of this step, the person receiving help can share his or her reframes based on new thinking. The final step in this phase is a commitment to action based on new insights (for example, gathering more information, checking out assumptions, or behaving in new ways). This prepares the way for phase 3, that of disengaging.

Phase 3: Disengaging. During the final phase, the learning coach, a member of the group, or the person who has been helped summarizes key discoveries, reviews commitments, and checks for alignment. As Figure 14.1 shows, doing so enables a feedback loop in which feelings and attitudes experienced can be informed by new insight and knowledge, which gets fed back into the way the person frames and engages the situation through action.

APPLYING ALC AS A HEURISTIC

We have used ALCs as a heuristic to guide the design and implementation of the Columbia Coaching Certification Program (CCCP), a strategic partnership between faculty at Teachers College and the executive education unit of the Columbia Business School. In today's global environment, characterized by exponential technological advances, learning demands have never been greater. Professional and executive coaching has emerged as a field to help people "speed-up the learning curve in acquiring the skills needed to navigate" the constant change characteristic of the new knowledge economy (Davison & Gasiorowski, 2006, p. 189).

There is little agreement about how coaches should be developed and the competencies at the heart of their practice. CCCP was designed to fill that gap. ALCs play a central role, along with perspective transformation (Mezirow, 1991), to design and redesign the coach development program and create ALC-based coaching protocols that graduates of the program can use in their work. The overall objective of CCCP is to develop a theory and research-based foundation for coaching and provide opportunities for intensive practice and feedback. Our goal is to help each participant chart a path toward an individualized coaching approach. Participants are introduced to the three phases of coaching: context (the where, when, who, and why of coaching), content (the what of coaching), and informed action (the how of coaching).

CCCP extends over a period of eight to ten months. It begins with a five-day face-to-face intensive, followed by a supervised practicum in which coaches apply what they have learned. During the practicum, participants engage in regularly scheduled online group coaching sessions; observe coach demonstrations; maintain a learning journal to integrate learning from the experience of coaching clients, online sessions, and assigned readings; and complete their own coaching project. The program ends with a five-day residential intensive, after which the participants obtain coach certification.

During the intensive beginning, ALCs are used in two ways. First, participants use the ALC process in a step-by-step fashion. Phase 1 is introduced and used on the first full day of the program. New skills are added on the second day, after which participants revisit phase 1 and add phase 2. On days 3 and 4, participants revisit and practice addressing challenges using all three phases of ALCs. Second, ALCs are used as a heuristic to guide curriculum design. The ALC structure—introducing and exploring a challenge; iterative cycles of asking questions, examining assumptions, and reframing; and taking action informed by this cycle—is used as the overall framework for each five-day intensive.

CCCP and the coaching process, in which participants are trained, are built around critically reflective practice and the principles of perspective transformation. As Conger and Benjamin (1999) note, reflection and feedback are what differentiate AL from ordinary task accomplishment; yet programs often commit the serious mistake of including reflection in only one session on the last day of the program. By contrast, in the CCCP, we explicitly integrate various forms of reflection—as Mezirow (1991) recommends, reflection on content (the what), process (the how), and premises (the why)—into the curriculum.

Furthermore, given that effective coaches must own and refine the use of self in relation to their work (the self as an instrument), they must often transform many of their own taken-for-granted assumptions about the process of helping others in general and the coaching process in particular. One common perspective targeted for transformation is moving from seeing coaching as giving others advice to a view of coaching as helping others discover their own truths and solutions. For this reason, Mezirow's (1991) phases of perspective transformation informed our work to help participants discover their signature coach presence and approach.

We further illustrate the way we use ALCs by elaborating on the design of the front-end five-day coaching intensive.

Prework and Gathering

The reflective process begins with prework that helps participants understand self as instrument, assess their current capabilities as coaches, and identify challenges they are facing on which they can work during the program. Participants identify high and low critical incidents in their lives that shaped their work as coaches. They gather on the afternoon of the first day to map their individual experiences and then create "group life maps" that help them understand their common experiences as coaches. Life history work prepares the group for critical reflection using ALCs by making them aware of their individually held and collective values, beliefs, and meaning schemes.

Participants also begin to identify challenges in their coaching practice that they will use throughout the program in ALCs. As is always done in AL, participants work on real problems or opportunities. We do not use off-the-shelf case studies or role plays. We think the potential for transformative learning is greater when work is based on participants' real, lived experience.

Day One

The learning theme for the first full day is understanding one's coaching mind-set. We start by developing a clear baseline description of how the learners currently understand and practice coaching. Central to this is coaching in triads on real challenges that is taped, viewed, and critiqued. ALCs are introduced and modeled by a lead faculty. Participants then review their recorded baseline coaching conversations. The emphasis is on inquiry rather than advice giving. Participants discover for themselves the insights embedded in their thoughts, feelings, impressions, behavioral patterns, perceived risks, fantasies, hopes, and fears that were at play during the actual taped conversation yet were not available to them in action.

Self-examination, prompted by reviewing the tapes, often triggers a disorienting dilemma. For example, participants give advice more than ask questions; they make judgments and focus on their personal agenda, not the client's. Overall, the image on the tape does not align with what they had envisioned their coaching skills to be. This disconnect triggers a wide range of feeling and emotions, including embarrassment, shame, resistance (they might say, "We were not given enough time"), uncertainty about their capabilities, and disappointment. Participants try to understand these emotions as they then reflect on content (the what of coaching), process (the flow of coaching), and, importantly, premises (guiding assumptions about effective practice). Participants begin to realize that their personal discontent is shared and to question taken-for-granted assumptions about effective coaching practice.

Day Two

The focus of the second full day of the intensive is on building four core coaching competencies: relating, coach presence, questioning and listening, and testing assumptions. The theme of the second day is using the self as instrument to facilitate the learning and change process with clients. For each competency, participants are provided with a description and behavioral examples of the skill in action. They then plan for and work with peers to try out each skill during taped coach conversations. Faculty members provide support but also encourage participants to drive their own process.

The ORID framework is used as tool for developing listening skills and progressive-questioning skills. A Kolb-based learning style inventory, linked to ORID steps, helps people make connections between coaching and learning from experience. The ladder of inference is introduced as a tool to test assumptions (one's own and those of others). Participants work together in triads to use ALCs as they try on skills associated with core coaching competencies. The formal part of the day concludes with a recorded integrated coaching conversation designed to pull together the competencies learned.

This day continues the process of fostering perspective transformation as participants continue self-examination of their practice, triggered by additional taped coaching conversations and review. People continue to wrestle with their personal views of what constitutes effective practice in coaching. They see that they are not alone in their discontent; it is shared. They occupy a place of "in-between-ness": having discomfort with old ways of doing and being, yet not quite sure how to replace these patterns. A shift starts to occur as opportunities to try out alterative approaches are presented.

Days Three and Four

During these two days, participants practice coaching one another in triads using ALCs. We also make the learning more public by providing feedback on taped conversations that take place in a "fish bowl" (coaching taking place in the center of a circle of observers). Next, faculty lead a review of the coaching conversations by first asking the client and coach what worked for them and what they might do differently in the future. Peers provide both oral and written feedback.

A major shift often occurs during these two days. Participants become much more focused on exploring new options; planning new courses of action, knowledge, and skill acquisition to support their plan; and opportunities for practice and feedback. They begin to find spaces during breaks and planned leisure time to continue their work with peers. They also complete the last taped coaching conversation of the week, which is combined with the baseline coaching conversation and becomes the focus of early work during the coach supervision component of the practicum. The tapes help make explicit the learning that occurred during the week, along with specific developmental priorities. Participants seem excited after the final taping as they reflect on the growth they have observed in themselves and others.

REFLECTIONS

We have become aware by writing this chapter of how deeply the underlying design principles of ALCs have become a heuristic for us in designing different kinds of learning environments and engagements. We realize how unconsciously we use the building blocks of ALCs to undergird our design work even when the ALC is not explicitly used. The duration of the event and capacity to become a holding environment are key and change with the context. We might compare this to differences between visiting a foreign country or culture versus living in that country or culture over an extended period of time. In both cases, we might surface and confront disorienting dilemmas because others think and act differently than do we. But in a short visit, we do not have to work through the implications and consequences of those differences. Similarly, using the ALC protocol for a limited period of hours, say, a four-hour half-day session, can involve critical reflection on assumptions, but even though it may lead to reframing one's challenge, the depth of reflection is limited by trust in the group, willingness to disclose, time to challenge one's thinking, and many other factors.

Deeply transformative learning, by contrast, requires a climate of both affective and cognitive trust, something that usually develops over weeks or months, often spread over time, and involves both the head and the heart. In such situations, we can see that we intentionally use repetition and frequency of the ALC protocol, combined with creating a safer "holding environment," to provide intensity of learning in ways that trigger transformation.

No matter the ALC duration, starting with a writing task to identify personally important challenges helps us earn the right to ask people to engage in a process that, from the start, feels awkward at best. Working on issues that are real and relevant helps to lessen the resistance to structured reflective processes, given the press for time and action.

ALCs are powerful in part because peers learn from one another, pool their knowledge, and gain direct experience of perspective taking. This is enhanced by combining challenge with a safe space to try out new roles and approaches. Engaging in a process that facilitates perspective transformation can trigger a wide range of emotions including surprise (or even shock), anger, and often rejection during the early phases. Use of the ALC protocol might not trigger unmanageable feelings because learners choose what to self-disclose, but when used as a heuristic over a longer time frame, strong emotions do emerge and are addressed. A safe environment needs to be created by faculty or ALC coaches (O'Neil & Marsick, 2007). One powerful strategy is for the faculty team to model the way.

We now see that opportunities for transformative learning differ in a shorter, half-day ALC versus a day versus several days. As facilitators, we have become more attuned to the learner and less concerned with whether learners are "doing it right." Our only goal becomes trying on the protocol at its most basic level to get as much as possible, given where one is, even if someone does not follow all the steps exactly as prescribed. For example, if a person cannot reframe, we suggest that this is not a failure, and it is okay if his or her original thinking is simply reconfirmed. This is a reframing of the process for us.

In longer programs, we have time to deepen the learning through layering of the capabilities embedded in each of the ALC steps. For example, early work with the ORID framework necessarily centers on learning the steps of the protocol. While listening is important, learners focus more on asking different kinds of questions. But over a longer period of time, we might emphasize the flip side of the coin, listening, which enables people to better hear new ideas. In subsequent cycles, we might show how learning style shows up in preferences for asking one kind of question over others or paying attention only to one kind of data.

The power of ALCs is both simple and nuanced. In every cycle, we go more deeply by layering the way we use the tools. We build on what is learned in earlier cycles and may use different tools in different ways as participants learn from their own and others' experiences.

REFERENCES

Adams, M. G. (2004). *Change your questions, change your life.* San Francisco: Berrett-Koehler.

Argyris, C., Putnam, R., & McClain-Smith, D. (1985). *Action science.* San Francisco: Jossey-Bass.

Butterfield, L. D., Borgen, W. A., Amundson, N. E., & Maglio, A. T. (2005). Fifty years of the critical incident technique: 1954–2004. *Qualitative Research, 5*(4), 475–497.

Conger, J. A., & Benjamin, B. B. (1999). *Building leaders: How successful companies develop the next generation.* San Francisco: Jossey-Bass.

Davison, M., & Gasiorowski, F. (2006). The trend of coaching: Adler, the literature, and marketplace would agree. *Journal of Individual Psychology, 62*(2), 188–201.

Flanagan, J. C. (1954). The critical incident technique. *Psychological Bulletin, 51*(4), 327–358.

Kolb, D. (1984). *Experiential learning.* Upper Saddle River, NJ: Prentice Hall.

Maltbia, T. E., & Power, A. T. (2008). *A leader's guide to leveraging diversity: Strategic learning capabilities for breakthrough performance.* Burlington, MA: Butterworth-Heinemann.

Mezirow, J. (1991). *Transformative dimensions of adult learning.* San Francisco: Jossey-Bass.

O'Neil, J., & Marsick, V. J. (2007). *Understanding action learning.* New York: AMACOM.

Revans, R. (1989). *The golden jubilee of action learning.* Manchester, England: Manchester Action Learning Exchange, University of Manchester.

Spencer, L. J. (1989). *Winning through participation: Meeting the challenge of corporate change with the technology of participation.* Dubuque, IA: Kendall/Hunt.

Yorks, L., O'Neil, J., & Marsick, V. J. (1999). *Action learning: Successful strategies for individual, team, and organizational development.* San Francisco: Berrett-Koehler and the Academy of Human Resource Development.

CHAPTER FIFTEEN

Transformative Learning in Adult Basic Education

Kathleen P. King, Barbara P. Heuer

Adult basic education (ABE) and General Educational Development (GED) classrooms have rarely been explored as sites of transformative learning. Adult learners in these settings are usually evaluated by quantitative norms or task completion. Although these are appropriate gauges for ABE curricula and GED programs, a broader perspective considers the possibility of transformative learning. When educators and adult learners implement strategies to encourage transformational learning, they capture additional gains that ABE and GED learning can have on student lives. This chapter extends the reach of a transformative research model (King, 1998). After a brief discussion of the development of this model, two adult learning settings serve to illustrate evidence of transformative learning and highlight three strategies that contributed to this deep learning.

This chapter draws on research regarding transformative learning (King, 1998, 2005; King & Wright, 2003; Mezirow, 1991). Among other settings, we have studied the learning experiences in the GED and ABE classrooms and workplace professional development for over ten years. From this research, an integrated model for instruction, the contextualized model of adult learning, has emerged. It builds on the adult learner's individual and comprehensive context as the starting point for transformative learning. Acknowledging resistance and discomfort, the model suggests that with support and modeling, adult learners can move to greater understanding and authentic action. The extensive evolution of this specific research over the past ten years and the different models, which have emerged are documented in full in King (2009). However, in this chapter, we introduce the model as a framework for considering effective instructional strategies rooted in transformative learning research.

TWO CONTEXTS

To set the stage for a discussion of three strategies that fostered transformative learning, we briefly describe two contexts. The first focuses on adult learners in a suburban adult literacy center where the first author and a colleague observed and interviewed adult learners across nine months. The second targeted group was a group of ABE teachers in an urban school system. These latter educators were involved in a year-long professional development initiative, which included eight workshops where the teachers came to a university campus and were visited monthly at their school sites. Mention of the duration of these efforts is relevant because it underscores the significance of the process for transformative learning over time.

In the first ABE suburban setting, most of the nineteen students had been attending the program for between three and six months. Many of them were on public assistance and were required to attend the class thirty-five hours a week to maintain this funding. They were diverse in nationality, race, and ages, with most from the United States, a few from Jamaica, and one from Cuba; over half self-identified as African American, a quarter as non-Hispanic white, and a quarter as Hispanic. Roughly a third were between the ages of thirty and thirty-nine, a third between ages forty and forty-nine, and 20 percent between ages twenty-one and twenty-nine. These students were categorized as social and academic failures. They were all in the same physical classroom at the center and tested below an eighth-grade level in math and a tenth-grade level in reading.

In the second case, 101 teachers and administrators were part of a system of alternative high schools in a large urban area undergoing extensive systemic reorganization to address needs of pre-GED and GED educators and students. Their teaching and advising experience ranged from five to twenty years. Sixty percent of the participants were European American, and 40 percent were African American. These instructors represented vocational and educational programs for pregnant teenagers, the incarcerated, early offenders, and low literates. Teachers from these programs who had been selected by their administrators met for day-long professional development workshops on our college campus for three workshops in the summer, two in the fall, and three in the spring. They also received on-site mentoring each month at their schools.

Evidence of transformative learning came in many forms. GED students in the first suburban setting showed their preference for participatory learning by their attendance and participation. Their confidence grew as they determined how they would learn. For the second group, teachers in alternative high schools, the progression from discomfort in the face of change, pessimistic expressions of their situations, reluctant exposure to new resources and viewpoints, reflection, and uneven but strong new attitudes and actions was palpable. They spoke and wrote about this journey vigorously. The passive, threatened group who started the workshops finished the academic year as energetic, outspoken practitioners who were comfortable trying new strategies and techniques, even incorporating new technologies, with their adult students.

We felt this outward sign reflected a shift in many of the participants' internal dialogue. They were questioning long-held perspectives and received information, and they were creating their own insights. While analyzing scenarios in one workshop activity, the educators compared their students to the ones described, often getting so passionate they engaged as if the fictional characters were real. Their dedication to their students was obvious and now expressed. In role plays, they were able to act out concerns about administrators and difficult students. After a few months, the teachers moved from skepticism to new perspectives. For example, in a major reversal of action and beliefs, teachers who had been convinced their students could not cooperate in small groups began to create more group activities. These same educators also described their own learning experiences as empowering, revitalizing, and encouraging. In a system that had provided little structure and support, educators turned their personal situations around and found they could be responsible for new visions and possibilities.

STRATEGIES

In the course of working with these two groups, we were often challenged to find the most effective strategies and techniques to meet their needs. From the many methods at our disposal, each was adapted to these learners' unique situation. They all, however, rested on our own adult learning values. In the following sections, we describe how we used the instructional approaches of learner centeredness, safety and trust, and facilitating and modeling across adult learning contexts

Learner Centeredness

Learner centeredness took many physical and curricular forms. The alternative high school teachers met in a well-appointed, carpeted, windowed meeting room. Tables were arranged in the center in a U-shape with tables for small group discussion around the perimeter of the room. Name tags, folders, and pens were provided for each participant. This setting projected respect for the learners and indicated that they would be listened to here.

On entering the classroom for the first session, many participants expressed surprise and commented on how spacious and comfortable the room was. The arrangement of tables, audiovideo equipment, flip charts on easels, and refreshments indicated that these would be interactive workshops where the teachers' needs would be met and their voices heard. Adult educators who worked in marginalized programs, often in secondary spaces like basements or K-12 classrooms, appreciated these surroundings. This environment communicated at least two critical differences in our approach from what they were used to: we as faculty developers respected them as professionals, and we expected that they would participate in important work.

A difficult change for the GED teachers at first was the collaborative learning and project-based learning activities we incorporated. We wanted to model these strategies because we knew it was the most effective way for them to understand the delivery details and the benefits. Yet the educators did not believe the strategies could work with their students, and so we confronted obstacles and resistance in the first few sessions. By taking time to discuss their concerns, learners and contexts, and participating in the projects, they gradually understood the potential of these strategies for themselves. However, the learner-centered focus of our work with the teachers was indispensable in allowing this shift to happen: we had to give space for them to be heard and be responsive to their needs. The message was clearly communicated: our instructional plans and strategies could be modified based on their needs.

Similarly, the ABE class we studied also took a decided departure from institutional practice. The rest of the adult learning center's classes were traditional and teacher centered. The classroom we observed, in contrast, was a learner-centered one where students entered, gathered their materials, and went to group tables. This collaborative classroom setting and approach resulted in adult learners' wanting to be in this instructor's classes for the whole day instead of for only her content subject. Over several years, a few students did elect to leave her class because they wanted a more traditional approach. This finding is consistent with what we know about adult learners' different learning styles and comfort levels with nontraditional education. While many adults want to have some voice in how and what they learn, many others prefer to be told what to do at various stages of their learning or for various subjects or contents.

When the ABE students entered their classroom, they often found the instructor and other learners at tables throughout the room, deep in conversation, gathered around assignments. The teacher worked as a facilitator to help students identify goals and suggest resources. Students also helped each other understand reading passages or solve math problems.

The students supported one another as peer facilitators working on individual assignments, readily assisting one another, and seeking assistance from the teacher and one another throughout the day. They used texts and workbooks; however, the instructor also used individual and group activities she had developed to incorporate everyday applications, dialogue, reflection, role playing, and simulations (Campbell & Malicky, 2002; Tout & Schmidt, 2002).

Another dimension of learner focus that fostered transformative learning was making teachers aware of resources beyond their schools. In workshops with the GED teachers, as we introduced professional associations, Web sites, and publications that directly related to what these teachers did each day, we saw how excited teachers became when they discovered the support and practical guidance available to them.

Safety and Trust

Making adult learners feel safe is a multidimensional prerequisite for transformative learning. For example, we soon realized that many of the adult high school teachers had concerns ranging from their centers' reorganization and their part in a new hierarchy to their own teaching skills and getting new textbooks. They also indicated a distrust of professional development efforts in general and a vague uneasiness about why they were "chosen" to participate. These layers of anxiety affected their involvement in the workshops. In order for significant learning gains to be achieved, including transformative learning, such obstacles needed to be acknowledged and validated. We created many opportunities for them to be expressed. Such dialogue and respect powerfully addressed the emotional and personal sides of learning (hooks, 1994; O'Sullivan, 1999).

These teachers obviously had different comfort levels in expressing their fears and exploring uncharted territory. In order to demonstrate and cultivate sincere respect of their insights and opinions, even when we did not have the ability or authority to resolve many concerns, we tried to respond by giving many opportunities for communication. From the first workshop, participants could, at any time, get up and record their question, concern, or observation on a flip chart without signing their name. Role playing and scenarios were other strategies that allowed teachers to express themselves safely.

At the end of each day's session, evaluation forms asked the teachers what they learned that was useful, what was not, and what else they needed. Providing an agenda at each workshop, meeting in a well-equipped meeting room, and scheduling the workshops over a full academic year were other ways we tried to make participants feel safe.

We even addressed urgent needs for advocacy and facilitation in a safe environment. At site visits, we served as the paid professional consultant-developers and advocates. We met with administrators, program directors, and the teachers and discussed classroom, program, student, and teacher needs in ways that might support teachers and yet be receptive to program needs. In several cases, we facilitated dialogue among teachers and administrators to seek answers regarding questions about textbooks, technology access, and technology support.

Facilitation and Modeling

Facilitation techniques were embedded in the supportive approach of the ABE instructor we observed who was humanistic and constructivist. This teacher held a master's degree in adult education and had been teaching in the ABE system for over ten years. Being a humanistic teacher, she supported the belief in building on the potential of her students, giving them freedom and autonomy and yet using a cooperative rather than competitive environment (Elias & Merriam, 1995). Her constructivist roots were evident in her commitment to having students engaged in hands-on and problem-based learning experiences in order to develop their understanding of concepts (Fostnot, 1996). The ways in which we facilitated the workshops for the ABE teachers provided at least two crucial factors. First, we modeled the learner-centered classroom in our choice of activities, our tone, our listening, and our responsiveness. Second, from the start, we tried to compare ourselves with our students and establish that we are all adult learners. The way they learned a lesson had important implications on how their students learned.

We tried to build in many opportunities to make these connections and realizations. For example, before one workshop, we asked participants to think about a time that they learned something out of school. We asked them to take brief notes on what they had learned and what they remembered about the experience. Then we went on with the workshop. Later we revisited this memory exercise, asking for volunteers to share their anecdotes. In describing experiences like learning to drive from an anxious parent, or learning to fish from a loving uncle, they identified the conditions that contributed to their learning. They noted the impact of negative comments and being shown different ways to do something. In reflecting, they made connections between their own learning and that of their students.

Regarding the facilitators' learning this was a deepening experience in learning to teach transformative learning to a different population, a successful collaboration in a stressful setting, and the creation of an environment of success and empowerment. We gained a different understanding of how to explain transformative learning to classroom educators who had no prior background in adult learning. We also honed greater collaborative skills together as a team in being able to read situations moment by moment, the needs of the educator-learners, or the progress of the session, and with this information we quickly adapted our plan of action with minimal communication between us. Our fundamental beliefs and values of our own roles as adult educators were supercharged through this experience. The work with the GED teachers was a year-long project, so it was a continuing challenge for a long period of time. We wanted to assist these educators, but it was stressful for all involved because of the outside pressures on the entire school system.

Finally, we were already greatly committed to cultivating safe and empowering climates for our students, but in no situation has it been more critical, more daunting, or more powerful than with the alternative high school teachers. Faced with participants who were internally resistant, fearful, and angry and outwardly passive and fatalistic, we had to work hard to build their genuine trust and keep it. The final transformation of their attitudes and behavior was so dramatic that it was an emotional situation for us. By the end, we saw those who once fought participation become active, enthusiastic participants and those who had distrusted us seek and offer assistance. The experiences with these learners changed our belief of what is possible through creating transformative learning opportunities.

The pace of the ABE workshops was brisk to engage the adult learners, appeal to different learning styles, and address a variety of goals. In the morning of some workshops, teachers participated in a short, reflective exercise about their own learning, discussed as a whole group, received information about resources available to them, developed a lesson plan, critiqued a literacy article, and posted questions on flip charts. These workshops actively engaged the educators in multiple relevant and practical activities. Participants were expected to produce a relevant lesson plan or poster or analysis to present to their peers. Whole group and small group discussion and activities and short presentations were interspersed with presentations of resources, vocabulary, and concepts. Formal formative evaluations conducted as large group discussion, open-ended surveys, and individual feedback concluded the first day. Adjustments were made throughout the workshops to improve pacing, maintain momentum, and address teacher needs, concerns, and content areas. Summative evaluations were gathered at the completion of the second day using structured focus groups and open-ended surveys.

Our original expectations of how the professional development would transpire did not materialize. The reality was that it was not received enthusiastically at first; it was misunderstood and resisted. We, in response, had to be extraordinarily dynamic and formatively adaptive. We had a tremendous opportunity to model transformative learning strategies and grow through the experience.

REFLECTIONS

Extending transformative theory to this audience contributes to the viability of the theory and the research on ABE and GED learning. Although it did not surprise us that adult learners responded to respect and support, this truism too often gets pushed aside, especially when positions of power are ingrained. Based on these results described, programs have to be designed and facilitators focused on moving core values of learner respect and support into primary and explicit instructional experiences.

Finally, what strikes us is the potential and importance of transformative theory to professional development and ABE and GED learning. While contextual and political issues presented students who on the surface were most interested in working in the system, we found that over time in these initiatives, these same adults claimed their own growth and voice. The role of modeling in the adult learner classroom is invaluable in assisting them in making connections between theory and practice (Belenky, Clinchy, Goldberger, & Tarule, 1986; Giroux, 1988; hooks, 1994; Schön, 1987). We witnessed expressions of possibility, empowerment, ownership, and new awareness. As one seasoned educator in the alternative high school system exclaimed, "I get it! You're doing what I can do!" These shifts were attitudinal and emotional in nature, and they were exciting for the educators and learners alike. Our preliminary research evolved from an approach of gathering data about transformative learning (King, 1998, 2002, 2005, 2009; King & Wright, 2003) to how to help educators understand the theory and to use it in the classroom based on their setting. This extended research has contributed to the development of the contextualized model of adult learning (CMAL; King, 2009; King & Heuer, 2006). We have used this model to help adult educators understand transformative learning in their general context and for their learners' needs more specifically.

Through our work, the focus on context has become important in connecting with practitioners with no prior knowledge of transformative learning to validate their experience, connect learning with their situation, and help empower them to create strategies for their learners. Gaining their trust, modeling, and walking alongside them through the process is indispensable. As the educators are transformed, they realize the possibilities for their learners. This comprehension enables them to create the best understandings, interpretations, and applications for their learners and contexts. The CMAL is a guide that is dynamic and interpretative. We believe it is consistent and grounded in the basis of the transformative learning experience itself.

Reflection on these experiences as educators provides additional thoughts. We are continually amazed at the depth and breadth of adult learning experience. Although we would never seek to force someone to be "transformed," we often invite adults to take that journey by creating transformative learning opportunities (King, 2005). To see educators and ABE learners released from prior constraints and adopting new perspectives renews our belief in the human spirit of possibilities.

We also recognize the difficult work involved in this teaching and learning experience (Giroux, 1988). It takes careful investigation, creativity, and collaboration to create contextualized programs to meet learner and program needs, and negotiation with organizations and individuals can be difficult when they bristle against change or reflection. Still we hold the vision ahead of us, and collaboration has been empowering for us as well. As learners transform, they have transformed us.

REFERENCES

Belenky, M., Clinchy, B., Goldberger, N., & Tarule, J. (1986). *Women's ways of knowing: The development of self, voice and mind.* New York: Basic Books.

Campbell, G., & Malicky, G. (2002, Spring). The reading strategies of adult basic education students. *Adult Basic Education, 12*(1), 3–19.

Elias, J. L., & Merriam, S. B. (1999). *Philosophies of adult education* (2nd ed.). Malabar, FL: Krieger.

Fostnot, C. T. (1996). *Constructivism: Theory, perspectives and practice.* New York: Teachers College Press.

Giroux, H. (1988). *Teachers as intellectuals: Toward a critical pedagogy of learning.* Westport, CT: Bergin & Garvey.

hooks, b. (1994). *Teaching to transgress: Education as the practice of freedom.* New York: Routledge

King, K. P. (1998). *A guide to perspective transformation and learning activities: The Learning Activities Survey.* Philadelphia: Research for Better Schools.

King, K. P. (2002). *Keeping pace with technology: Educational technology that transforms.* Cresskill, NJ: Hampton Press.

King, K. P. (2005). *Bringing transformative learning to life.* Malabar, FL: Krieger.

King, K. P. (2009). *Handbook of evolving research approaches in transformative learning: The Learning Activities Survey* (10th anniversary edition). Charlotte, NC: Information Age Publishing.

King, K. P., & Heuer, B. (2006). Empowering literacy workers through learner-centered environments. *International Journal of Learning 12*(9). Retrieved August 21, 2007, from http://ijl.cgpublisher.com/product/pub.30/prod.861.

King, K., & Wright, L. (2003). New perspectives on gains in the ABE classroom: Transformative learning results considered. *Adult Basic Education, 13*(2), 100–123.

Mezirow, J. (1991). *Transformative dimensions of adult learning.* San Francisco: Jossey-Bass.

O'Sullivan, E. (1999). *Transformative learning: Educational vision for the 21st century.* New York: Zed Books.

Schön, D. A. (1987). *Educating the reflective practitioner.* San Francisco: Jossey-Bass.

Tout, D., & Schmitt, M. J. (2002). The inclusion of numeracy in adult basic education. In J. Comings, B. Garner, & C. Smith (Eds.), *Annual review of adult learning and literacy*, Vol. 3 (pp. 152–202). San Francisco: Jossey-Bass.

CHAPTER SIXTEEN

From Tradesperson to Teacher

A Transformative Transition

Patricia Cranton

I have had the privilege of teaching in a unique program in Canada for the past twenty-five years. In the New Brunswick Community College system, instructors are hired based on their experience in the field rather than on their educational background. The New Brunswick Community Colleges prepare people for work in the trades, technologies, hospitality industry, and some areas of health care. A condition of employment for instructors is that they participate in the instructor development program. Part-time instructors and those wanting to find full-time employment in the colleges may also take the program. The program consists of two intensive three-week summer sessions, a practicum that takes place between the two summer sessions, and three other course electives from the undergraduate adult education program. Many courses are available online as well as face-to-face, but the summer sessions are offered only face-to-face. By taking three additional courses, students can obtain a certificate in adult education, and for those who want to go on to a bachelor of adult education degree, credit can be transferred into that program.

Every year I have taught the session that takes place in the second of the summer sessions. During the first session and also as a part of their practicum, participants learn the skills and techniques of teaching. They practice making presentations in a microteaching format, create course outlines and objectives, and develop tests for their students—the nuts-and-bolts of teaching. When they arrive for the second session, most people are relatively comfortable with the basics of classroom and shop or field teaching, though there are always more topics they want to explore in these areas.

My summer session meets from 8:00 A.M. to 1:00 P.M. five days a week for three weeks. Participants come from around the province, so some commute two hours or more (one way) each day, and others stay in the university residence during the week. Those who commute generally car-pool. It is essentially the same group as in the first summer session, so people know each other, and the group has formed. The average class size is about twenty people, though in some years there have been as few as twelve and in other years up to nearly forty. The numbers vary depending on the hiring done in the colleges in a particular year, and that, in turn, is based on the needs of industry for more individuals in certain trades or technology areas. For a few years, in response to a severe shortage of tradespeople in the province, we held two sections of both the first and second summer sessions. The majority of the participants are male, and there is little cultural or racial diversity in the group, reflecting the nature of the population of New Brunswick. The participants range in age from late twenties to early sixties, with most being over age forty, as the colleges prefer to hire instructors with considerable experience in their field.

I see transformative learning as an appropriate framework for understanding the process in which the instructor development program participants are engaged for several reasons. What generally has not yet happened is that these new instructors have started thinking of themselves as teachers. They see themselves as welders, carpenters, and mechanics who are passing down their practical skills to another generation of welders, carpenters, and mechanics. When I ask them to say something about themselves in the opening class, they typically say, "I'm a welder," not "I'm a teacher." They are in the midst of a transition from a life of working with their hands and bodies to a life of working with their minds and voice.

Many come from a culture that scorns the soft hands of an "office person" and values strength, calluses, and muscles. The men come from a working context in which they most often work only with other men. Many of their previously held habits of mind are called into question during their participation in the instructor development program. This may be less the case for the women in the program, who usually come from a background of being in the helping professions or service industries (nursing aides, radiation technicians, hospitality industry). However, the women in the group are also becoming college teachers, a change that can challenge their perceptions of themselves and their lifestyle.

Educators who have a goal of facilitating transformative learning in their practice can only set up an environment and create activities that have the potential to challenge participants' habits of mind and engage in critical self-reflection. There are no guarantees that anything we do will lead to a transformative experience for others, nor should there be. It would be ethically questionable to attempt to force transformation on others and probably not possible to do. With that in mind, I outline the strategies I have used in the instructor development program to foster and support critical self-reflection, learner empowerment, and potentially transformative learning.

PARTICIPATORY PLANNING

Participants come into their second summer session having already learned about the basic techniques and skills of teaching and having practiced these skills for at least one year. This allows me to use participatory planning to design the three-week session. On the first day of the summer session, following an introductory "tell a story about your teaching" activity and a discussion of the course process and philosophy, we plan, as a group, the topics and activities for the next six classes. There are fifteen classes in all, each one five hours long. A second planning session is conducted midway through the summer for the last part of the course.

The course is called Methods and Strategies in Adult Education, so our only boundary is that we stay within that broad title. Depending on the size of the group, the initial part of the planning is done in two or three subgroups to ensure that everyone's ideas are heard. I suggest that people brainstorm their ideas and record everything that everyone suggests. They then go back over their list and talk about what each one means, with a goal of coming to consensus on their top five or so topics. I describe why consensus is important to the process, and mostly the groups work hard to achieve it. During this time, I am available for anyone who wants me, and I often sit for awhile with each group and add an idea or two of my own.

The subgroups reconvene, eliminate redundancies among their lists, and try to come to consensus as a large group on the topics. Sometimes at this stage, we resort to a voting procedure, but most often, we are able to create a list that everyone is satisfied with. There are a few common themes from year to year (for example, how to evaluate learning in a shop setting or how to work within the constraints of mandated curriculum), but there are always unexpected, innovative, and interesting new topics. We then discuss strategies for working with the selected topics. I participate fully in these discussions but do not control them. A discussion leader may emerge in the group, or a few people share leading the discussion.

Sometimes resistance to the process arises, and we then discuss the process itself. The usual concern is that they are "missing something important," and they may turn to me for that. Depending on what choices they have made, I may say, "You have an interesting array of topics," or I may say, "There's nothing about evaluation [or whatever else is not there]. Did you want to include that?" I point out that there will be another planning session, and by that time, they will be conscious of missed topics. I take away their lists and create a course schedule for the next six classes. I usually determine the order of the topics and the amount of time required for each.

This strategy contributes to people's feeling of empowerment, and I believe that empowerment is simultaneously a prerequisite for and an outcome of transformative learning. The participatory planning process creates enthusiasm and even excitement regarding the upcoming classes. It also challenges their perspective that the teacher always needs to be in charge of content. Although the use of participatory planning means that the educator may need to scramble around to find the appropriate resources and design learning activities, it is well worth the effort when learners know they have designed "our course."

ACTIVITIES FOR CRITICAL SELF-REFLECTION

I essentially follow Mezirow (2000) in seeing critical self-reflection as central to transformative learning, although I also believe that this does not preclude intuitive, relational, social, and affective transformative learning (Cranton, 2006). I see the process of transformative learning as being different for different individuals to some extent and also varying in its nature depending on context. Having said that, I deliberately include and design activities that have the potential to encourage critical self-reflection. The precise nature of the activities depends on the topics participants have chosen, but here I describe some typical examples.

The key to starting the critical reflection process is to expose people to alternative perspectives. This can be done through reading, discussion, movies, and a variety of experiential learning activities. With the instructor development program, I tend more to experiential activities as they are more comfortable than reading for most of the tradespeople in the course. For example, if we are discussing ways to help students feel motivated, I may ask if someone in the group has a negative critical incident related to the topic—a time when they feel they failed to motivate students. We then role-play the scenario and switch roles so that the teacher becomes the student who was not motivated. This allows the participant to be in the shoes of the unmotivated student and see the situation from that perspective. We might create several such scenarios, each with different underlying assumptions, so that everyone who wants to can experience being his or her own students.

Critical debates provide a similar experience. If an issue comes up in class where there is considerable controversy within the group (attendance policies and late policies in the college system, for example), we divide up according to who is for and who is against the issue. Then we organize a debate where each team argues for the side they are really against. Time is taken for preparation during which people come up with as many arguments as they can for something they do not agree with. The debate is timed, someone chairs it, and there is a rebuttal period.

Critical reflection can be sparked by engaging in a completely different and unplanned activity. If it is a hot day in our building with no air-conditioning and people are languishing in the heat (there is not a lot of hot weather in New Brunswick, so folks usually do languish when it does arrive), I may say, "Let's go to the art gallery [or the movies or the museum]." Most people in the group have never been to an art gallery, so we take some time to figure out how we can link this to our course. This can be quite a simple thing, such as finding a painting that represents some aspect of an individual's philosophy of teaching or more complex team projects. Critical reflection is encouraged by the activity itself (finding something that reflects one's teaching) and by breaking with routine. The bonus is that the art gallery has air-conditioning.

ARTS-BASED ACTIVITIES

For people who have not had much opportunity to engage with art (and probably also for those who do), arts-based activities have the potential to foster transformative learning. We do this in a variety of ways. For example, in a discussion about learning styles, we decided to create collages or drawings that represented each of Kolb's (1984) four learning styles. People ran around the building asking for old magazines; they scrounged through the bulletin boards looking for appropriate outdated posters and announcements. I collected scissors, glue sticks, colored paper, and markers from the general office. Four groups formed, one to work on each of the learning styles, and people roughly grouped themselves to reflect their own preferred style. Both the process of finding or creating images and the creation of the collage itself led to a deeper examination of learning style, and the ensuing discussion in the whole group led us to question the premise of the concept of learning styles and challenge the idea of creating teaching methods to support each learning style.

Even simple drawings using colored markers and flip chart paper can help people understand a concept in a different way and possibly critically question the concept itself. For example, when we discussed the meaning of instrumental, communicative, and emancipatory knowledge and how those kinds of knowledge were relevant (or not) in their practice, I suggested that participants work in small groups and make a drawing that represented the interrelationship among the kinds of learning. Among other things, they drew a tree, the roots being instrumental knowledge, the trunk being communicative knowledge, and the leaves being emancipatory knowledge; and a sailboat, where the water was instrumental, the body of the boat communicative, and the sails emancipatory. Using their drawings as metaphors, participants then talked about kinds of knowledge in their subject area—for example, where emancipatory knowledge comes into carpentry or communicative knowledge into mechanics. Of course, this is not necessarily a transformative experience, but it has that potential. If a person has always thought of his area of expertise as consisting solely of technical skills and then comes to see that there can be an emancipatory aspect (learning to build things or fix things can lead to a certain freedom from constraints), this change in thinking can lead to a revision of a habit of mind about the trade itself. We left the drawings on the wall for the duration of the course and used them now and then to sort out an issue about kinds of learning.

In addition to the in-class activities and discussions, participants are required by the university to do some out-of-class work. In most courses, this takes the form of a traditional paper. In our course in the instructor development program, the learning projects, as we call them, are completely open in terms of content, format, and purpose as long as they relate in some way to the course. I provide examples of learning projects and encourage people to try an arts-based project, especially if they have never created art before. Participants create representations of their teaching or of themselves as teachers, and in doing so, they reflect deeply on what teaching means to them and what it means to be a teacher. Over the years, almost every art form has shown up in the learning projects from our course: paintings, watercolors, sculptures, CDs of music, collages, scrapbooks, photography, quilts, stained glass, and poetry.

SELF-EVALUATION AND SELF-GRADING

From the first day of the course, participants are aware that I hope they will evaluate and grade their own learning. This is a part of our opening discussion about the course process. Now and then, we refer back to this, and often by about midcourse, people are thinking about their learning projects and starting to feel anxious about evaluation. When that happens, we spend some time talking about what everyone is doing or is planning on doing for a learning project, and inevitably questions arise about my expectations. "How long should it be?" they ask, and "What do you expect in terms of an explanation of my art work?" "If I give a presentation, do you want to see my notes?" And so on.

It is an uncritically assimilated assumption in most educational contexts that students submit work to teachers, who then say how good it is and assign it a grade. Students might have their own opinions about their work and even disagree with their teacher or argue for a better mark, but essentially it is assumed that the teacher is the expert and is thereby able to judge the quality of the student's work. The student may be expected to learn from this process, but often commentary or discussion is minimal, so it is more of a judgment than a guide to improvement. Also, the teacher judges the quality of the product—the exam, the paper, the presentation, the book review—and makes the assumption that the product represents the learning. A student might say or think, "I really learned a lot, even though my paper wasn't as good as it could have been."

Participants in the instructor development program share the social norms about what teachers and students are supposed to do. So at this point, when participants begin to question my expectations (What do I want them to do?), we start to articulate and question our assumptions and values about the teacher role. The nature of this discussion varies with the group, of course, but there are some things we may question. We discuss how one person can judge the quality of another person's learning. In what contexts is this possible, and in what contexts is it not possible? What kind of learning can be counted or measured objectively? What kind of learning cannot be seen by another person? How is our course (learning about teaching) different from and the same as a course in trades or technology? How does the proportion of instrumental, communicative, and emancipatory learning vary in different contexts?

By the end of the course, most people comfortably engage in self-evaluation and self-grading. I ask them to think about their learning from all aspects of the course—readings, discussions, class activities, learning project—and to select a grade that best represents that learning. If they wish, they can set specific criteria, or they can engage in the process in a more intuitive or holistic manner. I ask them to write a short description of how they came to select that particular grade. This process usually leads people to meaningful and critical reflection on their learning. Now and then, of course, someone thinks, "Okay, this is an easy A," but I do not think it happens often. And if someone feels he or she simply cannot do this and wants me to do the evaluation, I will. To force self-evaluation seems like something of a paradox, but this rarely happens.

Self-evaluation is potentially transformative on two levels: thinking about the meaning of evaluation and who can evaluate whom, and reflecting on participants' learning during the self-evaluation and grading process. People are taken outside the stereotypical teacher and student roles.

REFLECTIONS

I have kept a daily reflective journal about my teaching for many years. At the end of each day, I write about the day's events, think about what happened and why, speculate about the meaning of what participants said. I sometimes record a dialogue from memory and then analyze and question it from different perspectives. I also usually reread the entries from the previous day or two to set the current day in its context. I have on occasion shared some journal entries or excerpts from them with the course participants, but I found this made me self-conscious about what I wrote, so I tend not to do that now. (This also helped me to understand how students might feel about keeping journals that their teachers will then read.)

In preparation for writing this chapter, I reread four years of teaching journals from the summer course, each journal about thirty to thirty-five pages in length. Many stories from this course have made their way into my writing in general (the students love to pick out stories that are about others in the program), so I did not expect to be very much surprised or entertained by rereading my journals. But I was. What surprised me was that each journal was a complete story: a story with a beginning, a cast of characters, a plot, various unexpected happenings in the plot, an end. When I was in the middle of the story, I was too close to see it. And all I have really done since then is to pull out various anecdotes to illustrate some point I wanted to make in a discussion of something else.

I started to think about courses as stories during this rereading and during the writing of this chapter. Was I the author of the story? I wrote it down. It was my reflections and my recording of the dialogue and my descriptions of the participants that made up the story. Does this mean I controlled the story? By no means. I wrote about a story that I witnessed, participated in, and contributed to. But someone else could have written quite a different story from mine about the same event, and, in fact, participants who kept journals as their learning projects did just that. So each course was several stories, of which my version was just one. Some of those stories were transformative; others were not. Some of the unwritten stories were transformative; others were not.

Then I started to wonder if there were patterns across stories. Is there a meta-story for the instructor development program summer school? This, I was thinking smugly, would be a fine way to end the chapter, and I thought about this for some time. There is a pattern in the context: people come to the same place for the same course for the same general reason. There is a pattern in the participants: they are all instructors for the New Brunswick Community Colleges. There are some patterns in the content: people do tend to choose some of the same topics from year to year, though there is less overlap there than one would expect. There is a pattern in my style as a teacher: I tend to be open, flexible, calm, and supportive, but always with a goal of challenging people's perspectives in my fairly quiet way. There is a pattern in the plot: people tend to become more responsible for their learning and the evaluation of it, more confident of their ability to teach, and they tend to make the transition to thinking about themselves as teachers.

The problem is that this is not a very interesting story. Once the individuality of each group and each group's process is stripped away to find the common ground, the skeleton that is left is boring—it is just another skeleton. People go to class, they have a certain type of teacher, and they learn something. There is no inspiration there. This is not what brings joy to my life as a teacher. This is also not what transformative learning is about for me.

In my practice as a classroom teacher in higher education, transformative learning is about the individual stories—the breakthrough moments, the recognition of a long-held unquestioned assumption, the dawning of an understanding of a new perspective, the opening up to alternatives, the seeing of self in a new way. In the instructor development program, because of the transition that people are making as they became teachers of their trade or technology and because of their fears and uncertainties in a new environment, the potential for transformation is great. I can create conditions where that transformation can happen, but each person's transformative experience is unique and to be treasured for its uniqueness. I think I already knew this, but writing this chapter, working with my teaching journals to do so, and preparing this final reflection on the process helped me see it in a new light.

REFERENCES

Cranton, P. (2006). *Understanding and promoting transformative learning: A guide for educators of adults* (2nd ed.). San Francisco: Jossey-Bass.

Kolb, D. A. (1984). *Experiential learning: Experience as a source of learning and development*. Upper Saddle River, NJ: Prentice Hall.

Mezirow, J. (2000). Learning to think like an adult: Core concepts of transformation theory. In J. Mezirow & Associates, *Learning as transformation: A critical perspective on a theory in progress* (pp. 3–33). San Francisco: Jossey-Bass.

PART FOUR

TRANSFORMATIVE LEARNING AS COMMUNITY AND SOCIAL CHANGE

The chapters in Part Four focus on transformative learning and the role it plays in making sense of explaining learning and guiding practice when fostering community and social change. It opens with Chapter Seventeen by Elizabeth Lange, who introduces the process of developing a learning sanctuary, a deliberative pedagogy, for adult sustainability education. It is followed by a discussion from Catherine Hansman and Judith Kollins Wright in Chapter Eighteen on popular education and transformative learning in a community education program involving women and legal education in Cochabambia, Bolivia. Susan Meyer describes in Chapter Nineteen transformative learning through journaling and coaching in a personal empowerment program for women in East Harlem. Next, Peter Easton, Karen Monkman, and Rebecca Miles examine in Chapter Twenty a participatory nonformal community empowerment program for women in rural West Africa designed to help women "identify and achieve change at the local level." Chapter Twenty-One emerges from a similar setting, rural Africa: Deborah Duveskog and Esbern Friis-Hansen introduce us to farmer field schools that are designed to provide farmers the means to meet regularly and engage in an action learning process about the everyday management of small farms. In Chapter Twenty-Two, Lucia Alcántara, Sandra Hayes, and Lyle Yorks introduce the practice of collaborative inquiry as a means to educate community activist and social justice workers to become co-inquirers, working with people to "help them develop strategic, conceptual, and creative thinking." Chapter Twenty-Three, by the European-American Collaborative Challenging Whiteness, discusses a form of action research involving the exploration of people's perceptions about privilege, race, and racism.

CHAPTER SEVENTEEN

Fostering a Learning Sanctuary for Transformation in Sustainability Education

Elizabeth A. Lange

Being a transformative educator is part of my identity, shaping my living and recursively my teaching, whether I am engaged in university courses, school classrooms, or in the community with immigrants, social service professionals, or church folk. I first encountered transformative learning in my teacher training through visiting professor Paulo Freire and later in my graduate studies through conference speaker Jack Mezirow. Such a fine introduction to transformative learning, as a body of theory and practice, resonated with my stance as a searcher for life meaning, a critic of status quo norms and social structures that silence and imprison, and an educator with an ethical commitment to nurture a socially just and environmentally sustainable society. In this chapter, I describe my own journey to transform my teaching practice, my current approach to learning encounters, specific practices developed for a university extension course on sustainability, and my reflections on the challenges and key lessons.

One of the greatest challenges facing humanity today is the choice between a sustainable and socially just future or maintaining the status quo. While the term *sustainability* is often co-opted, I have defined a sustainable society to be one that satisfies its needs without diminishing the prospects for the health and well-being of self, other peoples, future generations, or the environment. I adapted Lester Brown's definition (1981) to incorporate personal and community sustainability along with environmental sustainability and social justice. As I sought to implement sustainability education in my teaching, one important lesson has been that deep transformation, which changes our ways of being, doing, and thinking in a profound way, requires the creation of a learning sanctuary for both facilitator and participants. A learning sanctuary is constituted through three elements: a paradoxical relationship between a deliberative pedagogy while holding the space open for often unseen transformative processes to occur; providing new relational experiences with both the social and natural worlds that can prefigure new ways of being, not just thinking; and creating a safe space for committed peer relationships that allows participants to ask deep internal questions and probe broader societal realities.

While describing my facilitation of a transformative pedagogy, I am also resisting the modernist approach of instrumentalist prescriptions for effectiveness and linear technicist (that is, an educator as a technician) descriptions of theory into practice. Rather, I hope you will read this in the spirit of how creative potential can be unleashed through a deliberative pedagogy while recognizing the ultimate indeterminacy of educational work. Pedagogies for engagement (Briton, 1996) focus the purpose of adult education more on the meaning of living, where life becomes the fundamental subject matter, and less on making a living. Schapiro (1995) best describes this educative stance as the "mystical nature of the relationship [educators] enter into with learners . . . a creative space, . . . the sphere of the imagination, . . . the realm of the sacred. . . . It is in this encounter with others that we continuously awaken to the meaning of life" (p. 45).

As a facilitator, then, I enter the learning space with my own commitments and some content and processes to engage learners; however, transformative learning is what happens underneath this. It is intervening in the process of life to unsettle and inspire, unleash curiosity and hope, help learners "decipher the limit situations of why things are the way they are" (Freire, 1997, pp. 105–106), and explore alternatives beyond. There are no guarantees or "certainties of the find, but [a] movement in search" (Freire, 1997, p. 106), which is ultimately mysterious and, as I have learned, cause for deep humility.

RECONCEPTUALIZING TRANSFORMATIVE LEARNING

> *Once you wake up, can you wake up*
> *any more?*
> —Sue Monk Kidd (1996)

In the mid-1990s, after fifteen years of teaching—first as a high school social studies teacher preparing young people for active citizenship, then as a development educator in a social justice movement dedicated to educating citizens for social action related to international issues—I was disillusioned. With my colleagues, the typical educational approach was to frame the issues in such a compelling way as to move middle-class learners to take up their citizen responsibilities and act. We tried to appeal to people cognitively through well-researched factual information and social analysis and emotionally through content about negative impacts and by bringing people face-to-face with visitors who spoke of the suffering of their people. However, as many educators and social movements discover, the step from education to social action, and an enlivened citizenship and more vibrant democracy, is not natural or inevitable.

For me, a critical juncture was reached when historical events, including the dismantling of the Berlin Wall and freeing of Nelson Mandela, coalesced with a personal experience of leading a study tour to El Salvador. In retrospect, I was experiencing my own disorienting dilemma (Mezirow, 1991), prompting a critique of my basic educational assumptions. This coincided with teaching adult education courses in a university faculty of extension as well as the rise of neoliberal economic policies. The learners I faced had either lost jobs or doubled workloads due to restructuring and cutbacks. Given the intensity and pace of change, learners stated their desire for a transition toward life-giving rather than life-depleting work.

In a process of critical self-reflexivity and a desire to be responsive to learners, I probed my assumptions about transformative learning, realizing their Western Enlightenment origins. My first notion, that transformative learning is about challenging worldviews, with the implication that individuals and society are improvable and reconstructible, gave way to the understanding that people are repositories of conflicting social interests when confronted with social issues and that the change process may be as much about transforming ways of being as it is reconstructing a worldview. My second notion, conceiving of transformation as a rational, cognitive process involving a change of mind, gave way to acknowledging the role of a knowing body, intuitive knowledge, normative symbols, and a sense of place (Spretnak, 1999). My third notion, that individuals are autonomous beings who must form common purpose with other autonomous beings to create social change, gave way to a view of individuals as fundamentally individuals-in-social-relations and a living systems view of social change (Capra, 1996). My fourth notion, that transformation is progressive and incremental and that people will transcend self-interest to embrace larger social interests, gave way to an acknowledgment that people may desire to do good and have good intentions, but there are powerful pressures of social and economic conformity mediating the change process and shaping individual will. As Shor (1992) puts it, "Knowledge is not exactly power. Knowledge is the power to know, to understand, but not necessarily the power to do or to change" (p. 90). Finally, I agreed with the premise of radical ecology (Merchant, 2005) that human suffering and ecological degradation are manifestations of one system of injustice and that a transformative space can enable participants to experience new patterns of production (work), reproduction (life), and consciousness (personal and collective), all anticipating a more livable, just world. I began to see teaching as a "living practice" (Carson & Sumara, 1997, p. xv), where learning emanates from the living of it, with potential to transform all involved.

CREATING A RESPONSIVE PRACTICE OF TRANSFORMATIVE LEARNING

Transformative teaching for me has become organic teaching, where the themes and experiences brought into the educative space derive from the social reality in which we live. So after rethinking the assumptions built into my educational practice, the second step was undertaking an investigation of the issues most occupying learners' minds. From here, I identified generative themes and then problematized them in relation to the course content (Shor, 1992). These themes are chosen not because they are "relevant," which implies they are external and must be made relevant, but because they are integral aspects of our experience but often remain tacit. As an educator, I not only needed to challenge my assumptions but to carry out a social analysis of dominant ideologies and material practices as they related to course content.

Briefly the key issue that surfaced for these learners was work, and how work profoundly shapes all other aspects of living. Learners shared their discontent with the dominant work ideology—"staying competitive," "increased efficiency and productivity," "working smarter, not harder"—and their disillusionment with the needs to "stay marketable as a commodity" and "sell their self." They described their weariness from negotiating the conflicting demands of work and home life, and their yearning for serenity and balance in the crush of a frenetic lifestyle. In my social analysis of these material conditions, these were all manifestations of neoliberal globalization, particularly in Alberta, the initial Canadian microcosm for government and corporate restructuring. Albertans were given moral injunctions to tighten their belts through lower wages or job loss, show self-discipline with use of public services, and increase volunteerism as community services were cut. Health care, education, and other social services were cut significantly, doubling the ranks of the poor, as reflected in high rates of food bank use, child poverty, and homelessness (Harrison & Laxer, 1995). Learners in my classes were expressing the human cost of this politico-corporate will that drove them back to the adult classroom with anger and anxiety.

My third step was to search diverse literatures for potentially transformative ideas and activities that could speak to these realities, offer an accessible social analysis, and convey feasible alternatives. It became clear that a holistic concept of sustainability had power to foster cultural critique and new possibilities for living and working. From this research, I developed ten principles of sustainability that formed the backbone of a new course, entitled Transforming Working and Living (Lange, 2001; Edwards, 2005; Merchant, 2005). The course description indicated that participants would have the opportunity to rethink the purpose of work, develop principles to guide their working and living, understand the impact of the global economy on daily life, and develop an action plan. The stated purpose was transforming work in ways that were personally meaningful, contribute to community needs, balance family and individual well-being, and respect the natural world.

FOSTERING SANCTUARY IN ADULT SUSTAINABILITY EDUCATION

As the host of an educative experience, I believe that at its best, we create a learning sanctuary together—a place of immunity from the full weight of social forces. As the *Oxford Dictionary* (2007) suggests, a sanctuary is a special place set aside as a refuge of protection and shelter, enabling growth. Thus, to be transformative, adult education ought to provide a protective sanctuary for a deep encounter with self (mind, spirit, and body), social relationships, habits of thinking and living, and the conjoined individual and social myths that constrain human freedom and justice. This becomes a container for the dialectics between a pedagogy of critique and a pedagogy of hope. In relation to sustainability education, this encounter can enlarge the sense of self, from seeing oneself as separate and autonomous to seeing one's embeddedness in a web of living relations, both human and nonhuman, constitutive of an ecological consciousness (O'Sullivan, 1999).

After probing my assumptions, carrying out a social analysis, and investigating concepts that hold transformative potential, I designed a course to foster a learning sanctuary where learners could safely explore root causes of their discontent and a range of sustainable alternatives. In all the offerings of this course, most participants have found the concept of sustainability powerful for rethinking their working and living and for creating change. I typically meet with participants for sixteen three-hour sessions, once a week over three months, including four sessions as a weekend retreat. The course is divided into three iterative moments that spiral in a way to revisit and deepen previous learning. Deborah Barndt (1989) derives the term *moment* from Gramsci's idea of conjuncture, where conjunctural relations, such as in the classroom, are temporary and fluid relations, whereas larger structural relations are relatively permanent.

THE TEACHING AND LEARNING PROCESS

The introductory sessions enable participants to state the issues that brought them to the course, usually through a pictorial collage, and to begin a social critique of their stress and pressures. This constitutes an immersion into their own reality, creating an opportunity for Freirean problem posing or, rather, a reflection process to position their experiences within a larger socio-political-historical context. This reflection is facilitated as they tell their work stories, usually through drawing a work genealogy, to identify the key principles by which they work and live. Participants identify the Protestant work ethic, especially the idea of hard work before leisure or pleasure, as a key principle that is both a positive and a problematic cultural message. I then introduce sustainability to contrast the what is with the what is possible as a critique of incessant doing and workaholism that compromises health and relationships.

Rather than the typical process of deepening the social analysis at this point, I take the participants into the community to meet individuals who are exemplars of sustainability. We visit an organic farm family who sells at a local farmers' market and who designed a simple and effective home that is off the energy grid. We visit a woman who makes tree-free paper by recycling old clothes and locally available plant matter, the way paper was historically produced. We visit an outdoor equipment and clothing store that has adopted sustainability in all of its sourcing practices, building materials, energy practices, and employee relations. We meet at an organic restaurant, visit an environmental activist who shares his low-impact approach to living focused on social (not material) wealth, visit a brewery that recycles 99 percent of all the products it uses, and hear from a man operating a thriving company that uses straw bales for home construction. Meeting these people is one of the most powerful aspects of the course as participants discover that such people are not "out there" but simply people like them—except that they have structured their work around specific principles, including sustainability, to enhance their quality of life. This nourishes the formation of hope beyond perceived limit situations and provides realistic possibilities for sustainable working and living. Generally these visits foster high energy, excitement, and new principles for work they would like to explore further.

The next sessions are entitled Sustainable Living and Sustainable Working. In these sessions, participants engage in a cultural analysis by undertaking a self-audit assessing how they spend their time (every minute of each day for several weeks) and money (every cent for a month, if possible) and plotting their overall habits of consumption, relationships, and work (based on Dominguez & Robin, 1992). This heightens their consciousness of ingrained cultural myths that shape their daily habits and their thinking about what it means to be successful, happy, productive, and secure. To help repattern ways of living away from stress and anxiety patterns, I suggest simple, largely noncommodified activities like walking every other day in a wild area that is not manicured and monitoring body and emotional impact. Another activity is to slow down and mindfully enjoy the sensual pleasures of eating an apple, drinking a glass of water, playing with young children, or having a bath. As we debrief their surprise and joy, I present the history of the consumer society as well as research that illustrates the inverse relationship between consumption and happiness. It appears to be important to build a collective sense of hope and provide opportunities for self-critique before moving into the process of socioeconomic critique. This seems to avoid the resistance, despair, and sense of futility that typically develop when social analysis occurs early in the learning process.

Only at this point do I engage them in a broader socioeconomic analysis that illustrates linkages between North American consumption habits and the global impact on other people and the environment. Participants do an ecological footprint of their lifestyles by calculating their consumption level and converting that into an ecological footprint of how much land it takes to support their lifestyle. We then compare this to consumption levels in other countries and how many planets are needed to support their consumption levels, and examine this as a social justice issue. I also ask them to trace the life cycle of one consumer product, such as a pair of jeans, T-shirt, tomato, or banana, which quickly makes these global interconnections apparent and unveils the global structures of production and work: who benefits, who does not, and why. These sessions end with a redefinition of "good work" and voluntary simplicity (Elgin, 1993), including some questions: What work could I do that would most benefit the local and global community? How could I transform my working and living to be nonharming and, more important, life giving?

In the final action planning sessions, participants coalesce their previous learnings, what changes would manifest the principles they now want to live and work by, and then brainstorm what changes are actually possible. This is a crucial point in the course where sanctuary is required to foster a deep attentiveness to self and a meditative discernment process for choosing between alternatives. Thus, I invite the participants on retreat to a comfortable log lodge located on acres of undisturbed native aspen parkland where the hosts believe in wholesome food and hospitality. We engage in various relaxation activities to distance ourselves from immediate concerns and in a guided visualization to assist the discernment process. An environmental educator joins us to lead experiential activities in the natural world and build ecological literacy (Orr, 1992). Whether sitting against a swaying tree, lying on the peaty earth in tall grass watching clouds, coming to understand the life cycle of a tree and the energy and matter cycles in a forest, or studying the story buried in layers of fallen snow, they reconnect with themselves, others, and the natural world in profound ways. Using art, creative writing, music, and movement activities, they create a set of principles and intentions they wish to manifest in their lives, out of which flows a concrete action plan. Throughout the course, I weave in small rituals and symbols. At one retreat, some barren November dogwood branches were a focal point to symbolize how courage and new ideas are born in hibernation, in deep resting. By retreat's end, the warmth of the lodge caused the branches to leaf out, to the delight of participants, who interpreted it as a symbol of their renewal and reemergence.

The final sessions respond to the issues that arise when implementing change at home. We discuss fear or barriers they encounter at work or with family and friends. We develop affirmation statements, role-play their conflicting internal and external interests, practice nonconflictual methods of engagement based on living systems theory, and discuss how to withstand counterpressures and sustain the change process. The course closes with a celebration of their journeys, a sharing of plans, and symbolic candle lighting as hope for a new global future. They often meet thereafter, and some participants have started the Fireweed Institute to continue their learning and friendships supportive of the individual and collective change initiatives.

ADULT EDUCATION AS SANCTUARY

In retrospect, a learning sanctuary is created in three ways that augment the transformative impact of the course. First, while I deliberately plan a pedagogy, paradoxically, a sanctuary space is created as I suspend my educator desires and old assumptions. I approach this space with a respect for the deeper learning that occurs beneath any pedagogical plans, beyond what I can know in terms of each individual, the personal journeys and relationships, and the collective impact of changes. It is clear that the activities are conduits to deep learning that goes beyond what I plan and even beyond what is conscious, rational, or even identifiable. I simply try to hold this space open for the needed dynamics to occur, a risky place to inhabit.

This leads to the second element of a learning sanctuary, particularly related to sustainability education. David Abram (1996) suggests that "humans are tuned for relationship," where all our bodily gateways receive nourishment from the sensuousness of our natural environs—whether the brush of a butterfly, the dance of clouds, the pungency of rolling ocean waves, or the fluttering of aspen leaves. We engage in what Abram refers to as a "many-voiced landscape," part of a conviviality that makes us human. When we directly encounter the natural world and come into contact with ground and sky, a space is created where the living world can teach us of our embeddedness and where relationships are (re)membered. "Being" in these relationships, even momentarily, can prefigure a new way of daily being that heightens awareness of body and intuitive knowledge, foregrounding what is often only a background reality. This direct encounter challenges anthropocentric worldviews, initiates a growth in literacy about this ecological place, and catalyzes glimmers of a new ethical sensibility toward the more-than-human world. For instance, readings from *The Universe Story* (Swimme & Berry, 1992) help to provide a new understanding about the human place in a living cosmos and the implications of multiple interdependent relations. In this way, cognitive worldviews are shifted not through rationality only but through bodily experiences of a new way of being in the world: slower, peaceful, reflective, tangibly embedded in a web of life. Becoming a body memory, this way of being can be repeated until it is a rhythm of living, ultimately transforming daily life. Thus, I simply bring people into relationship with the natural world, where it can speak directly and revitalize ancient human memories.

A third aspect of creating sanctuary is the deeply committed relationships participants develop with each other and various facilitators. They (re-)experience what it means to talk deeply from the heart, to be mentored, and to be part of egalitarian relations. They analyze culturally shaped relations that can be threatening (driving a car, fast food, suburb design), test out new ideas, express emotions, and discern and articulate what they more deeply desire. As Kate (self-chosen aliases) explains, "Support of my colearners was very important, and I feel as if a new network/community of friends has been started.... I felt supported and nurtured by each member and was able to share my vision and to hear their vision of the world they would like to create." Gena and Jennifer recognized sanctuary: "I loved the honoring rituals you wove in"; "I appreciated your efforts to ensure a comfortable, safe environment at a time when one sometimes felt exposed." Dan states, "Within three classes, you feel as if you are dealing with a friend and equal as opposed to a 'teacher.'" Jennifer agrees: "Besides being instructors, you became participants in the course...allow[ing] us to strengthen our relationships.... I think this helped make this an excellent opportunity for exploring new pathways." Ky appreciated the responsiveness: "As the course content was flexible, changes were [made]...to meet the personal needs of participants." Thus, learning sanctuary honors participants; creates space for compassion and hope on the life journey; models relations of equality, responsiveness, interconnectedness, and depth; and engages the whole person.

REFLECTIONS

Despite this approach, when one inhabits the position as "teacher-participant," sometimes one misses obvious gifts within the group or, at times, must be humbly taught by the participant-teachers. Two very spiritually rooted participants, one of whom has since passed away and is dearly missed but to whom this chapter is dedicated, gave me a strong message that took time to learn: social and personal change is not about individual will; it is about intentionality. Individual will in transformation is about exerting power over your future and wrestling it into the shape you desire, associated with a new cognitive framework. Rather, their approach was to set intention and let the dynamics of a "creative cosmos" (Spretnak, 1999) enable this to manifest, often in unforeseen and unexpected social and personal ways. Both of them believed in mandalas (drawing and tracing spiritually symbolic diagrams) and meditative walking of a labyrinth as a physical way to "live into" a new future. This is confirmed by others who report the action plan does not come to fruition as planned, but changes revolve around the underlying intentions that informed those plans. Thus, my transformative learning coemerged with the participants.

Another significant learning was coming to understand the consistent emotional rhythm of the course. There is now a predictable point in the process when one or more people will project their anxieties, confusion, or anger onto me. I have learned to maintain my own spiritual practice to hold on to groundedness and openness to emotional intensity. As Angie expressed, "The only problem I had is that this course opened up so many questions for me that I was struggling with the enormities of the imbalances in my life." The course destabilized many aspects of their lives simultaneously, leaving participants vulnerable and with little as a solid foundation. The natural response was to target me as the catalyst. This is how I came to realize that restorative learning, connecting individuals to their deepest ethical principles, is crucial (Lange, 2004). If early in the course, participants identify their personal principles and submerged knowledges, such as childhood dreams, for their life or early experiences of being awake to the natural world as a refuge of serenity and joy, this provides a touchstone when so much else is fluid and questioned. Angie also highlighted the vital importance of visiting models of sustainability, who were hopeful exemplars: "It leaves people with little hope for their future if they have not explored the alternatives first." So restorative and transformative processes work hand in hand.

A third key learning comes from Kim, who was trying to integrate reiki, a practice of channeling energy through one's hands for healing, into her nursing practice. After presenting my tentative research findings to the participants, Kim challenged me: "Do you see the butterfly come out of the cocoon or do you see the worn-out, useless cocoon?'' In a further e-mail interchange, she wrote:

> Perhaps transformation is like a butterfly; to want to examine a butterfly fully and its fine details, we kill it. Then, we don't really have a butterfly. For a butterfly is about its flight, its dance in the light and its delicacy.... I hope to retain the mystery aspect of transformation. The profound is to be experienced...our words are limited, linear, and bound in space and time.

She encouraged me to read new science about relativity theory, quantum mechanics, complexity theory and Gaia theory, (Capra, 1996) to ponder my reductionist, linear way of thinking. Perhaps in naming elements of transformation, we disenchant the process or ignore the fruits of transformation. David Bohm (1994) posits that we do not take into account the complex, unbroken processes that underlie our experience of the world and how our thought patterns shape our images of reality. This is what I hope to convey through the concept of learning sanctuary: a protective space held open for bidden but unseen processes. Furthermore, he suggests that thought and knowledge are collective, not individual, phenomena comprising changes in communal meanings flowing between people. Thus, transformation is inherently collective and mediated by much more than a course or learning process. This challenged my assumptions about transformation, social change, and what can or ought to be known.

And so the teacher is taught. From my own disorienting dilemma, to rethinking my educational assumptions, to researching and engaging in a living practice of sustainability education, my transformative learning continues to coemerge alongside the participants through the collective creation of a learning sanctuary. As they have taught me, our energy for change is collectively rippling out into the world through our daily intentionality as we live and dance mindfully into the personal and social reality we yearn for.

REFERENCES

Abram, D. (1996). *The spell of the sensuous*. New York: Vintage Books.

Barndt, D. (1989). *Naming the moment*. Toronto, ON: Jesuit Centre for Social Faith and Justice.

Bohm, D. (1994). *Thought as a system*. London: Routledge.

Briton, D. (1996). *The modern practice of adult education*. Albany, NY: SUNY.

Brown, L. (1981). *Building a sustainable society*. New York: Norton.

Capra, F. (1996). *The web of life: A new scientific understanding of living systems*. New York: Doubleday.

Carson, T., & Sumara, D. (1997). *Action research as a living practice*. New York: Peter Lang.

Dominguez, J., & Robin, V. (1992). *Your money or your life*. New York: Penguin Book.

Edwards, A. (2005). *The sustainability revolution*. Gabriola Island, BC: New Society Publishers.

Elgin, D. (1993). *Voluntary simplicity*. New York: Morrow.

Freire, P. (1970). *Pedagogy of the oppressed*. New York: Seabury Press.

Freire, P. (1997). *Pedagogy of the heart*. New York: Continuum.

Harrison, T., & Laxer, G. (1995). *The Trojan horse: Alberta and the future of Canada*. Montreal: Black Rose Books.

Lange, E. A. (2001). *Living transformation: Beyond midlife crisis to restoring ethical space*. Unpublished doctoral dissertation, University of Alberta.

Lange, E. A. (2004). Transformative and restorative learning: A vital dialectic for sustainable societies. *Adult Education Quarterly, 54*(2), 121–139.

Merchant, C. (2005). *Radical ecology: The search for a livable world*. New York: Routledge.

Mezirow, J. (1991). *Transformative dimensions of adult learning*. San Francisco: Jossey-Bass.

Monk Kidd, S. (1996). *The dance of the dissident daughter*. San Francisco: HarperSanFrancisco.

Orr, D. (1992). *Ecological literacy*. Washington, DC: Island Press.

O'Sullivan, E. (1999). *Transformative learning: Educational vision for the 21st century*. London: ZED Books.

Oxford University Press. (2007). *Oxford English dictionary online*. Retrieved September 20, 2007, from http://www.oed.com/.

Schapiro, R. (1995). Liberatory pedagogy and the development paradox. *Convergence, 28*(2), 28–47.

Shor, I. (1992). *Empowering education*. Chicago: University of Chicago Press.

Spretnak, C. (1999). *The resurgence of the real*. New York: Routledge.

Swimme, B., & Berry, T. (1992). *The universe story*. San Francisco: HarperSanFrancisco.

CHAPTER EIGHTEEN

Popular Education, Women's Work, and Transforming Lives in Bolivia

Catherine A. Hansman, Judith Kollins Wright

W e believe that education may provide the opportunity for people to view themselves and their worlds differently, transforming their perspectives, and thus opening the possibilities of helping learners effectively promote social justice and action. As Cunningham (1988) and others have argued, adult education programs may help learners acquire the necessary skills and knowledge that will allow them to work toward social justice. However, the educational process is complex and often compounded by the sociocultural context in which the learning and the social change are taking place. In Latin America, some formal models of education have largely given way to popular education, leading to the implementation of transformational learning and critical theory (Merriam & Brockett, 2007). Popular education "strives to develop among targeted social sectors a critical social awareness and understanding of how society functions" (Fink, 1992, pp. 174–175). It is often combined with skills training in which two levels of knowledge are valued: (1) the traditions, knowledge, abilities, and experiences of the participants; and (2) the transmission of new technical skills and information (Fink, 1992).

The concept of popular education relies on assumptions that unofficial community knowledge is more valuable than outside "expert" knowledge as a resource for problem solving on an individual and societal level. Popular education methods often draw on art forms of an individual culture, incorporating theater, dance, storytelling, music, and art into education in order to stimulate reflection and analysis (Merriam & Brockett, 2007). When popular educational models are implemented that take into account the daily lives within local cultures, true learning and change can be seen. In particular, when women are an integral part of these programs and projects, individuals, organizations, and national groups can be transformed (Fink, 1992).

The Education Department of the Oficina Jurídica Para la Mujer (Women's Legal Office; OJM), a community-based popular education organization in Cochabamba, Bolivia, works with women in the Legal Promoter's Course to address personal, legal, and policy issues through local leadership training and popular education methodology. The OJM has developed creative initiatives to reach out to women and community members. Women who participate in these workshops have often faced domestic violence in their personal lives and historical marginalization in the traditionally male sphere of social action. This chapter describes the Legal Promoter's Course as a model for women's popular education and as a program that prepares participants to be educators in the family, workplace, and community. The purpose of our chapter is to examine the methods and practices of this popular education program in Bolivia and the critical role that participants within this program have played in its development and implementation.

Our work comes from a qualitative study (Kollins, 2002; Kollins & Hansman, 2005) we conducted several years ago that examined how the Legal Promoter's Course affected and transformed the lives of its participants. We started this work as a result of coauthor Judy's participation intensive field study in Bolivia in the OJM's Legal Promoter's Course. Her work in this internship program was coordinated through the Foundation for Sustainable Development, "a non-profit organization that supports the efforts of Latin America and African grassroots development organizations that are working to better their communities, environments, and the economic opportunities around them" (Kollins, 2002, pp. 13–14). Judy's participation in Bolivia for three months as an observer and assistant to program leaders in course activities formed the basis for this research. As a full participant in the workshop, she became immersed in the program, developed personal relationships with the staff and program participants, observed organizational activities, and conducted a series of interviews. The data illuminated the support and challenges of the program and the strength of its participants, revealing a direct connection to the concepts of transformational learning, women's learning, and critical consciousness through popular education.

As researchers, we understood that our status as outsiders in the Legal Promoter's Course may have limited our ability to truly understand the program and its facilitators and participants. However, we believe that the close relationships Judy developed with the facilitators and participants allowed "honesty and open discussion in the interviews and in casual conversation, providing a more personal perspective" (Kollins, 2002, p. 14). As we reflect on this research and its limitations, our interests in the program were to understand how popular education programs can facilitate the transformation of participants that may help them challenge existing social norms in order to transform their lives.

TRANSFORMATIONAL LEARNING

Transformational learning is taken to an active political level when individuals understand past experiences within the context of critical theory (Mezirow & Associates, 2000; Cranton, 2006). Cunningham (1988) argues that when teachers make the decisions of what knowledge is necessary and valuable, education becomes no more than a mechanism for enforcing hegemonic values and social control. However, when knowledge is viewed as socially constructed, spanning formal educational skills like literacy, practical abilities such as street smarts, and emancipatory awareness (Kilgore, 2001), the acquisition of knowledge is no longer simply a mastering of tasks. Rather, it is a multifaceted entity that each learner plays an active role in creating. Mezirow (2000) has described this process as transformational learning. As learners become aware of their abilities to participate in the creation of knowledge, their perspectives of themselves and their worlds change. Taylor (2000) maintains that context, culture, and readiness to change are all factors that directly influence whether transformative learning takes place.

When individuals understand experience within a sociopolitical context, transformative learning is informed by critical theory. Critical theory explores the symbiotic relationship between the awareness described in transformational learning and the realm of action. Freire (1970) contends that if learning takes place within the context of real life problems and if the learning process is a shared practice between students and teacher, students develop critical consciousness, or conscientization. The burden of past failure shifts away from the learner, allowing him or her to understand different ways to challenge existing power structures. In this context, education is explicitly political; thus, the teacher's job is not to impart information but to challenge students and ensure that the voices of the marginalized are fully engaged (Merriam & Brockett, 2007). The teacher or facilitator becomes a cocreator of knowledge.

It is our belief that the OJM and the Legal Promoter's Course facilitate transformation of participants, helping them challenge the social norms in their daily lives. Furthermore, the programs offered through the OJM and the Legal Promoter's Course help students develop critical consciousness about the personal and societal structures in their lives that are oppressive. Finally, in our view, the programs foster individual, community, and societal change and transformation.

THE OJM AND THE LEGAL PROMOTER'S COURSE

The OJM is an innovative nongovernmental organization conceived in 1984 as an option for poor women who needed training in the defense of their rights and protection from family and societal violence. The organizational history of the OJM can be divided into three stages. During the first stage, 1984 to 1988, the organization emerged and institutionalized the idea of working from a gender and class perspective. The staff adopted the methodology of popular education that allowed them to work with themes related to the situations of the women. From 1989 to 1992, the second stage, the social program of the OJM intensified, and the ideological and political stance of the organization developed. The legal and education departments expanded to include seminars, conferences, and international forums. Since 1993, the OJM has consolidated its ideological identity, allowing it to participate in the modification of discriminatory laws, defending the rights of women, and working for the elimination of gender discrimination.

The mission of the OJM is threefold: to change power relations in Bolivian society in order to eliminate social, economic, political, and cultural injustice; eliminate all forms of discrimination against the women of Bolivia and the rest of the world; and construct a truly democratic society that respects life, peace, liberty, and diversity (Montaño, 2000). Currently the OJM participates actively in planning and carrying out educational programs, modifying discriminatory laws, and maintaining its strong position in defense of the rights of women and the elimination of gender discrimination. To carry out its mission, the OJM is divided into three defined areas: the Legal/Psychological Department, the Communication and Documentation Department, and the Education Department. It is OJM's Education Department and one of its programs that is the focus of this discussion.

The principal function of the Education Department is training women from marginalized and rural areas of Cochabamba and other Bolivian states in the knowledge, use, and defense of their rights (Montaño, 2000). The goal of this combination of access to services, information, and training is to provide women with the tools they need to begin to take more control of their lives and education. The work of the Education Department is guided by the principle that if women are aware of their rights and are taught within the context of their experience, they will be motivated to exercise their rights. The participants in programs often include male and female adolescents, teachers, community organizers and leaders, and police officers.

Popular education methodology at the OJM is used in all areas of work but is particularly notable within the Education Department. The concept of popular education relies on assumptions that unofficial community knowledge is more valuable than outside "expert" knowledge as a resource for problem solving on an individual and societal level, often drawing on art forms of an individual culture and incorporating them into educational programs in order to stimulate reflection and analysis (Merriam & Brockett, 2007). In the OJM Education Department, courses are planned to expand on the existing knowledge that women have, regardless of their previous formal education and, in doing so, reduce their tolerance to the violence and discrimination they often face.

One of the early obstacles the OJM faced was language. There are three official languages in Bolivia: Spanish, Quechua, and Aymara. Quechua and Aymara are indigenous languages commonly used in rural areas and until recently were not taught in the schools. Early OJM programs were in Spanish and resulted in poor attendance by community women because they did not know Spanish and the program presenters did not know native languages. The OJM addressed this problem by using the native language of its participants. Urban area courses are taught in Spanish, while rural area courses use the native languages common to residents in these areas. Educators also learned to use simpler terms and language to help participants, many of whom had little or no formal education, comprehend legal concepts. The OJM values the concept of popular education and relies on the community knowledge of its participants to address critical issues in their lives and communities.

THE LEGAL PROMOTER'S COURSE IN COCHABAMBA, BOLIVIA

The OJM's Legal Promoter's Course focuses on teaching skills while at the same time promoting social change and justice through its course methodology. The course was developed in 1990 and has been an important aspect of the Education Department of the OJM ever since. The OJM developed the program in response to the urgent need to advance the knowledge of the law and legal rights among women leaders in the community. The program philosophy is to increase the effective exercise of human rights from the perspective of gender, class, ethnicity, and age, deconstructing patriarchal power mechanisms through leadership and sustained action. This philosophy translates into three specific goals: to defend and strengthen the women of Cochabamba in the exercise of their rights; influence a transformation of norms in terms of gender equality and the adoption of public policy, and promote the knowledge and exercise of women's rights, thereby contributing to women's insertion in places of power and influence on gender politics (Kollins, 2002; Kollins & Hansman, 2005).

Course participants are trained to provide legal assistance to women, particularly those with limited resources, and to refer them to the OJM for further free legal assistance. The development of the course includes both legal and educational training, preparing participants to be educators in the realms of family, workplace, and community. By training legal promoters, the OJM seeks to create opportunities for the active defense of human rights within community organizations (Montaño, 2000).

All participants in the program are leaders in their organizations or communities in some capacity. Many come to the program after hearing OJM advertisements concerning the course on several radio stations in and around Cochabamba. Others are invited because they are identified as potential leaders by legal promoters who participated in previous sessions. Still others are recruited to the course through invitations to organizations and institutions. The average number of participants in each course is forty, and the majority are women, although a few men participate in each session. The common goal for participants is that they are all committed to improving their own lives as well as the lives of the women around them (Kollins, 2002; Kollins & Hansman, 2005).

Course Curriculum

The curriculum of the Legal Promoter's Course is constantly revised and enriched according to the perceptions of the facilitators, the needs of the participants, and social conditions. The course is organized into twenty-eight workshops in the classroom, three institutional visits, two workshops of evaluation and reinforcement, and special events as they arise, such as seminars and field trips.

The content of the course is planned strategically to fall in the most effective time frames. For example, in order to prepare for elections, the workshops regarding the electoral code and political participation were moved to the early part of the course because that was when the electoral period fell. The section encompassing violence against women and the Law Against Family or Domestic Violence was originally one of the first workshops of the course, but it was moved toward the middle of the course because the reflection exercises regarding this problem, which affects the majority of women in the course, are more powerful and open when the group feels they can trust each other (Kollins, 2002). This need for trust and a cohesive group experience reflects the perception that women in particular need a sense of community in a learning environment (Flannery & Hayes, 2001), and it allows the participants to speak more freely and share their experiences.

Although the workshop agenda varies from week to week depending on content, there were some consistencies. Each week began with a debriefing of the previous week's session and a discussion of current events. The course we observed took place at the OJM office in central Cochabamba. Every workshop, even the field visits, included a snack and beverage; these refreshment breaks also served as a way for participants to build relationships and a sense of community within the course.

Course Methods

The format of the course consisted of weekly programs from February through October each year. The methodology of the program was "participatory and living," as one student said, making use of role plays, small group work, story-telling, presentations, field visits, and research homework. A primary method of learning was through reflection and discussion, which caters to women's developmental style and way of learning, using dialogue, communication, and expression (Flannery & Hayes, 2001). Students actively participated in developing the course, suggesting new projects and challenging each other to find creative ways to spread information. For example, in one workshop, several suggestions were made for course projects, including writing a play for their communities and organizing self-help groups for their peers.

Complicated legal topics, such as divorce, separation, and child custody, were presented using participatory methods to make them easier to understand. When studying these topics, students split into small groups and used a didactic workbook to answer questions about laws and policies. The groups met together and then reported their understandings of these policies back to the larger group. Multimedia tools were also used to aid comprehension; for example, participants in the course viewed a video that dealt with family roles and responsibilities and challenged them to examine their own roles within families, eliciting strong reactions and generating extensive discussion on this topic.

Role playing was another important tool used in the course. The experience of becoming a character, acting out experiences, and exploring stereotypes releases tensions and allowed students to express themselves. For example, in a workshop focusing on the role of the police, the course participants split into small groups. In one of the groups, every person had dealt with the police on a personal issue, and participants shared their reasons for police interaction and the treatment they received. One person had been arrested for hanging posters for the popular presidential candidate. Others told stories that ranged from simple to awful to funny, including incidents of robbery and physical violence. When the large group reconvened, this group presented a skit of personal experience with the police. The presentation made everyone laugh, but it also presented a serious commentary on the common abuse of police power and engendered a productive discussion of the rights and limits of police authority.

In addition to in-class work, there were weekly homework assignments, which usually consisted of questions or workbook assignments about an upcoming topic for the course. The questions often asked students to reflect on their own personal experiences. Students completed this work in order to prepare for the next session of the course.

The final part of OJM's methodology was an action component, reflecting the theory of critical consciousness and the ultimate move toward action in education. Because the concepts discussed in the course are dynamic parts of the women's lives, the course planners tried to find situations in which the women could get out of the classroom environment and relate their experiences to the real world around them through field visits. The objective of field visits was for the students to become familiar with institutions that work for the defense and promotion of human rights and the application of justice. For example, the group visited the Mother of God Women's Shelter, an alternative for women who have experienced domestic violence, and the Police Family Protection Brigade station. They also attended a play at a local theater that focused on AIDS and sexuality.

Facilitator's Role in the Legal Promoter's Course

In the framework of popular education, the facilitator must view the participants as equals, taking into account their life experiences. In the Legal Promoter's Course, facilitators learn to manage a group very diverse in terms of experience and educational level. When working with the difficult topics that are typically presented in the course, the facilitators must be sensitive to the balance of power between student and teacher. This is critical to the success of the program. For example, in a class focusing on the cycle of violence often present in abusive relationships, the facilitator created a visual discussion instead of lecturing, using drawings and role playing with participants to involve the students in the concept. Through these kinds of activities, everyone can participate and understand the concepts regardless of their individual backgrounds. In contrast, another session, focusing on the recently revised Bolivian Penal Code, was facilitated by a lawyer who used complicated legal terms without explaining them clearly and requested little interaction from the participants. The skewed balance of power was evident as people hesitated to ask questions during the workshop, preferring instead to speak privately with the lawyer at the end of his presentation. However, when the discussion shifted into Quechua, the primary among several indigenous languages of that region of Bolivia and as the lawyer spoke to the group in Quechua, the students began to participate and ask questions. Once the group realized that the lawyer was able to communicate with them in their own language, the power imbalance was lessened and the environment became more open, illustrating the importance of using native languages and the manner in which they can facilitate a breakdown of the traditional student-teacher power relationship.

Another example of the facilitators' integrating action components into the curriculum involved a rape case on trial during the time of the course. A public official had raped one of his employees and impregnated her, and a team of OJM lawyers was representing the victim. Although DNA tests and witnesses confirmed the official's guilt, the lawyers feared that they would lose the case because of the public official's political power and economic influence. The week of the trial, one of the lawyers came into the Legal Promoter's Course and explained the case. Sentencing was scheduled for the following day, and the facilitator explained that part of the course is the active defense of women's rights and that this was an opportunity to be active and promote justice. It was also an opportunity for the participants to learn about Bolivia's newly redesigned judicial system. In response, thirty of the Legal Promoter's Course participants attended the sentencing to show solidarity with the victim and put pressure on the jury. The rapist received a sentence of six years in prison, not the ideal punishment the defense attorneys hoped for, but a sentence that was longer than they had realistically expected. They attributed the sentence to the strong community presence within the courtroom. The facilitators found that compelling course participants to action, followed by reflective activities, enhanced learning and transformation among participants. Neither the education nor the action ended with the conclusion of the course, as all of the participants began working in their communities as resources for legal information and assistance.

REFLECTIONS

Much time has passed since Judy went to Bolivia and we first wrote about the Legal Promoter's Course and its participants. However, writing this chapter made the experience and its participants come alive for us again and allowed us to reflect on the program and the lived reality of its participants. For us, our reflection included rehearing the participants' stories, which illuminated the strengths and the challenges of the Legal Promoter's Course in their lives.

Through reflection, what becomes clear to us is the connection to the concepts of transformational learning, women's learning, and critical consciousness through popular education. In rehearing participants' stories, we see their shifts in attitudes and self-images. For example, Aide, a graduate of the program, described her transformation and how it affects her life:

> I have changed. Two years ago I was a shy, fearful person. Now I am not afraid of anything. I know that I can confront things. Becoming a legal promoter has given me a lot of courage. It has taught me to honor myself. Now my husband doesn't mistreat me, and I don't mistreat him. He respects my decisions, and I respect his. When I started to value myself, he started to value me.

While Aide discussed her personal transformation, Irma, a course facilitator, elaborated on her perceptions of the power of community outreach and how participants can transform communities and organizations:

> There are some who join the course as leaders. But after the course, they go to their organization, and they are more powerful. They move higher up in the leadership. This integration of legal promoters in leadership positions in organizations, institutions, school boards, women's groups, and so forth motivates other people's reflection and critical consciousness about the situation of women in Cochabamba, in Bolivia, and in the rest of the world.

The failure of the traditional education system in the lives of the participants in the Legal Promoter's Course and the importance of a sense of community in an educational setting emerged as essential to transforming their lives. The educational methods employed in the course, including community learning, use of native languages, and reflection and action, integrated the learning experiences into the daily lives of the learners. Furthermore, the use of participatory methods, discussions, and real-world examples led the learners to develop a critical consciousness about themselves and the context and society in which they live. The methods used by the program were strengthened because the women were not held in the domestic sphere, but instead participated in a place in which men and women could work together in a process that included a balance of power between teachers and students. Through the use of these educational methods, participants were allowed the space to challenge societal structures, and their perspectives shifted as they became critically aware of the societal forces that shaped their personal and political experiences, and furthermore, realized that they themselves are the creators and cocreators of constantly changing knowledge.

The collaborative nature of the work in which Judy and the other participants of the Legal Promoter's Course engaged allowed participants to reach technical and personal understandings of their lived experiences, often leading to perspective transformation and transformational learning (Mezirow & Associates, 2000). Through the work in the course and the telling of their stories, the program participants reached a point of critical consciousness in which they stopped blaming themselves for their problems and began to look outward at unjust social conditions that oppressed them. This examination led to active participation and efforts to create change, starting at the personal level but advancing to addressing community and societal issues. Through the interactive activities in the Legal Promoter's Course, participants were encouraged to question current societal norms, calling for a demystification of the law, and were given opportunities to practice the needed skills to challenge the widespread use of the legal system as a method of reinforcing their subordination.

We believe that the Legal Promoter's Course, with this combination of personal and large-scale structural and political change, can serve as a guide for popular education programs that seek to empower women and create long-term social change. Many programs throughout the world seek to end domestic violence, teach human rights, and facilitate gender equality. The Legal Promoter's Course, by operating within the larger category of popular education, was able not only to address the immediate needs of the participants but train a force of critically conscious educators.

REFERENCES

Cranton, P. (2006). *Understanding and promoting transformative learning: A guide for educators of adults* (2nd ed.). San Francisco: Jossey-Bass.

Cunningham, P. M. (1988). The adult educator and social responsibility. In R. G. Brocket (Ed.), *Ethical issues in adult education*. New York: Teachers College Press.

Fink, M. (1992). Women and popular education in Latin America. In N. P. Stromquist (Ed.), *Women and education in Latin America: Knowledge, power, and change* (pp. 171–194). Boulder, CO: Lynne Rienner.

Flannery, D., & Hayes, E. (2001). Challenging adult learning: A feminist perspective. In V. Sheared & P. Sissel (Eds.), *Making space: Merging theory and practice in adult education* (pp. 29–41). Westport, CT: Bergin & Garvey.

Freire, P. (1970). *Pedagogy of the oppressed*. New York: Continuum.

Kilgore, D. W. (2001). Critical and postmodern perspectives on adult learning. In S. B. Merriam (Ed.), *The new update on adult learning theory* (pp. 53–61). San Francisco: Jossey-Bass.

Kollins, J. M. (2002). *The role of women in popular education in Bolivia*. Unpublished master's project, Cleveland State University.

Kollins, J. M., & Hansman, C. A. (2005). The role of women in popular education in Bolivia. *Journal of Adult Basic Education, 15*(1), 3–20.

Merriam, S. B., & Brockett, R. G. (2007). *The profession and practice of adult education: An introduction* (new ed.). San Francisco: Jossey-Bass.

Mezirow, J., & Associates. (2000). *Learning as transformation: Critical perspectives on a theory in progress*. San Francisco: Jossey-Bass.

Montaño, J. (Ed.). (2000). *Annual report*. Cochabamba, Bolivia: Oficina Jurídica Para la Mujer.

Taylor, E. W. (2000). Analyzing research on transformative learning theory. In J. Mezirow & Associates, *Learning as transformation: Critical perspectives on a theory in progress* (pp. 285–328). San Francisco: Jossey-Bass.

CHAPTER NINETEEN

Promoting Personal Empowerment with Women in East Harlem Through Journaling and Coaching

Susan R. Meyer

This chapter focuses on the use of journaling and coaching for transformative learning in the LIFTT (Living for Today and Tomorrow) program, which I developed for STRIVE. STRIVE (Support and Training Result in Valuable Employees) was created in East Harlem in 1985 to help people who face significant barriers in employment achieve economic independence through work. The STRIVE Program is an intense four-week attitudinal training program focused on skills necessary to obtain employment. Although there had been a fatherhood program for men in place since the organization's inception, there was no program for women. LIFTT was created in 2004 to fill that void.

LIFTT was a nine-week, coaching-based, experiential workshop, incorporating the completion of a life history and weekly journaling, that helped women make the transition from lack of work history or underemployment, substance abuse, spousal abuse, charges of child abuse, public assistance, or incarceration to school or work. Whereas STRIVE focused on basics like professional demeanor, attire, and good work habits, LIFTT focused on personal empowerment and choice.

Twelve cycles of the workshop were offered over a twenty-six-month period. Group size ranged from four to twenty-two, with a typical group size of ten. The ages of the participants ran from seventeen to mid-fifties, with the bulk of the participants in their mid-twenties to early thirties. Most participants had at least one child, and a few had grandchildren. The groups were ethnically diverse, with a majority African American or Hispanic, including a range of Caribbean and African Caribbean women (Hispanic and non-Hispanic), Central and South American women, and African, Central European, and Caucasian women. Some participants had no work experience at all. Some had neither completed high school nor passed the GED (General Educational Development) exam. A few had undergraduate and graduate degrees, and a few had credentials from their countries of origin that they were not able to use in the United States.

Creating possibilities for transformative learning was essential to the program. Many participants had low self-esteem and interpersonal skills appropriate to their current circumstances but inadequate for their aspirations. They often not only did not see the possibilities open to them, but did not feel entitled to possibilities. They did not see themselves as deserving of or capable of creating a better life. Most were extraordinarily strong women who had faced and overcome multiple obstacles in life. Yet they did not recognize their strength and were reactive rather than proactive in their approach to life decisions. Few participants were long-range planners. These women were trapped in old stories and a parochial outlook; a big part of our work together centered around reinterpreting those stories.

The women received a stipend of $150.00, paid in three installments, plus weekly stipends for child care and transportation. Groups met for three hours one evening a week for nine weeks. The first seven weeks were content centered, the eighth focused on professional appearance and attire, and the final session was a graduation ceremony. Each session began with dinner, creating a space for reporting achievements and challenges and for general coaching. The second hour began with a review of journal entries about the previous topic, followed by discussion and exercises addressing the new topic. This was followed by an hour of group coaching around the evening's topic. Participants were provided with a workbook containing all program materials and a spiral notebook in which they were to write their life histories. A list of suggested categories and topics was provided as prompts. The workshop topics included creating a vision and life history, identifying roles and managing multiple roles, identifying a support network and building teams, communication, stress management, goal setting, and life planning.

PROGRAM GOALS AND ACTIVITIES

LIFTT helped women focus on what they wanted to achieve and engage in planning. Life plans were based on each participant's life history, supplemented by focused journaling, exercises, and action planning. Structured or focused journaling assignments were developed based on Progoff's (1975) assertion that this work was "capable of rechanneling a person's energies in terms of new patterns of behavior'' (p. 29). Exercises and journaling assignments to document skills practice in each session created time for the women to reflect on their practice and the underlying assumptions. For example, one structured journaling assignment involved observing and writing about family interactions as part of a discussion of support networks and family as team.

These journaling assignments served as a basis for one component of the group coaching process. Coaching is the process of guiding individuals that increases competence and confidence, establishes goals, and eliminates negative thought patterns and behaviors. Hudson (1999) defines a coach as one who "facilitates experiential learning that results in future-oriented abilities" (p. 6). Group coaching, in this context, was a facilitated discussion where the coach asked provocative questions, drew out and integrated participants' experiences as a way to help them redefine their premises, and guided them in selecting other courses of action. It included aspects of peer coaching in that participants provided each other insights, suggestions, and support. In sharing their experiences, participants were able to validate the changes they were making in their lives.

Participants use a series of exercises to identify and group skills. Following concepts developed by Richard Bolles (1987), participants identified and categorized all the skills mentioned in their life histories. These were ranked so that the women could see which skills they wanted to use, ignore, or develop. The information from this two-tiered process provided categories to be researched for new careers. This process is especially powerful for women who see themselves as having no marketable skills or have a narrowly defined skill set.

Engaging in follow-up coaching based on focused journaling also allowed reconstructing a life in an understanding of, and at the same time freedom from, the influences of others on decisions and actions. The workshop engaged participants in an ongoing process of self-discovery. To allow this to happen, the facilitator established a safe and supportive environment with conditions that encouraged reflection and experimentation with alternative meaning schemes. For these participants, who were slow to trust others and slower to reveal themselves, it was crucial to create a safe environment and encourage peer support. At the graduation, women consistently said that they had never before had female friends. They had come to depend on the other women in the group and looked forward to the sessions as a break from the rest of their lives.

OPPORTUNITIES FOR PERSONAL TRANSFORMATION

Mezirow and Associates (1990) suggest a variety of techniques for assisting or prompting the transformation process, including reflective journal writing, composing life histories, metaphor analysis, and conceptual mapping. These techniques bring the basic assumptions developed through a lifetime of negative messages and carried by the participants into their daily understandings and interactions, into conscious awareness, thereby creating opportunities for new interpretations and actions.

In LIFTT, the pairing of coaching and structured writing encouraged participants to reflect on their experiences and examine mind-sets and increased possibilities for transformative learning. Writing put the individual in touch with the past and offered an opportunity to revisit people, influences, and events and, in the revisiting, reinterpret and reinvent the past. Coaching guided and supported the individual in this exploration.

Using life history to promote self-exploration is useful with women who have made life choices that are not consonant with their self-perceptions (Meyer, 1986). This dissonance played out in a variety of ways in LIFTT participants. Most were struggling with negative messages received at home, in school, and in their community that contradicted their personal belief that they could achieve something. For example, Carin (all names are pseudonyms) wanted to learn computer repair and was told by her family that she couldn't because "girls don't do that" and, besides, she would never get into the program (she could and she did).

This kind of conflict is wearing when it is conscious. For some, the roots of negative assumptions were so deeply buried that the woman was no longer aware of their existence. This can be even more wearing, as she may not understand why she is feeling depressed or disconnected. Surfacing assumptions through journaling is the first step to clarifying a disconnect between one's own and others' perspectives, or what Mezirow (1978) calls a disorienting dilemma, and the possibility of transforming ways of thinking and acting. Coaching allows the individual to examine premises and create alternate assumptions, alter habits of mind, and choose different actions in the future.

WRITING ABOUT ONE'S LIFE THROUGH JOURNALING

Writing one's own history is a powerful act. Numerous sources speak to the power of writing about one's self (DeSalvo, 1999; Dominice, 2000). Because journaling unlocks the past and allows writers to view events in a different, more concrete way, there may be a dissonance between the narrative and the consciously remembered experience that provides a different frame for the writer. This dissonance creates the conditions that enable or encourage reflection and opens a space for personal transformation. Coaching provides safe conditions for reflection and support and assistance in probing for a wider range of alternative beliefs. Individual behaviors can be owned rather than attributed to others or to extenuating circumstances. Isolating behaviors from influences in a protected environment gives some clarity as to deliberate choices and convenient or culturally driven choices.

For example, April chronicled her history of drug and alcohol abuse in her life history and then dropped out of LIFTT. She returned in the next cycle feeling ready to deal with what she had written. She was coached around how substance abuse allowed her to suppress her feelings and around what other choices she might make. While addicted to drugs, she had numbed herself to avoid the pain of the loss of her mother and brother, feeling that she was not strong enough to deal with the situation. During the program, April had a chance to test her strength when she learned her aunt had terminal cancer. April wrote about her visits with her aunt. She built a powerful connection, supported this relative, and in the process was also finally able to grieve for her mother and brother. As she shared portions of her narrative, coaching supported her in the process of choosing to feel her emotions rather than suppress them and helped her discover that she was strong enough to face grief and loss without drugs.

Two separate but related writing processes shaped the LIFTT experience. As for April, writing a life history assisted the women in not only remembering their stories but in reinterpreting them in an organized, meaningful way. Structured journaling, for many others, created a focus on specific meaningful events. The data from both can be viewed in terms of creating different meaning schemes. Cell (1984) reminds us that both primary thinking and secondary reflection shape our understanding of the events of our lives. Both forms of writing capture our primary thinking or initial reaction to remembered events, foster ownership of life events, and provide the distance that promotes secondary reflection. This facilitates the process of isolating, identifying, and examining assumptions. Kelly (1963) views the individual's life as being made up of a series of constructions of reality that shape a worldview and personal schema for interacting with the world. Journaling and life history both promote the close examination of those constructs by making them more accessible. As DeSalvo (1999) writes:

> We are the accumulation of the stories we tell ourselves about who we are. So changing our stories . . . can change our personal history, can change us. Through writing, we revisit our past and review and revise it. What we thought happened, what we believed happened to us, shifts and changes as we discover deeper and more complex truths. It isn't that we use our writing to deny what we've experienced. Rather, we use it to shift our perspective [p. 11].

These were compelling reasons to include in the LIFTT process both a full life history, kept private by most participants, and structured journaling assignments, shared on a voluntary basis during group sessions. A decision was made to allow participants a greater sense of confidentiality by not requiring that the life history assignment be monitored. Some participants chose to share their entire life histories. For the rest, pieces of the life history were replicated in journaling exercises in success stories, family relationship stories, and communication stories.

Participants used journaling and coaching to deconstruct old messages and replace them with more accurate self-perceptions. A big part of the coaching process was simply asking, "Is that really true?" or "What evidence do you have of that?" One coaching exercise that asked participants to write three ways in which they were perfect just the way they were brought some participants to tears. They had never thought of themselves as special in any way. Writing positive statements and then saying them out loud had an immediate, strong impact.

Brookfield (1987) points out that we can become caught in our own constructed and narrowly constraining paradigms, that is, the frameworks of understanding through which we make sense of the world. Journaling opens up the possibility of painting small pictures of pieces of our lives and in reviewing and rearranging them, like constructing a patchwork quilt or creating a mosaic, making something beautiful and valuable out of events that, when viewed discretely, may not seem to have meaning. For April, this was an opportunity to revisit and reframe a painful period in her life.

Adding coaching discussions around structured exercises provided a third way to look at alternate constructions of reality. Opal, for example, was profoundly affected by an exercise that involved creating a pie chart to demonstrate how she was using her time and how she wanted to be using her time. After completing the chart, this mother of four, who was juggling court-imposed counseling, court dates, supervised visits with her children, and a job search, left the room in tears and was unable to return for some time. When she finally was able to speak, she said that she had never realized how little control she had over her own time, how much time she spent doing things she did not want to do, and how much she wanted to spend her time mothering her children. We used this realization to talk about how she could begin to control more of her time, and she was able to create a plan to shift her perspective about her many appointments as impositions to steps on a time line to regain custody of her children. She attended her graduation with her children at her side.

Structured journaling combined with coaching also provides a way to examine a group of feelings and experiences in relation to a particular set of life skills. Ira Progoff (1975), creator of the intensive journal process, asks workshop participants to list stepping-stones—the significant or marker events in their lives—as a prelude to looking at the choices they have made. Structured journaling creates a similar vehicle to reposition seemingly unconnected events to reveal patterns. Analysis of these patterns provides the opportunity for reflection and potentially for change.

Bolles (1987) and Progoff (1975) describe the power of documenting one's own achievements through a full life history or shorter, focused journaling assignments. This power of knowing what you can do or that you know how to do anything has great significance for women with low self-esteem. It gives reality to the woman's existence, validates her experiences for her, and allows her to see them in a different way. For the LIFTT participants, who have had few opportunities to generate alternative perspectives, group coaching around the journaling was a vehicle to hear and consider other perspectives. Simply hearing someone else's interpretation of an event was helpful to many of the women. Other participants would find strength where the author saw only weakness. These sessions validated the women's experiences and reduced feelings of isolation and helplessness.

CONNECTING JOURNALING AND TRANSFORMATIVE LEARNING

Transformative learning involves reexamining one's mind-set. If, as Levesque-Lopman (1988) suggests, this mind-set is devoid of an owned personal image, the very act of writing one's life must be transformative. For the women in LIFTT, making their lives real through journaling seemed to be increasingly important in direct relation to how removed they felt from being part of mainstream society. For women like Iris, who had completed a prison term for homicide, journaling about success provided an opportunity to reconnect with an earlier version of herself. Coaching helped her pull threads of that old forgotten self into the present and to use them to weave a new, more confident self. When she appeared at graduation in a designer suit, the group felt as if they were meeting a new person. Her new confidence helped her get her own apartment and return to regular employment.

Daloz (1986) found that in order to see how ideas different from our own exist in their own legitimate framework, it is necessary to leap out from our shell of absolute certainty and construct a new world based on some other person's ideas of reality, other assumptions of truth. The women of LIFTT tended to live in an absolute uncertainty created by negative views of reality. They needed coaching to discover multiple ways to sort and interpret information, through reflection and experimentation with alternate meaning schemes or perspectives. In order for transformative learning and personal change to occur, new material needs to be interwoven with old.

Structured journaling exercises enabled the LIFTT participants to organize their responses and separate past fears from current realities. It provided a framework for identifying and examining the origins of distorted thinking that limited their range of responses to situations. It also clearly identified the influence of self-fulfilling prophecy. The creation of individual action plans (that is, next steps) and follow-up sessions assisted participants in integrating new behaviors into their lives.

Structured journaling is especially effective for those who feel powerless. The narrative helps them claim the power in their own lives—to see their own achievements and get in touch with their strength. The power of the written word appears to make these women's experiences real and valid. It appears to be similar to the process that Belenky, Clinchy, Goldberger, and Tarule (1986) described as "coming to voice." LIFTT encouraged alternate interpretations of reality in which participants could examine the constructs of their lives free from other-imposed norms. This can be especially important for minority women who are struggling to define themselves through multiple layers of negative norms about women, poverty, and minority status. Levesque-Lopman (1988) points out that "what are clearly missing are women's self-definitions. As long as the images that women have of themselves are largely the product of men's perceptions and endeavors, they will continue to be perceived and to perceive themselves as objectified, simplified, and dehumanized" (p. 10).

A common thread in writings about journaling is the need to provide ways to document and validate personal experience before an individual engages in reflection. Cell (1984), Dominice (2000), and Gould (1990) speak of the need to concretize and organize experience. The purpose of journaling about specific life incidents is to encourage exploration of multiple influences and multiple perspectives. Dominice (2000) says that "life history narratives can reveal the ways in which living systems form a web of life. They can make it increasingly clear that the personal and societal aspects of life are connected" (p. 6).

Coaching helped participants examine their stories through multiple lenses, explore multiple interpretations, and select those that best fit their new life choices.

CHALLENGES WITH JOURNALING AND COACHING

Because the women came to the program from so many different backgrounds, at such different levels of education, different levels of preparation, and different reasons for participation, maintaining group cohesiveness and creating a productive environment was the biggest challenge in facilitating the program. Other challenges arose from differences between myself and the group and between members of each group.

Nonparticipation

Some women did not actively participate in any part of the process, and a few were disruptive. Talking, joking, and bluster often covered a fear of looking too closely at their own lives. The women came to the group for a wide variety of reasons, including simply having a social experience. Some participants should have been screened out, and for a few others, readiness was the issue. This lack of readiness made these participants resistant to coaching. These women generally left the program unchanged by the experience.

Need to Dominate

Because of the wide age range in the group, among other factors, a few women felt a need to dominate the process. In groups where there was a wide age disparity, the older women tended to see the younger women as their children. They would often preface unsolicited advice with, "When I was your age..." This had the dual effect of discounting the life experiences of the younger members and turning them off to what was often valuable information. It limited the level of peer coaching in some groups.

Time for Coaching

Initially coaching was restricted to the dinner hour. Some participants came in having reflected on the previous week's content and were eager to jump into discussion. Some needed time to decompress from their workday and move slowly into being part of the group. Others needed a longer time to feel ready to discuss their concerns. A shift to providing time for coaching at both the beginning and the end of the session provided a greater time span for reflection and increased participation in peer coaching.

Sense of Loss

This was a big issue for many of the participants because moving to something better meant giving up something familiar. Some participants missed aspects of their old selves. They had been allowed to remain passive, and other people had taken care of them, although often not very well. In a few cases, choosing a new life meant a significant loss of income. Some of the women had been involved in highly lucrative illegal activities, and their new choices meant moving into a different system and learning to live on a different scale. Coaching centered around examining sources of self-esteem associated with the new choices and acknowledging what was being given up in acting on the choice.

Threats of Change

Change was threatening not only for the participants but often for their families as well, so it was important to coach around changing relationships. When the participant was the family scapegoat, her relatives fought hard to keep her in that role. Some overprotective families did not want to see the participant step out in any way that might be painful, even if the ultimate gain was clear. Some put a great deal of effort into undermining the participant's efforts.

Creating and Maintaining an Environment of Trust

For some groups, building initial trust was difficult. I had to create compelling reasons for participants to trust and be coached by someone who was culturally very different from themselves. I engaged in a greater degree of self-disclosure with these groups than usual, both to model the behavior I hoped to see in them and dispel some of the assumptions they may have made about me. I also created an environment in which it was clear that the needs of the group superseded the agenda. We spent time role playing upcoming interviews, identifying resources, or arranging for support for appointments as needed. As participants reported back after these events, it became clear to the group how important trust and support were.

REFLECTIONS

I believe that coaching and journaling have great potential for fostering reflection and change. As I wrote this chapter documenting the process I used, however, I became more aware of the cautions about using this process. Focused journaling and exploration of life history cannot be confused with therapy. I was reminded that I was always aware of this thin line and the need to have systems in place to provide additional services. In this work, facilitators must understand that they may be unlocking powerful memories and must take care not to leave participants unprotected. DeSalvo (1999) cautions that individuals writing about their pain must be strongly supported in their efforts. Building coaching into the process helped me support the participants by creating norms for both sharing with and supporting others. Still, in some groups, it was not unusual to have more than one participant in tears at every session, and I went home both exhilarated and exhausted from the careful facilitation of exploration, discovery, and mastery.

Most of my reflections on the program are presented earlier in this chapter in the description of challenges. Documenting the experience provides me the opportunity to reflect on my own expectations for the participants. It was hard to remember that not everyone will have a transformative experience. My hope was, though, that every participant would learn or confirm something about herself. My hope was that as participants came to understand what was possible in their lives some would make substantive changes. I was also reminded that facilitators must manage their own expectations. I sometimes wanted more for participants than they wanted for themselves and was reminded of the need to refrain from managing or manipulating the expectations of others.

Writing this chapter has increased my admiration for the women who participated in LIFTT. Although each struggle was individual, collectively these women struggled with myriad obstacles including stereotyping, discrimination, poverty, and limiting local and global cultural norms. Despite this, more than 75 percent of the participants reached their stated goals: they found a better job, returned to school, moved out of shelters, or got away from court-appointed schedules. That so many were successful is a tribute to the courage and strength of these women to engage in and complete the process and to follow through on suggestions that eventually changed their lives.

REFERENCES

Belenky, M. F., Clinchy, B. M., Goldberger, N. R., & Tarule, J. M. (1986). *Women's ways of knowing*. New York: Basic Books.

Bolles, R. (1987). *What color is your parachute?* San Francisco: Ten Speed Press.

Brookfield, S. D. (1987). *Developing critical thinkers*. San Francisco: Jossey-Bass.

Cell, E. (1984). *Learning to learn from experience*. Albany: SUNY Press.

Daloz, L. A. (1986). *Effective teaching and mentoring: Realizing the transformative power of adult learning experiences*. San Francisco: Jossey-Bass.

DeSalvo, L. (1999). *Writing as a way of healing: How telling our stories transforms our lives*. Boston: Beacon Press.

Dominice, P. (2000). *Learning from ourselves: Using educational biographies with adults*. San Francisco: Jossey-Bass.

Gould, R. (1990). The therapeutic learning program. In J. Mezirow & Associates, *Reflection in adulthood: A guide to transformative and emancipatory learning* (pp. 134–156). San Francisco: Jossey-Bass.

Hudson, F. M. (1999). *The handbook of coaching*. San Francisco: Jossey-Bass

Kelly, G. A. (1963). *A theory of personality: The psychology of personal constructs*. New York: Norton.

Levesque-Lopman, L. (1988). *Claiming reality: Phenomenology and women's experience*. Lanham, MD: Rowman & Littlefield.

Meyer, S. R. (1986). *An investigation of self-concept change in black re-entry women*. Unpublished doctoral dissertation, Teachers College, Columbia University.

Mezirow, J. (1978). *Education for perspective transformation in women's re-entry programs in community colleges*. New York: Center for Adult Education, Teachers College, Columbia University.

Mezirow, J., & Associates. (1990). *Reflection in adulthood: A guide to transformative and emancipatory learning*. San Francisco: Jossey-Bass.

Progoff, I. (1975). *At a journal workshop*. New York: Dialogue House.

CHAPTER TWENTY

Breaking Out of the Egg

Methods of Transformative Learning in Rural West Africa

Peter Easton, Karen Monkman, Rebecca Miles

T ostan is a Senegalese nonformal education program that has achieved some remarkable success in fostering community empowerment and promoting the abandonment of female genital cutting (FGC) in sub-Saharan countries. The word *tostan* means "breaking out of the egg" in the Wolof language, and the program was originally designed as a literacy and empowerment activity for rural women in Senegal's central peanut farming region. Its methods bear intriguing similarities to those used elsewhere to facilitate transformational learning, a term that may itself take on quite varied meanings. There is not space here to go into the differing emphases of rational, psychosocial, personally anchored, and politically focused models of transformational learning in any detail. Suffice it to say that we find a common denominator to lie in their shared concern to better understand how "deep, structural shift[s] in [our] basic premises of thought, feeling and action" (O'Sullivan, 2003, p. 327) come about and their role as both cause and consequence of adult learning. Beyond that, we prefer not to opt for one approach over another, since the purpose of our examination of the Tostan experience in this chapter is in good part to explore just how such basic changes in outlook are understood in African cultures with histories and epistemologies that are quite different from the predominantly European American ones out of which most recent theories and methods of transformational learning have been developed. In this chapter, we therefore examine successively the setting in which the Tostan program took shape, the nature of the problems it has attempted to tackle, the evolution of its methods, and lessons that may be learned from its experience as a means of beginning, and elucidate what cross-cultural study of transformational learning experiences may have to offer practitioners and theoreticians.

Tostan's particular approach to transformative learning cannot be well understood without carefully portraying its development, because the program has been highly responsive to its environment and the inspiration of its participants. As a consequence, a good deal of the presentation that follows traces how practices emerged and evolved. From this chronicle of lived experience emerges a portrait of the program methodology. Much of the information for this chapter derives from our shared experience evaluating replication and adaptation of Tostan program methodology in Mali and the Sudan, a task that required frequent interchange with the program's Senegal-based staff. In addition, the principal author had worked with the Tostan director and Senegalese staff on several previous occasions and gained familiarity with program history and methodology reflected in earlier work (Easton, 1998; Easton & Monkman, 2001).

THE SETTING

Although for decades home to the capital of French West Africa, Senegal, like other countries of the region, remains predominantly rural (data in the paragraphs immediately following are drawn from Randle, 2004). Nearly 60 percent of the people continue to reside in small towns and villages, yet more than 80 percent of the wealth is concentrated in urban centers. Endemic poverty afflicts just under half (48.5 percent) of the country's population of 12.5 million and nearly two-thirds (62.5 percent) of those living in rural areas. In 2005, the female literacy rate was 29 percent, little more than half that for males. Girls' school participation rates, however, are now only marginally below those of boys, and primary school completion rates (42 percent versus 49 percent) are close to being comparable.

Like most other African nations, Senegal is multiethnic. The Wolof people account for the large plurality of the population (43 percent), and the Wolof language is a lingua franca for most of the country, since French (the official language) is spoken by only about a quarter of Senegalese citizens. But Senegal is home as well to a variety of other peoples, including notably the Pulaar (24 percent), the Serrer (15 percent), the Diola (9 percent), and the Mandinka-Bambara (7 percent). Almost 95 percent of the population is Muslim, and most of the rest are Christian, but traditional African religions continue to hold sway as well in virtually all regions of the country.

UNDERSTANDING FEMALE GENITAL CUTTING

The practice of female genital cutting (FGC), sometimes inaccurately referred to as female circumcision, is widespread in certain regions of Senegal and even more so in a number of other Sahelian countries (those situated on the southern border of the Sahara desert) and subjacent savanna regions. The area stretches from Mauritania and Guinea on the west to Ethiopia and Egypt in the east. The overall rate of incidence in Senegal is 28 percent according to the most recent estimates (World Health Organization, 2006b). It is lower than in many neighboring countries (rates in Guinea and Mali, for example, exceed 90 percent), thanks in part to the fact that few of the Wolof people observe the custom. But in the far northern, central eastern, and southwestern (Casamance) regions of the country, rates exceed 80 percent.

FGC involves partial or total removal of the female external genitalia and is usually performed on prepubescent girls, aged four to twelve, as part of their rites of passage, though cases are reported where local custom dictates performance as soon as baby girls reach two weeks of age. FGC is practiced for a variety of social and cultural reasons:

> The ritual cutting is often an integral part of ceremonies...in which girls are feted and showered with presents and their families are honoured.... The ritual serves as an act of socialization into cultural values and an important connection to family, community, and earlier generations. At the heart of all this is rendering a woman marriageable, which is important in societies where women get their support from male family members, especially husbands.... The practice [of FGC] is perceived as an act of love for daughters.... Because of strong adherence to these traditions, many women who say they disapprove of FGM still submit themselves and their daughters to the practice [Population Reference Bureau, 2001, p. 6].

The health consequences of this practice can be severe, though they are seldom connected in the popular mind with FGC. Hemorrhaging, trauma, and infection frequently occur and may even result in death of the young girl (World Health Organization, 2001). Longer-term effects include painful sexual relations and increased difficulty with childbirth and menstruation (World Health Organization, 2006a). International health agencies have condemned the custom for some time, stigmatized its practitioners, and promoted its eradication, all too little apparent avail. Tostan is one of the few programs to have apparently made real inroads on the practice.

ORIGIN AND GROWTH OF THE PROGRAM

Tostan was not created as a campaign against or even about FGC. Rather it grew out of the efforts of an American woman, Molly Melching, and her Senegalese colleagues to find a form of literacy training that would add up to genuine empowerment for rural women in that country. Melching originally came to Senegal from the University of Illinois in the 1970s to complete graduate studies, but remained as a Peace Corps volunteer and later as a nonformal educator. After several years of working on cultural enrichment offerings for out-of-school youth and noting how popular these programs were with their parents as well, Melching and colleagues decided to move operations from the capital city of Dakar to the rural community of Saam Njay, a Wolof village of three hundred inhabitants in central Senegal. They wished to try their hand at developing more effective and culturally appropriate nonformal education programs for adults and adopted principles that would be fundamental to the program's subsequent growth:

- Base all curriculum design on participatory research with the intended students

- Ground offerings in local culture and, just as with the out-of-school youth program, use a variety of simple media and dramatic formats to create interest and involvement

- Cultivate good relations with traditional and religious authorities, demonstrating respect for existing customs even while questioning their effects or broaching questions of change

- Adopt a holistic approach, blending literacy with information about issues of live interest to participants, discussion and dramatization of topics, practical skills acquisition, and community application

- Put participants in charge of running the programs and managing any follow-on activities

Piece by piece and through continual testing and dialogue with the villagers, a new style of programming was fashioned. It began with a module on problem solving in rural communities, then wove literacy in Wolof into succeeding units on practical concerns, like preventive health and project management, and it ended with participants, principally women at this point, identifying issues on which they particularly wanted to work and conducting a feasibility study to decide how to tackle them. Major emphasis was given to income-generating activities and local community development (CD) conducted for and by women. The participants, in fact, launched a series of projects and succeeded, with the center's help, in finding donor funding for them.

Over succeeding years, the program attracted growing interest, both locally and among donor organizations like UNICEF and USAID. The model was modified, implemented, and evaluated with participants in several neighboring areas of Senegal, reaching Pular, and Mandinka- or Bambara-speaking populations as well. In 1991, the program was incorporated as an American nongovernmental organization headquartered in Africa under the name of Tostan. At the same time, new modules on maternal and child health were developed, and staff were inspired by reading *Women's Ways of Knowing* (Belenky, Clinchy, Goldberger, & Tarule, 1986) to further adapt their pedagogy to the manner in which local participants framed issues. In addition, the entire method was increasingly imbued with a human rights and child welfare perspective that made both religious and cultural sense in the largely Islamic and entirely African environment.

Taken together, the new and old modules now were part of what Tostan called its community empowerment program (CEP), a holistic approach designed to help participants themselves identify and achieve needed change at the local level. To everyone's surprise, new units based on the human rights perspective—lessons that emphasized local democracy and women's health by linking respect of the vox populi with increased attention to the welfare concerns of the female population—broke all records for attendance and interest in rural areas. The ground was prepared for what turned out to be the signal breakthrough in the spread of the program.

THE PLEDGE OF MALICOUNDA-BAMBARA

Between 1995 and 1997, women and a few men in the village of Malicounda-Bambara, a community of three thousand people, took part in the program and worked their way through a curriculum highlighting democracy, women's rights, and local development. On completing the modules, the participants made an unanticipated decision. Their number one objective, they decided, was not to launch income-generating activities, establish well-baby programs, or start village hygiene initiatives. It was quite simply to get their village to abandon FGC once and for all. Bambara people are among the sizable minority of Senegalese ethnic groups that observe the practice. In the course of the training, women had shared with each other painful personal experiences on this taboo topic and had confronted the issue from the perspective of their heightened sense of women's rights (Easton, Monkman, & Miles, 2003).

As a consequence, they approached local authorities and other villagers to win their support for a common declaration of intent to abandon FGC, an initiative well attuned to cultures grounded in social convention and consensual decision making, if not necessarily a topic that others would have readily broached. In fact, they were successful. On July 31, 1997, the villagers of Malicounda-Bambara made a statement renouncing the practice in perpetuity in front of twenty Senegalese journalists invited for the occasion. The event made a minor splash, perhaps greater through local word-of-mouth dissemination than in print and audio media. There was some immediate vocal opposition to what the women of Malicounda had done, as much in reaction to the "shame" of talking so publicly about a taboo topic as to the substance of the declaration. Despite the controversy, a second nearby village also undergoing the Tostan training program, Ngerigne-Bambara, decided to imitate Malicounda-Bambara's example, led by a woman who was herself a traditional cutter; and yet another, Kër Simbara, began actively discussing the idea. Then a critical event occurred.

Breakthrough

The imam of Kër Simbara, a sixty-six-year-old religious leader, much respected in the region, became concerned at the events, and he came to talk with Tostan representatives and the women of Malicounda-Bambara. He was not opposed to the abandonment of FGC. In fact, the controversy had prompted him for the first time to talk to his female relatives about their own experience and feelings regarding FGC, and they gave him quite an earful. He ended up a strong supporter. But he felt that there were two major problems with the way in which things were being done.

First, a single village cannot do this alone, the imam said: "We are part of an intra-marrying community, and unless *all* the villages involved take part, you are asking parents to forfeit the chance of their daughters getting married." Second, there was a real problem of language and approach. These are taboo topics, he pointed out, and they should not be discussed lightly or inconsiderately. The people who crusaded against FGC in the past used terms that villagers consider unmentionable and showed images and pictures that shocked them. They treated the practice as a disease to eradicate and its practitioners as social pariahs. That is no way to change a culture or to help it change itself, the imam said.

A Pedagogy of Respect

The women agreed: it was time to think things through a good deal more carefully. Together they outlined a strategy:

- Go to all the villages in the intramarrying community. Start by reaffirming personal relationships.
- Do not tell the villagers what to do. Tell them what Malicounda-Bambara and Ngerigne-Bambara have done, and why. Then let them tell their own stories and make their own decisions.

- Avoid using graphic terms or demonstrations for taboo activities. Refer to FGC simply as "the custom." Everyone will know what is meant. (In Senegalese Bambara, "customs" in the plural refers to a whole set of cultural traditions; "the custom," in the singular, refers to FGC alone.)

- Avoid condemning practitioners implicitly or explicitly. They have been performing accepted cultural practices in good faith.

On the basis of these agreements, the imam set out on foot, accompanied by the woman cutter from Kër Simbara and his own nephew, to visit ten other villages in that marriage community. It was a ground-shaking experience. Women opened up and told stories of daughters who had died from hemorrhage and of others who had contracted infections or had long-term psychic distress from the FGC trauma. Those who performed the practice talked too about why and about changing customs. Men joined in with their reflections. "We never knew," they said.

Before it was over, all ten villages had decided to join the ranks of those declaring against FGC. With representatives of Malicounda-Bambara, Ngerigne-Bambara, and Kër Simbara itself, they met in the community of Diabougou, fifty Tostan participants and new advocates representing eight thousand villagers, and declared "never again" on February 15, 1998, before a crowd of local people and journalists from Senegalese media.

THE CONSEQUENCES

The repercussions of these events both changed Senegal and projected Tostan, and some of the cast from Malicounda Bambara, onto an international stage. The growth of the program within Senegal progressively accelerated. The Malicounda-Bambara experience proved in many ways contagious. Groups of women traveled among villages and between regions of the country, with Tostan's support, to reseed the movement for abandonment of FGC as well as the entire CCEP. In the Sine Saloum islands off Senegal's southwest coast, women literally canoed from island to island in order to spread the word (Easton et al., 2003).

At the same time, encouraged by Senegalese President Abdou Diouf, the country's Assemblée Nationale (Parliament) moved to pass a law abolishing FGC and dictating severe penalties for violators. The allies of Tostan were immediately concerned and went to Dakar to warn against the initiative—not, obviously, because they wanted to maintain FGC, but because they firmly believed official abolition and sanction were simply the wrong way to go. The law, they felt, should follow and model a change in practice developed in the field, not attempt to dictate it. As the imam from Kër Simbara put it in reference to his own ethnic group, "Try to tell Bambara people what they must do about their own customs, and you have a fight on your hands." The premonitions proved right. The law was passed, and a general outcry ensued. In protest, one traditional cutter in the region of Tambacounda made a point of performing FGC on no fewer than 120 young girls in the days following.

Despite such setbacks, the movement gathered momentum year by year. By 2007, Tostan calculated that nearly half of the approximately 5,000 villages in the country that practice FGC in one form or another—2,336 out of approximately 5,000—had joined alliances to abandon it and made public declarations (Molly Melching, personal communication, September 20, 2007).

Media attention to the program also rapidly gave it an international presence, and Tostan representatives were invited to a variety of venues in Europe and the United States, including committee hearings of the United Nations, to relate their experience. Wherever possible, local people were sent to these gatherings with interpreters. The imam and traditional cutter from Kër Simbara, for example, spoke in the British Parliament, while the cutter from Ngerigne-Bambara made a presentation at International Women's Day in Germany.

At the same time, Tostan was increasingly solicited to transplant the approach elsewhere. To date, replications or adaptations have been attempted in the Gambia, Guinea, Burkina Faso, Mali, the Sudan, and Somalia, and new projects are envisaged in Mauritania and Djibouti. To their credit and in conformity with their own principles, Tostan staff have made consistent efforts to adapt the methodology and materials to conditions within the target country; they have partnered with local nongovernmental organizations in its implementation and have systematically promoted exchange between program participants in all countries involved.

TRANSFORMATION OF A METHODOLOGY

In 2007, Tostan and the villages of central Senegal celebrated the tenth anniversary of the Malicounda-Bambara declaration, and the organization marked more than twenty years of work in the empowerment of rural women and communities. There is little doubt that people have transformed their lives in the process: in fact, a significant part of Senegal has been changed as well, and new seeds are sprouting in neighboring countries. That much is clear. It is more difficult to identify just what measures and methods are most directly transformative in a program that has been shaped by participants and events as much as it has shaped them. Examining what has changed in Tostan's approach, and what has not, should help to answer this question.

The first elements to stress are doubtless those that have not changed. The program remains largely true to the orientations and pedagogical principles described earlier in the chapter and continues to develop a holistic empowerment approach—one that (1) blends practical problem-solving strategies with beginning literacy and new information on issues critical to health and well-being, (2) uses an active pedagogy rooted in local culture and based on dramatization and discussion as much as skill acquisition, (3) gives a large measure of initiative to participants, and (4) promotes in its final phase the design and execution of self-directed income-generating and community development activities. As Tostan staff recurrently insist, it neither was nor is an "FGC" program. There is, in fact, still no module on FGC itself, though the topic is treated. The public declaration breakthrough and its spread were initiated by the participants themselves—proof, perhaps, of the program's transformative effects but not the root of them.

At the same time, some significant aspects of the methodology have changed or matured in the process. Although the FGC breakthrough was arguably the key to the organization's biggest triumph, the refinement of focus that this success both conceals and reveals is a progressive shift to prime emphasis on the paired themes of human rights and democracy. It was, in fact, the human rights theme that gave women the courage to speak out and take action about FGC. That strong note was soon matched, as a natural outgrowth of Tostan's early concern with creating local leadership for its spin-off activities, by an emphasis on promoting local democracy and translating that notion into meaningful terms at the household and community levels. Operationally this meant affirming everyone's right to decide how traditional culture should be interpreted and applied in daily life, as well as how domestic and community decisions are made; it resulted, among other things, in the development of an emphasis on reconsidering child marriage as well.

In the process, an underlying social strategy has emerged. Tostan manifested early on a clear understanding that personal transformation in an African setting had to be more than individual. As the story of Malicounda-Bambara illustrates, major personal decisions or changes in African cultures are also collective matters, having implications and entailing long-standing practices at the family and community levels as well, even—and perhaps particularly—when the substance of the change is itself highly innovative. By way of contrast, most of the existing transformational learning literature, excepting perhaps the older Freirean strands, puts preponderant emphasis on the dynamics of individual change. After the events of Malicounda-Bambara, staff were much inspired by the writings and direct assistance of Gerry Mackie (1996), a political scientist who has examined the renunciation of foot binding in China and its parallels to the FGC movement, basing his analysis on social convention theory, which focuses on the political-economic dynamics of behavior change and the feedback cycles within social groups that reinforce or cancel the change initiatives undertaken by individuals. His insights helped them give a name to this intuition and their related practices: for behavior to change radically in a milieu where people are as tightly interlocked and related as they are in rural Africa, buy-in must be obtained from a critical mass of those concerned. Transformations propagate once a tipping point or a requisite density of interactions has been reached. As a consequence, Tostan now carefully studies the social milieu, the intermarrying patterns, and other forms of close association in any region before introducing its program, and its implantation follows a strategy designed to favor new social alignments. At one level, the tactics are as reminiscent of Saul Alinsky's (1971) energetic strategies for community organizing and power leverage as they are of the somewhat more introspective or cognitive approaches of many transformative learning theorists (Mezirow, 1998; Merriam, 2004).

Tostan's perceptions of its clientele have also evolved. Of course the program has gone international, a fact that has entailed catering to many different situations and groups. But in a more immediate demographic sense, the identification of prime participants has fluctuated over time. Early experiments in Saam Njay targeted the entire adult population, but soon emphasis shifted toward women, given their particular needs and disadvantaged status. As the years wore on, however, and progress was made at this level, staff became aware once again that male participation was critical to the enduring effects of the program, just as men like the imam of Kër Simbara had been vitally instrumental to the success of the FGC abandonment campaign. In addition, special focus programs were developed for other disadvantaged groups, like Senegalese prisoners and the population of *talibés,* or Koranic students, who throng the cities of West Africa and are often rudely exploited by their masters. The program seems to come out with a more sophisticated and multidimensional approach that seeks to identify the special social functions and potentials of different actors in any imperiled milieu and to find roles for each, while stressing human rights and placing emphasis on the most disadvantaged as the leaven of change.

Finally, Tostan's pedagogical method and its curriculum have evolved as well, though the basic orientations remain valid. The organization no longer lays emphasis on discrete modules. Although a definite, if flexible, sequence of lessons is observed and included in the training given by facilitators, Tostan has simplified its characterization of the pedagogical strategy to two essential elements: first, the *Kobi* or social empowerment element (the term means "preparing the field" in the Bambara-Mandinka language), which includes the human rights and democracy themes, methods of problem solving, and lessons on hygiene and health; and second, the *Aawde* component (Pulaar for "planting the seed"), which includes literacy, math for management, and project direction. Significantly, literacy and math—the latter arguably the more important lesson, given Tostan's emphasis on local management—have moved to a second tier, though no less significant place, in the program. They are brought in when participants' movement toward local development and income-generating activities has created a need and an immediate field of application for their skills.

REFLECTIONS

Perhaps in Tostan's case as for King, "ripeness is all": the chronicle of its development and the portrait of its evolving strategy say more about the approach to transformative learning than a static inventory of its methods could, even if the story in fact continues to emerge. Looked at under the microscope and dissected, individual aspects of the curriculum and methodology, while laudatory and reflective of many of the virtues exhibited by good nonformal education programs over the past forty years, do not seem particularly exceptional. Yet running through them are some central inspirations that time has brought to the fore and that seem to have produced major effects. Four appear most important to us. First is the doggedly participatory approach and careful attentiveness to what the women themselves were saying, paired with deep respect for and confidence in the strengths of local culture. Next comes Tostan's willingness to break with doctrine in literacy and other areas of development and to experiment with methods that fit the circumstances in which they were working. Third is the program's adeptness in recognizing and enabling the collective as well as the individual dimensions of transformation—in fact, in pairing them and underwriting the mix with tools of organization and income generation. And the last and greatest might be their progressive adoption as central theme of a very personalized and localized version of human rights and democracy, addressed to the most disadvantaged groups in a disadvantaged milieu. Do these add up to personal transformation? It is our sense that they add up to something more important: creation of circumstances in which the participants learn and find ways to transform themselves individually and collectively.

At the same time, reflecting on the lessons of the Tostan story for transformative learning takes us beyond the experience of simply evaluating the program. An evaluation is necessarily focused on issues like fulfillment of objectives and program performance. Tostan's objectives clearly include personal and community transformation, but assessing their accomplishment did not automatically mean discerning just what fueled the events recorded or what they would mean for us, the more so as the work transpired across considerable cultural boundaries, even if ones we have negotiated before and have come to cherish. The insight and the challenges for practice that the experience of writing this chapter provided us may be best encapsulated in the Wolof definition of the program's name itself, "coming out of the egg," and the understandings of how such new birth transpires that lie in Tostan's two stages, the *Kobi* and the *Aawde.*

We ourselves have often interpreted transformation as a question of becoming something different, but both the Tostan program and its name put the emphasis on becoming what one is, on bringing to fruition what is latent within oneself and one's heritage or community — and this despite a context of development programming in Africa that is still largely oriented to externally driven changes. It is thus more a question of internally driven liberation than deliverance, of what Martin Luther (Erikson, 1962), a transformed person from an utterly different era and culture, once said must always "move from within." We find the practices that create space for and encourage that movement, and that challenge our own practice, well summarized by "preparing the field" (*Kobi*) and "planting the seed" (*Aawde*), particularly if one remembers that in African culture (and agriculture), seeds are most often things one has put aside in the family from previous seasons, if not those implanted by martial concourse from previous generations. How then shall we best enable people to discover within the seeds of new life that bear and transform their own cultural code?

REFERENCES

Alinsky, S. (1971). *Rules for radicals: A practical primer for realistic radicals.* New York: Random House.

Belenky, M. F., Clinchy, B. M., Goldberger, N. R., & Tarule, J. M. (1986). *Women's ways of knowing: The development of self, voice and mind.* New York: Basic Books.

Easton, P. (1998). Senegalese women remake their culture. *IK Notes, 3,* 1–4.

Easton, P., & Monkman, K. (2001). Malicounda-Bambara: The sequel. The journey of a local revolution. *IK Notes, 31,* 1–4.

Easton, P., Monkman, K., & Miles, R. (2003). Social policy from the bottom up: Abandoning FGC in sub-Saharan Africa. *Development in Practice, 13*(5), 445–458.

Erikson, E. (1962). *Young man Luther: A study in psychoanalysis and history.* New York: Norton.

Mackie, G. (1996). Ending footbinding and infibulation: A convention account. *American Sociological Review, 61*(6), 999–1004.

Merriam, S. (2004). The role of cognitive development in Mezirow's transformational learning theory. *Adult Education Quarterly, 55*(1), 60–68.

Mezirow, J. (1998). Transformative learning and social action: A response to Inglis. *Adult Education Quarterly, 49*(1), 70–71.

O'Sullivan, E. (2003). Bringing a perspective of transformative learning to globalized consumption. *International Journal of Consumer Studies, 27*(4), 326–330.

Population Reference Bureau. (2001). *Abandoning FGM*. Retrieved October 12, 2005, from http://www.prb.org/pdf/AbandoningFGM_Eng.pdf.

Randle, W. (2004). Senegal strives for millennium goals: Reducing poverty requires will, money and community action. *Africa Recovery, 18*(1), 16–21.

World Health Organization. (2001). *A systematic review of the health complications of female genital mutilation*. Geneva: World Health Organization.

World Health Organization. (2006a). Female genital mutilation and obstetric outcomes: WHO collaborative prospective study in six African countries. *Lancet, 367*(9525), 1835–1841.

World Health Organization. (2006b). *Female genital mutilation: New knowledge spurs optimism*. Geneva: World Health Organization.

CHAPTER TWENTY-ONE

Farmer Field Schools

A Platform for Transformative Learning in Rural Africa

Deborah Duveskog, Esbern Friis-Hansen

In a policy meeting, a Kenyan female farmer self-confidently expressed "Before I joined FFS, if somebody asked me what I do, I used to say, 'Nothing.' Now I proudly answer, 'I am a farmer.' " Triggered by the learning process in which she had been involved, her perspectives had been changed in such a way that she no longer looked on her role as a farmer with shame but with pride and dignity. Similar frequently observed expressions among Farmer Field School (FFS) participants have made practitioners increasingly realize that beyond the technical aspects of the learning process in FFS, a human transformation is going on, somewhat behind the scenes but equally as or even more important. Drawing on results from several interrelated research investigations in the East Africa context, this chapter explores transformative aspects of FFS in more depth and analyzes how the learning tools applied facilitate critical thinking and transformation of mind-sets among rural poor.

We have extensive experience and knowledge of the African rural small-holder context and FFS. Duveskog has for the past ten years been based in East Africa and worked as Farmer Field School advisor for the U.N. Food and Agriculture Organization and is currently carrying out doctoral research on farmer empowerment related to FFS. Friis-Hansen is a research fellow at the Danish Institute of International Studies and has, through a number of research projects and consulting assignments, been involved in program development, support, and evaluation of FFS programs in East Africa.

Since a majority of the poor derive their livelihoods from agriculture, farmer education and extension are important components for improving people's lives. However, existing approaches and methods have proven largely unsuccessful. In conventional agricultural training, farmers are pushed into preconceived behaviors and actions, often with a focus on uptake of externally designed technologies. Freire (1970) refers to this as education that is domesticating in nature as opposed to liberating, where participants and advisors together search for solutions to problems faced through reflection on experience.

Smallholder farmers in Africa operate in risky and disaster-prone environments and face a range of oppressive forces and exploitation, especially in relation to the sale and marketing of their produce. While liberalization has provided new market opportunities, smallholders are faced with continuing challenges, including massive price distortions, poor physical access to local and regional markets where the poor conduct most of their transactions, underdeveloped market information systems, and lack of innovation in financial services to facilitate marketing. Furthermore, while globalization expands markets for untraditional exports, it has also made an agenda designed to help the poor more difficult as falling commodity prices and more demanding and sophisticated commodity chains question the viability of traditional small-scale family farms (World Bank, 2008). Many policy observers argue that increased individual and collective agency among small scale farmers and their organizations is needed if broad-based agricultural development is to succeed.

However, decades of economic mismanagement by African governments and donor agencies have significantly eroded the level of trust and organizational capacity within rural areas. The sense of citizenship is low, and the general farming population has very little power in relation to other actors in society (Friis-Hansen, 2000). The FFS learning process fostering critical consciousness and decision-making skills can assist citizens in changing from being passive beneficiaries of services (if they receive them at all), into citizens who actively participate in society and decision making. Freire (1970) refers to "the practice of freedom," by which men and women deal critically and creatively with reality and discover how to participate in the transformation of their world.

THE FFS APPROACH

Farmer Field Schools (FFS) provide an institutional platform where farmers meet regularly in groups to study a particular topic and engage in an action learning process that includes making regular field observations, relating their observations to the ecosystem, and blending previous experience with new information to make improved crop or livestock management decisions. Apart from technical issues, group dynamics and sessions addressing special topics relating to broader livelihood issues are integrated into the learning process. Farmers meet regularly, usually weekly or biweekly, over a period of time on a schedule defined by the group members. A skilled facilitator guides the FFS learning process. This person is most often an extension worker, agricultural technician, or local farmer who has been trained in FFS facilitation skills and tools.

The FFS approach was developed at the end of the 1980s in Indonesia in response to the ineffectiveness of the conventional agricultural advisory system to address a rice insect outbreak affecting the country. Complex and site-specific integrated pest management practices were demanded. However, conventional methods of delivering messages were often inappropriate and too simple to deal with complex problems, and it proved necessary to ensure local decision making by farmers in their fields. The FFS approach, building on adult education and experiential learning principles as a process of sharing among peers and experiencing through hands-on practical learning situations, emerged as a means of facilitating critical decision-making skills among farmers to deal with complex farming problems.

In East Africa, the FFS approach was introduced in 1996 and has since been taken up by numerous actors in more than fifteen African countries. Topics addressed in FFS have gradually broadened out from crop-related aspects to a wide spectrum of farming and livelihood-related issues and lately with applications in the public health sector.

TRANSFORMATIVE OUTCOMES OF FFS

There are many indications that the learning process applied in FFS leads to transformative outcomes and human development (Braun, Jiggins, Röling, van den Berg, & Snijders, 2005). The sections that follow describe some of the changes observed among FFS graduates following their participation in FFS groups.

Change in Habits

Mezirow (1991) mentions that one of the most important areas of learning for adults is that which frees them from their habitual ways of thinking and acting. Changes in routine and habitual behaviors have been demonstrated in various ways among FFS graduates. Participants have learned to diversify their farming system and try new technological solutions to a higher extent than their average fellow farmers do. In particular, the traditional reliance on maize as the main crop changed following farmers' reflective analysis of the cost and benefits involved. Many farmers explain this learning as a big mind opener, as expressed by a farmer in Mwingi, Kenya, who stated, "Until now, I have never realized that I actually operate at a loss by planting maize. I always assumed that just by planting, I at least gain something."

Farmers have also been observed to gain confidence in experimenting with selling produce to higher levels of the value chain in the local market and mention that the learning process has been a process of change from a mind-set of risk minimization to opportunity search. A recent study in Soroti, Uganda, showed a significant correlation between membership in FFS groups and level of adoption of improved techniques for soil and pest management (Friis-Hansen, 2008). This study concludes that farmers' capability to detect and solve field problems has been enhanced as a result of a transformative learning process.

Perspective Transformation

Mezirow (1994) defines *perspective transformation* as the process of becoming critically aware of our assumptions and ways of viewing the world and asserts this as developmental: "Perspective transformation is the engine of adult development" (p. 224). Taken-for-granted norms and practices are confronted and challenged, and frames of reference become more differentiated, open, and inclusive. FFS has demonstrated an increase in self-confidence and in how farmers perceive their role versus the role of experts.

A recent survey among women FFS graduates showed a statistically significant difference in the feeling of "myself" as opposed to other people having the biggest influence to change aspects of life for the better (Duveskog and Friis-Hansen, 2009). The change of mind-sets and attitudes to be more differentiating and integrative of experiences is expressed by a local stockist (a vendor) selling agro-inputs (for example, seeds, fertilizers, chemicals) in Mwingi district, Kenya. He explained:

> Farmers often blankly used to come and ask me to advise on which seed to buy. However, among FFS graduates, I have noticed a fundamental change in that they often confidently come and ask for a specific variety, and when I inquire for the reason, the farmers are able to specify detailed justifications, usually based on reference to actual field experience.

Social Change and Collective Agency

Freire (1970) explains that liberating education leads to the ability to perceive social, political, and economic contradictions and stimulate action against oppressive elements of reality. Much of the social change experienced among FFS graduates relates to farmers' taking steps to deal with challenges and obstacles through reflective critical thinking and collective action, where farmers work together in groups to share information, reflect on experiences, discuss and test ideas, and define strategies for action. This often results in farmers who are increasingly challenging authorities. FFS graduates also tend to take a greater interest and more action in community decision-making processes. A survey among FFS graduates in Kenya (Duveskog, 2009) showed a statistically significant difference in relation to non-FFS members in participating in community meetings, voting in local elections, and holding leadership positions. Furthermore, farmer networks and associations have emerged as a follow-up effect of FFS, and these units have increasingly been breaking manipulative relationships with trade middlemen and thereby gaining access to more lucrative markets to sell their produce.

In Soroti district, Uganda, thirteen FFS groups have formed a sweet potato producer association in response to problems they faced with access to profitable markets. The association members share what they have learned from experiments carried out by individual FFS groups (for example, on vine multiplication and conservation, variety evaluation, and processing into diverse sweet potato products) and is now involved in joint marketing of sweet potato products: wholesale contracts of highly nutritious yellow-fleshed sweet potatoes for distribution in refugee camps and the sale of processed sweet potato products to supermarkets and traders, for example.

Similarly, the Kakamega and Bungoma FFS networks in Kenya have opened shops where they stock and sell agricultural inputs to member farmers at favorable conditions as compared to private retailers, and they have also engaged in collective marketing of produce among members. This is a large breakthrough considering that normal practice often entails farmers' being manipulated and exploited by market actors. Local traders have been unable to respond effectively to this challenge, which has further encouraged the farmers. Farmers attribute these achievements to the social bonding and trust building that take place within the FFS context.

THE REFLECTIVE LEARNING PROCESS IN FFS

Some key learning tools and exercises carried out in the FFS contribute to learning and serve as an aid for the facilitators to ensure participation, dialogue, and critical reflection. There are also some key concepts and slogans used to define FFS. Key to the approach is the concept that "the farmer is the expert"—in other words, the farmers are the ones who best know the local context (they are the experts of that particular system, and their knowledge and experience are central to the learning process), and they learn by conducting their own investigations; in the process, they become experts on the particular practice.

Another key feature is that "the field is the classroom." This relates to the notion that people learn most effectively when working on real-life problems occurring in their day-to-day setting. All learning in FFS takes place in a real-life situation, which in the agricultural context means the field, the pasture, or the livestock unit. Participants generate their own learning materials (drawings and posters, for example) based on their observations in the field. These materials are always consistent with local conditions, and learners know the meaning of them because they have created the materials.

Another central feature of FFS is that it entails "facilitation, not teaching," meaning that the role of the outsider or advisor is that of a facilitator. Facilitators offer help and guidance in the group learning process and stimulate dialogue and reflection for farmers to challenge their habitual ways of thinking and acting. This means that the teacher-student relationship is horizontal: where both parties are simultaneously teachers and students (Freire, 1970).

Critical self-reflections is a central element of adult learning and development (Mezirow, 1981; Freire, 1970). Learning links theory and practice through a cycle of immediate concrete experience that forms the basis for observation and reflection. These observations are assimilated into a theory from which new implications for actions or further experimentation can be deduced (Kolb, 1984). With FFS tools, such as agro-ecosystem analysis, exercises designed for discovering underlying concepts of technical challenges and practical field investigations help the group reflect on actual situations and provide a forum where knowledge is created through the assimilation of actual experience among participants rather than through learning theoretical concepts.

Discovery-based exercises form the basis for learning in FFS. These exercises are usually one to three hours long to fit into a regular FFS session and address the learning topic in a practical hands-on manner where farmers' experiences and reflections are the basis for learning. An example might be that the farmers collect various insects from the field and make an "insect zoo." They then observe the insects as a basis for discussion and conclusion in regard to how various species relate to each other in the ecosystem. These observations then related to farmers' own situation in their field in order to come up with recommendations for action.

In FFS, groups find their own solutions to problems through testing and experimentation. At the formation stage of FFS, a problem identification process takes place from which an experimental theme is derived. Thereafter, various technologies or practices to study and compare in relation to the theme are defined. These may be research-generated technologies or local farmer innovations or practices. Typical experiments in FFS may be the testing and comparison of drought-tolerant crop varieties, options for improved soil management, or types of poultry feed and housing. The group establishes field investigation trials where the identified options are compared over a longer time (for example, from seed to harvest or from egg to egg). The trials, whether crop or livestock, form the nucleus of the FFS learning since the physical site of the trials becomes the meeting point and learning space for the group. Apart from forming the basis for learning on the particular issue under investigation, the trials also more broadly build capacity among farmers to adapt to change and improve the way they manage their resources (that is, they generate innovativeness among farmers). The group engages the field experiments with discussion and reflection by using the Agro Eco Systems Analysis (AESA) exercise.

AESA, a field-based analysis of interactions observed in the ecosystem, is the cornerstone of the FFS approach. The exercise was developed in the FAO Programme for Community IPM Asia (www.communityipm.org), and the purpose of the exercise is for farmers to practice field observation skills, learn how to analyze problems and opportunities they encounter in the field, and improve their decision-making skills regarding farm management. The AESA process follows a cycle of observation, analysis, and action and is carried out regularly, at each group meeting in relation to the field investigations. In practice, this usually entails that each time the group meets, subgroups of four or five farmers visit the various plots or experimental sections of the crop or livestock enterprises. The subgroups make observations according to a predetermined format and discuss what they see. Typical observations include soil moisture levels, pests and diseases observed, and growth of the crops or animals since the last visit. The subgroups analyze their information, record their findings visually (as to aid to learning, especially for the illiterate), and draw conclusions as to what the reasons might be for the observed situation. Thereafter, the subgroups present their findings to the larger group and explore how to deal with the observed problems. Actions are agreed on through discussion comparing the findings of the different subgroups. For example, the farmers might conclude that the plot with soil cover might have handled the previous week's dry spell better than the plot with base soil, and this observation might lead to a recommendation to ensure soil cover at times of scarce rainfall in order to keep plants moist.

A skilled facilitator is needed in the AESA exercise to help rural people analyze and reflect on their livelihoods in a way that is empowering and transforming. In FFS, the facilitators are taught to take a back-seat role and let the farmers lead in all activities. The facilitator serves as more of a mentor, steering the learning process. FFS facilitators are encouraged never to directly answer technical questions but to use questions as a basis for probing and posing counter-questions in order to stimulate deeper thinking and reflection on the topic. For example, if a farmer in the field asks, "What insect is this?" the facilitator does not answer directly even if he or she knows the name but instead asks questions such as these: "Where did you find it? What was the insect doing when you saw it? Have you seen it before? When in the day does it appear? What do you normally do when you see it? What do other farmers do about this insect?" The FFS facilitator moderates the dialogue where the bulk of information comes from the group members, and in order to facilitate participation by all, small group discussions are commonly used. Effective facilitation means that learners are challenged to examine their previously held values, beliefs, and behaviors (Brookfield, 1986). This happens in FFS through sharing among participants, which provide exposure of different values and attitudes and thereby opportunities for participants to question their own views and perceptions.

To assist participants in feeling comfortable in sharing their own views, FFS has learned that it is important to provide a safe learning environment, where participants can experiment and try out new ideas without facing personal or economic risks. This is consistent with conditions that foster transformative learning (Mezirow & Associates, 2000). The safe environment allows participants to speak their mind or, as Mezirow (1991) says, it gives equal opportunity to "challenge, question, refute, and reflect and to hear others do the same" (p. 78). In FFS, the safe environment is developed by group cohesion, created by involvement in practical learning activities over a long period of time. When farmers meet regularly and are involved in hands-on activities with participants of various wealth-, gender-, and hierarchical-related groups, the differences between members become less significant, and trust and solidarity are nurtured. Also the fact that the learning space is the field rather than a formal classroom provides a more informal atmosphere where participants can feel at ease with each other. The informal atmosphere is further stimulated by the social and team-building aspects of the FFS, such as singing, dancing, and drama.

At each meeting, the host team (a subgroup of farmers that rotate responsibility for conducting the FFS sessions) leads the group in some kind of dynamic, such as singing or dancing. Theatrical skits and dramas are also prepared by the group and performed for the larger community during field days and graduation ceremonies. The theme for these skits is usually a humorous reflection on the learning process that has taken place in FFS and the outcomes experienced. Often sensitive issues are brought out in these skits such as aspects of HIV/AIDS, domestic violence, and alcoholism, and the skits thereby assist in breaking the ice for discussion of topics that normally are not addressed openly.

CONTEXTUAL CONSIDERATIONS

The FFS learning process can provide a platform for transformation of behaviors and worldviews. However, its effectiveness for social change is strongly influenced by the formal and informal context within which actors operate.

Experience from East Africa indicates that transformative learning through FFS can play a crucial role in social change, resulting in poverty reduction and passive farmers who become active citizens and engage in an ongoing relationship with the local government (Friis-Hansen and Kyed, 2008). In a context where authorities, both deliberately and unintentionally, hinder change and action by the poor, transformation might not have the same effect. Schugurensky (2002) argues that in the absence of a supportive social environment, "critical reflection alone is not only unlikely to lead to transformative social action, but in some cases may even lead to the opposite situation, with cynicism, paralysis, and a general feeling of helplessness" (p. 62). In Kenya there are several cases where farmers have mentioned feeling more powerless and unable to make significant changes in their lives after FFS participation. This is after trying to lobby for change with local authorities on issues such as water access and complaints of corruption and then realizing to what extent their views were ignored by the system, thereby engendering a feeling of helplessness.

Evidence from FFS, as well as from related studies in other agricultural extension contexts, highlights one of the biggest challenges for implementing demand-driven services as being behavioral and attitudinal change on the part of the actors involved, from farmers to bureaucrats. A top-down decision-making and control culture is widespread in the public sector institutions in most developing countries (Sen, 1997), and the institutionalization of participatory learning thus demands significant organizational, methodological, and attitudinal shifts among all partners. In such contexts, institutional learning and change in learning institutions do not occur unless individuals go through a learning process themselves and learn from their own experiences. Therefore, institutionalization of transformative learning relates not only to the participants' level but also needs to include learning among facilitators and supervisors of such programs. However, within the public sector, there is often resistance to the necessary change in institutional culture, such as basic attitudes toward farmers and reassessing work approaches. In most FFS programs, facilitators and direct supervisors undergo shorter training that includes learning tools for experiential learning and facilitation skills. However, this training is often inadequate to fundamentally change attitudes and perceptions. On-the-job mentoring and support of field staff to continue expanding their own learning and transformation thus becomes crucial.

REFLECTIONS

Current reforms of agricultural extension in Africa seek to shift the emphasis from a central public sector command approach to more demand-driven and privatized services. Such reforms assume that small-scale farmers, if given adequate institutional opportunities, will articulate informed demands and engage in governance processes. However, often such interventions fail, and instead of farmers being able to exercise choice, they become subjects of exploitation due to their often low levels of individual and collective agency. Reflecting on the experiences described in this chapter makes it evident that transformative learning through FFS can have a crucial role to play in fostering active citizenship among rural poor and thereby increase the effectiveness of rural service delivery, which can help ensure the success of reform programs.

However, as we realized during our close interactions with FFS participants, empowering education often takes unpredictable paths, and in the often weak democracies of Africa, many forces quietly strive to keep local communities relatively powerless. Standing up and fighting for change often means challenging authorities, something that may put individuals at personal risk, especially in the commercial sphere (for example, in the exposure of exploitation of farmers by market actors). Furthermore, the culture of top-down education is deeply embedded in people's minds, and teachers are traditionally connected with so much status that trying to depolarize the student-teacher relationship in FFS is sometimes felt as a personal attack on the integrity of these people. Also among the communities, a shift of attitude is required. The poor are so accustomed to a culture of handouts and expert advice that at the initial stages of FFS, they may not fully appreciate the new style of engagement that demands their active participation and reflection. There is as well a challenge to involve the most vulnerable sections of the community, such as those who are disabled and single mothers of many children, in the FFS learning process as they often are so deep in poverty that they cannot afford to spend time on learning if the economic returns are not immediate.

In Africa, FFS is rapidly gaining popularity, and there are efforts to scale up the approach on the national level. However, these attempts tend to focus on FFS as a successful means for increased application of improved farming practices. There is still among many FFS actors at all levels a belief in technological solutions to problems, and human empowerment is not being emphasized. There is a need to recognize the potential of FFS and farmer education to serve as a platform for transformation and action, with more attention given to the process of reflective learning. This will ensure that FFS and similar programs do not become a forum—for domestication of farmers' behaviors and practices; instead they truly stimulate critical reflection among people to become their own agents of change.

REFERENCES

Braun, A., Jiggins, J., Röling, N., van den Berg, H., & Snijders, P. (2005). *A global survey and review of Farmer Field School experiences*. Nairobi, Kenya: International Livestock Research Institute.

Brookfield, S. (1986). *Understanding and facilitating adult learning*. San Francisco: Jossey-Bass.

Duveskog, D., & Friis-Hansen, E. (2009). *Measurements of empowerment among Farmer Field School graduates*. Unpublished manuscript.

Freire, P. (1970). *Pedagogy of the oppressed*. London: Penguin Books.

Friis-Hansen, E. (2000). *Agricultural policy in post adjustment Africa*. Copenhagen: Centre for Development Research.

Friis-Hansen, E. (2008). Impact assessment of farmer institutional development and agricultural change: Soroti district, Uganda. *Development in Practice, 18*, 4–5,

Friis-Hansen, E., & Kyed, M. H. (2008). *Inclusive citizenship and social accountability*. Copenhagen: Danish Institute for International Studies.

Kolb, D. (1984). *Experiential learning*. Upper Saddle River, NJ: Prentice Hall.

Mezirow, J. (1981). A critical theory of adult learning and education. *Adult Education, 32*(1), 3–24.

Mezirow, J. (1991). *Transformative dimensions of adult learning and fostering critical reflection in adulthood: A guide to transformative and emancipatory learning*. San Francisco: Jossey-Bass.

Mezirow, J. (1994). Understanding transformative theory. *Adult Education Quarterly, 44*, 222–235.

Mezirow, J., & Associates (2000). Learning to think like an adult: Core concepts of transformation theory. In J. Mezirow & Associates, *Learning as transformation: Critical perspectives on a theory in progress* (pp. 3–33). San Francisco: Jossey-Bass.

Schugurensky, D. (2002). Transformative learning and transformative politics. In E. V. O'Sullivan, A. Morrell, & M. A. O'Connor (Eds.), *Expanding the boundaries of transformative learning* (pp. 59–76). New York: Palgrave.

Sen, G. (1997). *Empowerment as an approach to poverty*. Bangalore: Indian Institute of Management.

World Bank. (2008). *World development report*. Washington, DC: World Bank.

CHAPTER TWENTY-TWO

Collaborative Inquiry in Action

Transformative Learning Through Co-Inquiry

Lucia Alcántara, Sandra Hayes, Lyle Yorks

Good inquiry will only take place if
it is disturbing in some way.
—P. Reason (1992)

Collaborative inquiry (CI) is a strategy for learning from experience that is derived from the seminal work of John Heron (1992, 1996) on personhood and cooperative inquiry. Participants organize themselves into a small group to address a compelling question through repeated cycles of action and reflection for the purpose of creating new meaning (Bray, Lee, Smith, & Yorks, 2000). A sense of disquiet, problem, or interest felt by participants around an issue gives voice to the question. In any case, the inquiry question is framed by and owned by the participants, and participation is voluntary and consensual. This principle rests on the epistemic assumption that human experience is most validly understood when people are politically full participants in decisions so that they can most fully engage as their authentic selves leading to valid experiences (Heron & Reason, 2001).

Striving to operationalize these principles in practice is among the challenges of engaging in collaborative inquiry. CI groups function as a form of generative social space (Yorks, 2005). Like all other such spaces, collaborative inquiries are subject to the influences of personalities, assumptions, and context. Reflecting on these influences, as the group works its way through the experiences of convergence and divergence of meaning associated with the cycles of action and reflection, is central to the integrity of the process. The broader context

---

This chapter was written collaboratively. The authors are listed alphabetically, and the listing does not imply order of authorship.

of the inquiry, whether self-initiated, institutionally sponsored, or classroom focused, can make a difference in terms of realizing the principles on which CI is based.

COLLABORATIVE INQUIRY AND TRANSFORMATIVE LEARNING

Collaborative inquiry is aligned with transformative learning theory in three ways: establishing a social space that actualizes the conditions for engaging in effective discourse; following an epistemic framework that is holistic, integrating feeling with cognitive knowing; and fostering critical reflectivity on personally embedded assumptions and premises. Through sharing power equally, challenging and testing assumptions, and following group-adopted validity practices to explicitly avoid distorting meaning, participants in CI create a learning context consistent with the conditions traditionally argued as necessary for transformative learning—specifically, freedom from coercion (explicit or implicit), equality of access to information, and norms of inquiry that contribute to shared meaning through consensual validity testing (Mezirow, 2000). Indeed, a major contribution that CI makes to adult education theory and practice is its systematic structure for processes through which these idealized conditions can be realized.

Although Mezirow (2000) acknowledges the importance of multiple ways of knowing, rational discourse and analytical reflection remain central to his conceptualization of transformative learning. The holistic epistemology of Heron and Reason (2001) recognizes, but does not privilege, the role of rationality, and posits a healthy interdependence between the affective and the rational (Davis-Manigaulte, Yorks, & Kasl, 2006), that we would argue is essential for transformative learning. This is consistent with Taylor's (2000) observation that, "based on the research it seems quite clear that critical reflection and affective learning play a significant role in the transformative process" (p. 303). Finally, consistent with transformative learning theory, the focus of CI is on personal learning. The purpose of CI is for participants in the inquiry group to change themselves and how they are in relationship to the disorienting dilemma that is motivating their interest in the inquiry question (Kasl & Yorks, 2002).

For example, an inquiry group of community activists and social justice workers originally organized itself around the question, "How can we teach people to be more strategic, conceptual, and creative in their thinking?" (Kovari et al., 2005, p. 3). Through critical reflection on their own stories and experiences, they came to realize that the question needed to be reframed to, "How can we change how we are working with people to help them develop strategic, conceptual, and creative thinking?" Kovari et al. continued, "We came to understand the difference between training people to implement an action and developing their ability to think like creative and strategic leaders. We concluded that strategic, conceptual, and creative thinking is best developed through processes of inquiry that engage the learner. Importantly, we had to be engaged in the inquiry process itself"(p. 3).

The experiences of the co-inquiring community activists were grounded in their respective organizations. Their contexts provided ample opportunity to experiment with long-held assumptions around their practices as part of the cycle of action and reflection (Alcántara, Yorks, & Kovari, 2005). For this particular group, the CI experience led beyond experimentation to lasting changes in how they perceived their roles and undertook their tasks.

During the sixteenth-month-long inquiry, one co-inquirer changed positions from social change activist to a middle school teacher at a "last-chance school" in a predominantly immigrant school district in California. He tested his assumptions around the effectiveness and impact of his intentionality in creating new experiences for his students. In an effort to help his students be more conceptual or creative, he designed a hands-on experiment for measuring the density and buoyancy of water. As the more senior teachers urged him to "just tell them the density of water is one," he took a risk and did the experiment anyway. The students were actively engaged, and the lesson was well received. While engaged in collective subjective reflection in the inquiry group, he noted that the response he received from his fellow educators paralleled that of his social change colleagues: "As organizers, we are often like these experienced teachers. We feel so task oriented that we don't take the time to help people learn. We already know exactly how to do the next step, so we train people to do it, rather than creating a 'lesson plan' that helps them to discover how to do it."

Briefly, CI is one approach for *potentially* generating learning that is transformative in the sense of altering existing frames of reference (Mezirow, 1991, 2000). We italicize the word *potentially* because the learning that takes place during CI can take many forms. These forms include adding to existing frames of reference or creating new frames, all of which are enlightening, educative, and empowering but not necessarily transformative. Alternatively, the learning may lead to changes in points of view or a habit of mind (Mezirow, 2000) that are transformative. The learning that takes place may differ for participants based on different experiences and their developmental ways of making meaning. CI provides a structure for learning; the learning that emerges is a function of the engagement of the participants within that structure.

THE PROCESS OF COLLABORATIVE INQUIRY

Collaborative inquiry is particularly appropriate for pursuing questions that are professionally and personally developmental or socially controversial or require social healing. It has been used in dissertation research, as well as a strategy for inquiring into the practice of social justice organizing. Collaborative inquiry is a social process where the intention is to test systematically the assumptions and premises that the participants hold. New meaning is created through dialogue and critical reflection on experience and actions taken out in the world.

Bray et al. (2000) provide a four-phase framework for the CI process: forming the group, creating the conditions for inquiry, acting, and making meaning. This framework is especially appropriate for extended inquiries, such as those involving a group of doctoral students. Other collaborative inquiries that take place within a period of several months tend to merge the first two steps. Nevertheless, careful attention needs to be given to how a CI group is initiated. In initiating an inquiry, it is important to invest time in shaping the question and having an open conversation around expectations and commitments. Agreement on how many cycles of action and reflection will be initially undertaken needs to be reached, along with agreement on a willingness to test personal assumptions. Diversity of experience, and respect for that diversity, is critical to having an effective inquiry. A group inquiring into the question of, "How and when does art release, create, and sustain transforming power for social change?" noted, "The value of this group is that we are not [all] artists, said Nobuko, one of the artists among us. The artists saw their work through the eyes of organizers, and the organizers saw the transformative power of the community artists" (Aprill et al., 2006, p. 5). The common thread among the inquirers was that all were involved in community change.

Another inquiry group (Kovari et al., 2005) summarized what they found to be important characteristics of their inquiry process as follows:

- Having a compelling question that participants are hungry to answer
- Having a desire for inquiring into the question with the other participants
- Realizing there are no quick or guaranteed answers, but having faith that something valuable will come out of the process of inquiring with this group of people
- Accessing experienced facilitation
- Understanding that the process is organic and unfolds; the process cannot be scripted — getting in the muck is important
- Taking action and learning from experience
- Recognizing the value in diversity of practice
- Developing a product deepened the exercise and crystallized the learning

Inquiry groups are launched from two basic platforms: institutional and spontaneous. Spontaneous groups emerge as a result of a mutually compelling interest. These groups are generally initiated, designed, and self-directed by the co-inquirers themselves. Institutionally established groups are those formally construed under the aegis of an organization, which offers degrees of support and resources and boundary management while retaining vested interests in the outcome of the inquiry.

Power dynamics exist in all inquiry groups. In spontaneously organized groups, the power dynamics are rooted in the traditional sources of diversity. In institutionally sponsored groups, the power dynamics are doubly complicated because the institutional presence imposes influences and constraints on the group. The dynamic synergy present in the interaction between the inquiry groups and the sponsoring organization is rarely addressed, yet likely to materialize in different organizational contexts. An institutionally formulated inquiry group of social change leaders encountered tensions surrounding voice and validation of leadership. These issues presented challenges that ultimately had an impact on the relationship among the participants, cofacilitators, and the organization supporting the research. Embedded in these dynamics were tensions requiring facilitation.

FACILITATION OF COLLABORATIVE INQUIRY

Working successfully with the principles of CI is not always easy. Collaborative inquiry itself can be disorienting since "the contradictions between the collaborative paradigm and the 'real' world are powerful enough to impair the efforts of even enthusiastic and well-intentioned collaborators" (Oakes, Hare, & Strotnik, 1986, p. 545). Facilitation from within the group, or experienced CI facilitators invited in to serve the group, is useful as the group strives to learn and perhaps transform themselves and their practice. We believe a facilitator's effectiveness is enhanced by her or his awareness of the nuances of CI group facilitation. Below are some of the considerations of facilitating a CI. We draw from our own experience facilitating various collaborative inquiries over the past decade and a half.

Our experiences as CI facilitators align with the six dimensions and three modes of facilitation Heron (1999) identifies as core elements of learning facilitation (see Table 22.1). The six dimensions of facilitation are related to the issues involved with the ways facilitators can influence the learning process itself. The modes are related to the different ways the facilitator handles decision making. We found ourselves shifting through each of the modes, sometimes operating in the hierarchical mode by directing the learning process and thinking and acting on behalf of the group. At other times, we operated in

Table 22.1. **Modes and Dimensions of Facilitating a Collaborative Inquiry**

| | Modes | | |
Dimensions	Hierarchical	Cooperative	Autonomous
Planning	Decide on process and content of group members' learning	Negotiate and seek agreement on what participants will learn and the process by which they will learn	Affirm group as it plans its own learning process
Meaning	Illuminate and make sense of participants' actions and experiences for them	Partner with the group in the generation of understanding emanating from the process	Allow and support participants in the generation of their own meaning making
Confronting	Raise group's level of self-awareness by pointing out behaviors and other issues affecting their experience	Consult with group members, and invite them to raise each other's awareness of the dynamics affecting their process	Create a climate for group members to practice confronting and consciousness raising
Feeling	Choose the methods of managing feelings and emotions to suit the purposes of the group	Work with the group to elicit views on and handling of feelings and emotions	Give group space to manage its own affective dynamic
Structuring	Design and supervise group learning methods and activities	Construct learning methods and exercises with group members	Delegate group control over the design and supervision of their learning
Valuing	Initiate care for group members, and commit to creating a climate that values each person	Build a community of value and mutual respect with participants	Entrust to the group the affirmation of self- and others' worth

Source: Adapted from Heron (1999).

the cooperative mode when the power over the learning process was shared with the group. In the autonomous mode, we offered the group no guidance or assistance, allowing them full self-determination and responsibility for their learning.

The complexity that comes with facilitating CI groups becomes more apparent as we look closely at how each of the modes plays out in each of the dimensions. Within each of the six dimensions, the facilitative influence on the group's learning process is different. According to Heron (1999), in the planning dimension, facilitation is concerned with how the group will meet its objectives, whereas in the meaning dimension, the facilitative focus is on how the group participants are making sense of their experiences and actions. The confronting dimension is about challenging group participants to attend to what they are resisting and avoiding. How feeling and emotion are handled in the group is the focus of the feeling dimension. The structuring dimension—how the group's learning is shaped—and the valuing dimension—the climate of integrity and respect created within the group—are the other areas of facilitation influence and concern.

Consistent with our experience and as noted by Heron (1999), although the six dimensions are distinct and require the facilitator to attend to a particular aspect of the CI learning process, they are also entwined, challenging the facilitator to notice and respond to the varying dynamics in an organized yet fluid way. Moreover, given the six dimensions and the three facilitative modes that can be used within each dimension, we think it is important that the approach to CI facilitation be understood as a multifaceted undertaking. Table 22.1 offers a simplified adaptation of Heron's (1999) explanation and rendering of how the various dimensions and modes work together to influence the CI facilitation decisions we make and the decisions we believe have significance for facilitating CI—a potential transformative learning vehicle.

The modified version of Heron's (1999) modes and dimensions of facilitation we offer is only a partial view of what we believe a facilitator must keep in mind, especially to optimize the conditions for transformative learning. Traversing through the various facilitation options effectively requires a high level of critical reflexivity on the part of the facilitator. A critically reflexive CI facilitator examines the impact of his or her assumptions, values, and actions on others. When facilitating a group's inquiry, it is important to pay rapt attention to how we ourselves affect the group's experience.

One group we facilitated praised us for "getting out of their way" and letting them own their CI process. Another group, as the CI was coming to an end, expressed gratitude to us for using our knowledge to direct and hold the group. Their inexperience with CI and the ambiguity that comes from engaging in something new made it difficult for them to see how the process could foster learning and help them gain insight that would contribute to their practice. This was a group wrestling with how to integrate human rights, social justice, and ecological sustainability. It took purposeful and conscious cycling through the various combinations of facilitation dimensions and modes to work effectively with this CI group. With them and with each of the groups we have facilitated, critical reflexivity has been essential to our ability to foster a space for learning. Furthermore, we learned from our experience facilitating CIs within an institutional context, where funds and other resources were provided for the group, that practicing critical reflexivity enabled us to build and maintain the credibility we needed to work successfully with the group and the institution. Continually examining the impact of our assumptions, values, and actions on the group and institution was a way we were able to deal with some of the challenges and caveats associated with CI practice.

CHALLENGES AND CAVEATS IN PRACTICING COLLABORATIVE INQUIRY

Any learning strategy that holds the potential for stimulating transformative learning must be entered into with the recognition that while conditions supportive of transformative learning can be created and facilitated, ultimately transformative learning is emergent, not instrumentally produced. In the case of CI, this emergence is shaped by a number of challenges and supports. They include the diversity of the group, personal agendas that participants bring into the group, opportunities for action, and the context of the inquiry.

Our experience has been that diversity of skill, practice, and perspective is an important contributor to a rich inquiry. Diversity of skill sets and level of practice are significant contributors to the discursive aspects of collaborative inquiry. These two factors are essential in anchoring the co-inquirers' experiences and beliefs within the collective range of exposures. The group can then begin to explore what has informed their practice and how they arrived at their habits of mind (Mezirow, 2000). Another form of diversity lies in the participants' perspectives about their field of practice. Uncovering the underlying belief systems that contribute to their perspectives is the key to their becoming explicit about their closely held assumptions. In doing so, it provides opportunity for participants to become explicit about any preexisting premises, frames of reference, or habits of mind that they bring into the group.

It would be inaccurate to suggest that all participants are able to shelve their personal agendas at the gateway to the inquiry. More often, when participants arrive at the inquiry, they have given thought and perhaps have even been advocating around issues related to the topic. This signals a change in posture from advocacy to inquiry or vice versa; in doing so, the co-inquirers move toward clarifying intentions, an important part of the initial stages of

CI. Preliminary findings from research on critical factors affecting knowledge creation from inquiry groups indicate that most participants have no initial expectations of the inquiry process. However, this does not preclude them from holding personal agendas that they wish to expose among group members. Deeply seated feelings even marginally associated with the inquiry process, group membership, or perhaps the organization supporting the inquiry will manifest within the group dynamic. These agendas were a complicating factor in the inquiry on engaging and sustaining social justice movements that seize power.

While spontaneous CIs are independently initiated, institutionalized CIs take place within broader organizational settings. These settings can provide support and resources and offer an engaging alternative development strategy for members. An example is the work of Bray et al. (2000), who conducted a CI as an alternative form of professional development for high school teachers. A multinational philanthropy provided financial support for the CIs referenced earlier involving social activists. However, these contexts are also laden with potentially competing interests in the process of learning and producing outcomes. One place where these competing interests often surface is around questions of accountability and expectations about deliverables. Just as individuals can initially enter into a CI under the influence of the agendas they have traditionally advocated for, so too can sponsoring institutions have interests that they seek to serve. Expectations must be carefully established that the process is intended to be developmental and potentially transformative for the participants. The participants' needs, not the institution's, are the focus of the inquiry. This requires trust on the part of the institution that the participants' learning will result in organizational benefits. Similar considerations need to be taken into account when using CI as a course structure in an academic program or a dissertation.

REFLECTIONS

The collaborative process necessary to produce this chapter has taken us back to a time when we worked together and with others. Our role as facilitators was critical to the CI process. As humans, we are not infallible. As researchers, we must be observant of the process. As practitioners, we must make room for reflexivity. This chapter grows from an ongoing conversation among ourselves, with colleagues, and with the community. At the core lies the question, "What did we do, and why did it work so well, or not so well, with this group?" Some of our answers manifest in actions, others in words, and most of all in the intention to be fully present and in service to the group. We showed up with good humor and took kits replete with materials on adult learning, group dynamics, the topic being discussed, and sometimes even chocolate. We separated from the groups yet never left the CI process because it becomes an extension of our transformation as researchers, facilitators, and lifelong learners.

One reflection we had, as we gathered our thoughts for this chapter, was related to the idea that the CI process itself is rife with potential for disorientation and, therefore, transformative learning for the CI participants as well as for external facilitators and institutional sponsors of the process. As facilitators of several CIs, we were struck by how similar the group dynamics were to the forces we have each witnessed while facilitating learning in other group situations. Yet because CI encourages shared ownership of the inquiry, embraces both divergence and convergence in perspectives, and, importantly, is a process where learning occurs by holding an ongoing tension between understanding and ambiguity, we believe our facilitative practice has been sharpened. The dilemmas the groups faced while co-inquiring have influenced our views on learning facilitation by obliging us to be critically reflexive. We also note that the nature of CI, particularly the self-determining and the process versus product aspects of CI, was usually disorienting to sponsoring institutions. Writing this chapter, we were reminded that institutions that engage in critical reflexivity could generate learning that is potentially transformative.

Finally, academic writing, collaborative or otherwise, is itself a practice of extended inquiry and knowledge creation. As such, it reveals lessons about the epistemology in use of the writer. Questions of influence, the need for facilitating the space, reflecting on agendas and the presentation of self, and the practice of real reflexivity are disorienting and challenging. Theoretical knowledge (knowledge about) can be easy and often idealistic; engaging in firsthand application of practice (leading to knowledge of acquaintance) is disorienting, disquieting, and hard.

REFERENCES

Alcántara, L., Yorks, L., & Kovari, V. (2005). *Cooperative inquiry as a tool for transformative learning: Stories from community organizers who transformed their practice.* Paper presented at the Sixth Transformative Learning Conference at University of Michigan, East Lansing.

Aprill, A., Holliday, E., Jeffers, F., Miyamoto, N., Scher, A., Spatz, D., et al. (2006). *Can the arts change the world? The transformative power of the arts in fostering and sustaining social change: A Leadership for a Changing World Cooperative Inquiry.* New York: Research Center for Leadership in Action, Robert F. Wagner Graduate School of Public Service, New York University.

Bray, J. N., Lee, J., Smith, L. L., & Yorks, L. (2000). *Collaborative inquiry in practice: Action reflection and making meaning.* Thousand Oaks, CA: Sage.

Davis-Manigaulte, J., Yorks, L., & Kasl, E. (2006). Presentational knowing and transformative learning. In E. W. Taylor (Ed.), *Fostering transformative learning in the classroom: Challenges and innovations* (pp. 27–35). New Directions for Adult and Continuing Education, no. 109. San Francisco: Jossey-Bass.

Heron, J. (1992). *Feeling and personhood: Psychology in another key*. Thousand Oaks, CA: Sage.

Heron, J. (1996). *Cooperative inquiry: Research into the human condition*. Thousand Oaks, CA: Sage.

Heron, J. (1999). *The complete facilitator's handbook*. London: Kogan Page.

Heron, J., & Reason, P. (2001). The practice of co-operative inquiry: Research "with" rather than "on" people. In P. Reason & H. Bradbury (Eds.), *Handbook of action research* (pp. 179–188). Thousand Oaks, CA: Sage.

Kasl, E., & Yorks, L. (2002). Collaborative inquiry for adult learning. In L. Yorks & E. Kasl (Eds.), *Collaborative inquiry as a strategy for adult learning* (pp. 3–11). New Directions for Adult Learning, no. 94. San Francisco: Jossey-Bass.

Kovari, V., Hicks, T., Ferlazzo, L., McGarvey, C., Ochs, M., Alcántara, L., et al. (2005). *Don't just do something, sit there. Helping others become more strategic, conceptual, and creative: A cooperative inquiry*. New York: Research Center for Leadership in Action, Robert F. Wagner Graduate School of Public Service, New York University.

Mezirow, J. (1991). *Transformative dimensions of adult learning*. San Francisco: Jossey-Bass.

Mezirow, J. (2000). Thinking like an adult. In J. Mezirow & Associates, *Learning as transformation: Critical perspectives on a theory in progress* (pp. 3–33). San Francisco: Jossey-Bass.

Oakes, J., Hare, S. E., & Strotnik, K. A. (1986). Collaborative inquiry: A congenial paradigm in a cantankerous world. *Teachers College Record, 87*(4), 545–561.

Reason, P. (1992, April 24). [Meeting with thINQ, at Teachers College, Columbia University.] Unpublished raw data.

Taylor, E. (2000). Analyzing research on transformative learning theory. In J. Mezirow & Associates, *Learning as transformation: Critical perspectives on a theory in progress* (pp. 285–328). San Francisco: Jossey-Bass.

Yorks, L. (2005). Adult learning and the generation of new knowledge and meaning: Creating liberating spaces for fostering adult learning through practitioner based collaborative action inquiry. *Teachers College Record, 107*, 1217–1244.

CHAPTER TWENTY-THREE

Challenging Racism in Self and Others

Transformative Learning as a Living Practice

European-American Collaborative Challenging Whiteness

In this chapter, we describe a form of action research that is well suited to fostering transformative learning when self-identity is at stake. We refer to this practice as CI, an abbreviation that designates either cooperative or collaborative inquiry. Cooperative inquiry is an action research methodology developed over the past forty years by human potential theorist John Heron (1996). *Collaborative inquiry* is the nomenclature adopted by adult educators who advocate this action research process as a liberatory structure for adult learning (Bray, Lee, Smith, & Yorks, 2000; Yorks & Kasl, 2002; Chapter Twenty-Two, this volume).

We present a case example drawn from our personal experience as a group of white adult educators who have used CI to change our awareness about privilege, race, and racism. Because white people's awareness about our relationship to race is one expression of a meaning perspective that is profoundly intractable and difficult to transform, our case example is ideal for illustrating CI as a transformative practice in action. Before proceeding to the case description, we describe the intractable meaning perspective that engenders white people's perceptions about privilege, race, and racism.

WHITE SUPREMACIST CONSCIOUSNESS AS A MEANING PERSPECTIVE

White people's meaning perspective on race is rooted in a system of thought known as "white supremacist consciousness" (Delgado, 1995). Although the United States is increasingly multicultural and multiracial, cultural norms that dominate significant power structures continue to reflect the original colonizing powers of Great Britain and other Western European countries. Some U.S. scholars of color and white allies refer to this dominating system as white supremacist consciousness.

Although some people conflate the label "white supremacist consciousness" with "white supremacist," these phrases do not have the same meaning. In the United States, "white supremacist" refers to a person who believes that white people are superior human beings. In contrast, "white supremacist consciousness" refers not to a person but to a system of thought. Spelman College president Beverly Daniel Tatum (2000) explains how individual beliefs differ from systemic power when, writing about racism, she observes, "Many white people think of racism as a problem of individual prejudice and hatred," while many people of color understand racism as "an intricate web of individual attitudes, cultural messages and institutional practices that systematically advantage whites and disadvantage people of color" (p. 11).

In the United States, this web of attitudes, cultural messages, and institutional practices has become normalized, thus creating an implicit inference that the dominating culture's norms are superior to others' values and practices. Although the term "white supremacist consciousness" derives from the context of discourse about race, this consciousness permeates multiple realms of behavior and attitudes (Ani, 1994). White ways of being, such as dualism, individualism, or presumption that one's values are universal, manifest throughout U.S. society (Paxton, 2003). That this consciousness is often invisible to those who hold it strengthens it as a force for hegemony.

Looking at how white people in the United States perceive race, Ruth Frankenberg (1993) identifies three major perspectives. In *essentialist racism,* races are perceived as unequal within systems of white superiority. Individuals known as white supremacists think and act from this perspective. A second perspective encompasses two types of evasiveness. *Color evasiveness* denies race-based differences, and *power evasiveness* discounts the impact of historical factors and structural inequities. People who frame their worldview by evading the salience of race and power are purveyors of white supremacist consciousness, though, by definition, they are unaware of their complicity.

Within Frankenberg's third perspective, *race cognizance,* people consciously reject both white supremacy and white supremacist consciousness while engaging actively in efforts to decenter whiteness. Nevertheless, their actions often betray their conscious good intentions because limitations in their knowledge, imposed by the tenacious grip of white supremacist consciousness, remain invisible to them.

Each of these positions—essentialist racism, color or power evasiveness, and race cognizance—can be thought of as what adult learning theorist Jack Mezirow calls a meaning perspective (1991) or habit of mind (Mezirow & Associates, 2000). According to Mezirow, transformative learning is a process of making visible perspectives that have been invisible and coming to recognize the distortions and limitations in current meaning perspectives so that one is able to create and integrate more appropriate ones. The challenge of making whiteness and white supremacist consciousness visible to white people so that we can change our habits of mind is an ideal location and subject for transformative learning practice.

CI AS A PRACTICE THAT FOSTERS TRANSFORMATIVE LEARNING

In the CI process, described more fully in Chapter Twenty-Two (this volume), a small group of peers seeks to learn from personal experience about an issue that each group member finds compelling. In this chapter, we use our case example to focus on three of CI's important practices: repeated cycles of action and reflection, extended epistemology rooted in personal experience, and group learning.

Repeated cycles of action and reflection are designed by the group to yield information about what the group is studying. Actions can be carried out by the group as a whole or by individual members in the context of daily living. In either case, the cycle is completed through group reflection on the meaning of the actions and their perceived results.

The group's meaning making is grounded in an extended epistemology, which presupposes that meaningful knowledge is rooted in the knowledge makers' lived experience. For example, in this chapter's illustrative case, group members do not study white supremacist consciousness in others or white supremacist consciousness in U.S. society, but instead, white supremacist consciousness in ourselves. Furthermore, as with all other types of action research, the primary purpose of developing new knowledge is for taking action. In our case example, we describe how we use our deepening understanding of white supremacist consciousness to change personal behavior so that action in our professional and personal lives is more effective.

Heron (1996) describes CI epistemology as "extended" because it values four interconnected ways of knowing: experiential, presentational, propositional, and practical. Current educational practice heavily favors two ways of knowing, propositional and practical (Boud, Cohen, & Walker, 1993; Paxton, 2003). In contrast, CI's extended epistemology honors the equal importance of experiential and presentational knowing, which some adult educators identify as pivotal forces for personal transformation because these ways of knowing are the sites of emotions, intuition, and imagination (Yorks & Kasl, 2006; Paxton, 2003).

The context of group learning fosters individual learning by supporting several skills and behaviors: living in the inquiry, recognizing disjuncture between espoused beliefs and actual practice, practicing new behaviors, improving the ability to reflect in action, conceptualizing new ideas, and staying present to learning in the face of difficult emotional challenges (European-American Collaborative Challenging Whiteness, 2005a). In addition to creating a context that supports individual learning, groups learn as whole systems. They create complex knowledge that becomes a foundation for action and continued meaning making. The group often encodes this knowledge in key phrases or metaphor (Kasl & Marsick, 1997).

Although each of the practices just described (action and reflection, extended epistemology, group learning) is commonly found in adult education (Taylor, 2007), it is their synergistic interaction in the CI process that fuels their power for transformative learning and change. The following case example drawn from our personal experience shows this synergism at work.

TRANSFORMING OUR CONSCIOUSNESS ABOUT WHITENESS AND TAKING ACTION

We are a group of six white adult educators who, as individuals, practice in different institutional and community settings. Meeting monthly since 1998, we use CI practices to inquire into the impact of white supremacist consciousness. In the following case example, we show our personal and collective transformation with three snapshots, taken in 1998, 2002, and 2005. Our intention is to illustrate how CI looks and feels in practice.

1998: Seeing the "Good White Person" as a Friend and Enemy Within

At our first meeting, we discussed our individual interests in an inquiry about whiteness and our commitments to social justice. It struck us that our efforts to "be good" and "do good work" led us to distance ourselves from white people who seemed to us not to share our commitments or not to know as much about race as we perceived ourselves to know. We began playfully to talk about "good white people" and "bad white people." This conversation caught our imagination. We realized the potent irony: in trying to minimize our supremacist consciousness, we felt compelled to cast ourselves as superior (which is supremacist consciousness). We created our first CI action in order to explore the idea further: before our next meeting, we would each notice when we felt like the "good white person" and record our thoughts and feelings.

At our next meeting, Daniel told us about his experience in a social situation with Jane, a woman he had just met:

> She asked...what kind of work I did. I mentioned school and she enthusiastically asked to "hear all about it." When I explained I was studying what it means to be white and how I wanted to work on my racism, she leaned over the table conspiratorially and told me she thought that was important. "I have black friends.... When I was a girl my parents taught me to treat all people equally, no matter if they were black, white, green, or blue" [European-American Collaborative Challenging Whiteness, 2005a, p. 251].

Daniel looked around the room at each of us, shaking his head with self-deprecation as he reexperienced his dinner with Jane. He told us how smug he had felt, thinking he knew more about racism than Jane did because he imagined the phrase she used was self-congratulatory and offensive to people of color. He was afraid he was "stuck" having dinner with someone who thought she knew it all. Then, in a voice of wonderment, he described a moment of epiphany:

> As I was caught in the frustration of how to proceed with the evening, our inquiry group's action popped into my consciousness—"notice when you feel like the good white person." Whew! That stopped me in my tracks. It was as though our group were sitting there on my shoulder, paying attention so that I could pay attention.... With a sense of the surreal, I experienced myself as floating above the restaurant, looking down at the two of us. It dawned on me, "I AM her. She cares about racism, is naive about racism, and shows her ignorance when she speaks about racism. *I do all these things too!*" I was...overwhelmed with...tears of recognition....
>
> The surreal moment seemed to stretch out in slow motion.... I was hit with waves of new insights.... I noticed interconnection with Jane instead of separation. I replaced judgment of her with compassion for her, and in doing so replaced judgment of myself with compassion for myself. I was humbled by my awareness of the arrogance and superiority with which I met Jane [European-American Collaborative Challenging Whiteness, 2005a, p. 252].

Hearing Daniel's story solidified our interest in exploring the concept "good white person." Over the year, we gradually created a profile of the good white person's motivations and behaviors, enhancing our knowledge through additional actions such as "put yourself in a situation where your whiteness is very visible." Our evolving views of the good white person became a critical signifier for our meaning making.

2002: Learning More About Ourselves as White People

We continued to change our awareness and ability to act from that awareness with ongoing cycles of action and reflection. We also interviewed others who were using CI to learn about their whiteness (Barlas et al., 2000), wrote empirical papers, and designed participatory workshops. Because our experience piqued our curiosity about how to elicit reflections rich with detail and insight, we decided to try for ourselves a data collection strategy one of our members learned from a former colleague.

The life history methodology created by Matthias Finger (1986) helps people discern patterns. The first step is to choose categories for describing important influences on one's life. We chose people, places, historical events, critical personal incidents, and "other." The second step is to create material that can be used to make a visual representation of these influences. The process involves assigning each category of influence to a different color, then writing individual entries on separate colored sticky notes. For example, one might end up with a group of twenty pink stickies, each with the name of one person who had been an important influence; a group of twelve green stickies, each with a meaningful historical event; and so forth. The third step is to arrange the stickies into a collage that creates a visual representation answering the question for reflection—in our case, "What factors in my life account for my current understanding of whiteness, race, and racism?" Finally, the visual representation is shared with others.

Through telling the stories represented by our collages, we got to know each other on a deeper level. For example, as Daniel studied the way he had clustered important people from his life, he observed, "I realize how many people of color loved me enough to stick with me as I learned. Seeing all their names in one place helps me realize how much love is required in order to do this work." Andrew described tears in his mother's eyes as the car radio brought to life the violent events of Selma. "My idealism was shattered," he explained. "I was a little boy who suddenly understood that the world was not just." Rose revisited many memories, now painful, of how she learned racism from her parents' bigotry: "I remember watching my mother rewash any drinking glass that our African American maid had used. And my father's attitudes about Mexicans were so negative!" Robin explained how an incident from twenty years ago exposed her sense of superiority and entitlement. After arriving at an annual festival where she had served as a leader for several years, she found that an African American colleague had put her personal belongings in the desk that Robin had used in the past. Describing how she imperiously moved the colleague's belongings because they "appropriated" her work space, Robin told us, "I didn't see this as racism. I felt, 'How dare she take over my desk? This is where I always work.'" Remembering the subsequent fallout, Robin recalled, "It was a hard lesson, beginning to see the difference between my walk and my talk." The focal point in Victoria's collage was a volcano that represented a two-year period of rapidly escalating awareness. Pointing to a small stick figure being blown into the air by the volcano's force, she explained, "Everything I thought I knew didn't apply." Louise's voice became quieter and quieter as she described her collage. With tears welling in her eyes, she told us that she felt self-conscious about how her stories compared to others. Louise's feelings reminded us that we are as prone to judging ourselves as "bad white people" as we are to judging others.

The collage experience helped us become more vulnerable to each other, deepening our trust. It was an example of presentational knowing, defined by Heron (1996) as an intuitive grasp of patterns in our experience, discerned through use of graphic, plastic, moving, musical, or verbal art forms.

2005: Being a Good White Person Is a Process, Not a Destination

Embedded in all our interactions was the ever-present "good white person" whom we thought of as a person whose motives were sometimes suspect and whose actions were often ineffective because of self-righteousness of the kind Daniel felt when he had dinner with Jane. Group members used a common refrain, "There I go again. Thinking I am the good white person."

This signifier continues to guide our learning, as, for example, when a journal editor invited us to respond to an article about to be published. In the article, the author explored her personal learning about herself as a white person in a multiracial environment. Cautious about the delicacy of our task, we drafted a manuscript in which we tried to be tactful in suggesting that the author's consciousness was narrow and naive. When we discussed our draft, we realized that we had fully embodied the self-righteous "good white person" who strives to educate the less informed white person and, in the process, display his or her own superiority. We were dismayed by how grievously our practice fell short of our espoused values and intentions.

This experience heightened our efforts to learn how to be more effective in talking with people about white hegemony, white privilege, race, and racism. We encapsulated what we had been learning into a concept we called "critical humility," which we defined as the practice of remaining open to discovering that our knowledge is partial and evolving while at the same time being committed and confident about our knowledge and taking action in the world. Asking ourselves, "How can we get better at acting with critical humility?" we formulated questions to guide personal critical reflection about successes and failures with practicing critical humility (European-American Collaborative Challenging Whiteness, 2005b).

We soon had an opportunity to test our guiding questions. When Victoria shared an experience in which she failed to speak out when racism manifested at a meeting she attended, we decided to role-play how she might have acted with critical humility. Andrew and Daniel volunteered. When the role play was finished, Louise observed, "Even though they were trying to be humble, they still seemed to be showing the woman how she was wrong. It sounded patronizing to me." As both Andrew and Daniel agreed with Louise, we tried using the questions we had recently developed. With the questions and the group's supportive prodding, Daniel gained insight into his desire for approval from people of color, and Andrew described how he prevents himself from being genuinely vulnerable.

Seeking greater capacity to live critical humility as a way of being has absorbed our group's attention for the past two years and has led us to greater clarity about the "good white person." We now realize that by focusing on the behaviors and attitudes that white people often use with good intention but poor effect, we turned the "good white person" into another iteration of the "bad white person." Reflecting on our use of this signifier, Andrew observed:

> Actually, trying to be a good white person is a *good* thing. There is nothing wrong with striving to become a good white person. The problem comes when you start thinking you actually *are* a good white person and even more so if you think that you need do nothing in order to continue to be one.

SYNERGISM OF ACTION AND REFLECTION, EXTENDED EPISTEMOLOGY, AND GROUP LEARNING

Our intention with these snapshots is to provide rich illustration of how CI looks and feels in practice, in particular, how the CI process helps a group deepen its knowledge through the synergistic interaction of three practices: repeated cycles of action and reflection, extended epistemology using four interconnected ways of knowing, and group learning. Although our group's longevity enhances our learning, CI groups of shorter duration also experience synergistic interaction of the three practices described here (Yorks & Kasl, 2002).

To illustrate this synergy, we have described how our group complexified its meaning making, using a signifying phrase of "good white person," reflecting critically about distortions and limitations in our perspectives about the signifier, formulating a vision of "critical humility," and experimenting with how to actualize critical humility as a way of being. Each of these phases in our meaning making included multiple spirals of action and reflection, during which we used the four different ways of knowing: individual and group actions provided new encounters with experiential knowing (Daniel's experience of seeing himself as Jane, Victoria's experience of failing to speak out, the group's experience of bearing witness to the role play) that we explored and reflected on through the presentational forms of story, visual art, and role play. Through analytical discussions, we created new propositional understanding, which we formalized periodically by writing about our evolving ideas. We tested our practical knowing by striving to live our everyday lives in congruence with our new knowledge, setting off new cycles of reflection and action. Our collage experience demonstrates how presentational knowing engenders intimacy and vulnerability, which foster the conditions of mutual respect and trust that group learning requires.

REFLECTIONS

Reflecting on what we learned from writing this chapter, we continue to feel humbled by the fundamental paradox of our inquiry into white supremacist consciousness: the more we learn how to become conscious about this habit of mind, the more we see how our deep embeddedness keeps us unconscious. Evolution in the way we understand and use our signifier "good white person" provides a ready example. Our 1998 snapshot shows us engaged in dualistic thinking, contrasting the good white person with the bad, even as we noted ironically that the good white person might be the enemy within because of the way we sanctimoniously felt a need to set ourselves apart. Through our process of reflecting on our experience as we wrote the chapter, we became more aware of how our signifier reinforces dualistic thinking, which is not useful in the conduct of our inquiry. Critical humility is a practice and an aspiration that helps us keep going. We also note that our collaborative writing process is itself a form of action and reflection that develops our capacity for critical reflection on both our thinking and our practice.

In writing this chapter, we are reminded how important a sense of community is while doing this work. As Edward W. Taylor (2007) reports in his update on transformative learning theory, "It is ... trustful relationships that allow individuals to have questioning discussions, share information openly and achieve mutual and consensual understanding" (p. 179). The relationships in our group continue to be the foundation from which we take risks, share emotions, support and challenge one another, and develop shared language and understanding of our experiences with being white. In this context, we were able to move through our shame and guilt about our unearned privilege and come to new understandings of whiteness. Recalling some of our pivotal moments provided us with a sweet reminder of what our collaboration has brought to our lives and how love has fueled our continued willingness to meet and learn about a subject like white supremacist consciousness.

Finally, writing the chapter also helped us sharpen our awareness that presentational knowing has been a catalyst for some of our most transformative moments together. This awareness reaffirmed our long-held intentions to broaden our ways of knowing beyond the propositional and practical realms, to include more feelings and emotions in our work together by using art, movement, poetry, and storytelling. Although we espouse the power of the presentational, we see that we tend to work in a predominantly "white" fashion. We reflect on ourselves as adult educators who frequently advocate multiple ways of knowing to our students and colleagues, but get together and talk and analyze for hours. With this fresh reminder of how presentational practices have led to our most significant moments of sudden understanding, we have recommitted ourselves to engage presentational knowing more frequently and systematically.

REFERENCES

Ani, M. (1994). *Yurugu: An African-centered critique of European cultural thought and behavior.* Trenton, NJ: Africa World Press.

Barlas, C., Kasl, E., Kyle, R., MacLeod, A., Paxton, D., Rosenwasser, P., et al. (2000). Learning to unlearn white supremacist consciousness. In T. Sork, V. Lee-Chapman, & R. St. Clair (Eds.), *Proceedings of the 41st Annual Adult Education Research Conference* (pp. 26–30). Vancouver: University of British Columbia.

Boud, D., Cohen, R., & Walker, D. (1993). Introduction: Understanding learning from experience. In D. Boud, R. Cohen, & D. Walker (Eds.), *Using experience for learning* (pp. 1–17). Buckingham, England: Society for Research into Higher Education and Open University Press.

Bray, J., Lee, J., Smith, L., & Yorks, L. (2000). *Collaborative inquiry in practice: Action, reflection, and meaning making.* Thousand Oaks, CA: Sage.

Delgado, R. (Ed.). (1995). *Critical race theory: The cutting edge.* Philadelphia: Temple University Press

European-American Collaborative Challenging Whiteness. (2005a). When first-person inquiry is not enough: Challenging whiteness through first- and second-person inquiry. *Action Research, 3*(3), 245–261.

European-American Collaborative Challenging Whiteness. (2005b). Critical humility in transformative learning when self-identity is at stake. In D. Vlosak, G. Kielbaso, & J. Radford (Eds.), *Appreciating the best of what is: Envisioning what could be: Proceedings of the Sixth International Conference on Transformative Learning* (pp. 121–126). East Lansing: Michigan State University.

Finger, M. (1986). *A life-history approach to adult learning: Epistemological and methodological foundations.* Unpublished doctoral dissertation, University of Geneva.

Frankenberg, R. (1993). *The social construction of whiteness: White women, race matters.* Minneapolis: University of Minnesota Press.

Heron, J. (1996). *Co-operative inquiry: Research into the human condition.* Thousand Oaks, CA: Sage.

Kasl, E., & Marsick, V. (1997). Epistemology of groups as learning systems: A research-based analysis. In *Crossing borders, breaking boundaries, research in the education of adults, an international conference: Proceedings of the 27th Annual Conference of the Standing Conference on University Teaching and Research in the Education of Adults* (pp. 250–254). London: Birbeck College, University of London.

Mezirow, J. (1991). *Transformative dimensions of adult learning.* San Francisco: Jossey-Bass.

Mezirow, J., & Associates. (2000). *Learning as transformation: Critical perspectives on a theory in process.* San Francisco: Jossey-Bass.

Paxton, D. (2003). Facilitating transformation of white consciousness among European-American people: A case study of a cooperative inquiry. *Dissertation Abstracts International 64* (01), 297A (UMI No. AAT3078796).

Tatum, B. D. (2000, July 2). A conversation on race. *New York Times,* p. WK11.

Taylor, E. W. (2007). An update of transformative learning theory: A critical review of the empirical research (1999–2005). *International Journal of Lifelong Education, 26*(2), 173–191.

Yorks, L., & Kasl, E. (Eds.). (2002). *Collaborative inquiry as a strategy for adult learning: Creating space for generative learning.* New Directions for Adult and Continuing Education, no. 94. San Francisco: Jossey-Bass.

Yorks, L., & Kasl, E. (2006). I know more than I can say: A taxonomy for utilizing expressive ways of knowing to foster transformative learning. *Journal of Transformative Education, 4*(1), 1–22.

PART FIVE

REFLECTIONS

The final chapter is in keeping within one of the central themes of the book: encouraging a reflective practice. Like all the contributors who were asked in their chapters to provide a reflective discussion about new insights gained about transformative learning from writing about their teaching experience, this final chapter analyzes all of the chapters on practice, reflecting back and attempting to identify new insights and challenges that inform practitioners about transformative learning in action.

CHAPTER TWENTY-FOUR

Looking Forward by Looking Back

Reflections on the Practice of Transformative Learning

Edward W. Taylor, Jodi Jarecke

This chapter emerges from a content analysis of all the other chapters about the practice of transformative learning and identifies significant themes through a comparative approach. It was a messy and iterative process of discussing at length the dominant ideas of each chapter and working through multiple versions on a whiteboard. As the process evolved and themes were clarified, it was apparent how much was still left on the drawing table—creative strategies and illusive challenges found in the practice of transformative learning that would not be highlighted in this chapter. That being said, this final chapter is only an impression, a slice of meaning that emerges from these informative readings on fostering transformative learning. Its purpose is not only to look for shared ideas but to pique the readers' interest so they might go back to related chapters and read about them in greater depth. Furthermore, it adds new understanding to the core elements discussed in Chapter One and begins to identify new core elements emerging on the horizon of practice. Finally, this chapter is about raising questions concerning practice that have yet to be adequately addressed and should be reflected on as practitioners engage in the challenging task of fostering transformative learning.

The initial impression that emerges from the chapters was a vast array of purposes and settings in which transformative learning is being practiced. Beginning with the purposes, these chapters reveal a variety of educational agendas of which transformative learning is seen as a means to an end.

For example, there is Cranton's goal of helping tradespersons begin to think like teachers; Langan, Sheese, and Davidson's interest in having students in lower-division sociology courses "recognize and challenge the dominant ideological assumptions that are taken for granted in everyday discussion, and representations of social (in)equalities"; the European-American Collaborative Challenging Whiteness group efforts to change their awareness about privilege, race, and racism through collaborative inquiry; and MacLeod and Egan's goal of helping medical students develop empathy and understanding of patients who are receiving palliative care. In concert with these purposes is an equally wide array of settings in which transformative learning plays out. They include, for example, nonformal education programs in Senegal, West Africa, that are promoting the abandonment of female genital cutting (Easton, Monkman, and Miles); literacy programs in the workplace (King and Heuer); a faculty development program at the University of Johannesburg in South Africa (Gravett and Peterson); and exploration of transformative learning in an online context (Dirkx and Smith), to mention just a few.

Looking back over these various settings and agendas, it seems that while the experience of fostering transformative learning is shaped by context, in many ways as a practice it transcends context. More specifically, this book highlights the practice of transformative learning occurring in various settings, from the classroom to the workplace and from community gatherings to the online context. Likewise, it represents practice in various countries from the United States to Senegal and South Africa, from Canada to New Zealand. However, when considering the diversity of the contexts represented, what becomes apparent is that although each author's practices are shaped by the immediate setting (culture, resources available, learners' needs and interests), there are common practices. It is these common practices that are the focus of the remainder of this chapter. Although not an exhaustive list, we examine six practices: as a purposeful and a heuristic process, confronting power and engaging difference, an imaginative process, leading learners to the learning edge, and fostering reflection and modeling.

TRANSFORMATIVE LEARNING AS PURPOSEFUL AND HEURISTIC PROCESS

A shared theme that is most evident in these chapters is the purposefulness of fostering transformative learning, meaning that the authors not only have an educational, political, or social agenda as they engage transformative learning as a means to an end with their learners, but also transformative learning in and of itself is purposeful. When the goals are couched within a practice of transformative learning, something different is taking place—something more profound where learners are provoked to the "edge of learning" (Marsick and Maltbia; Gravett and Petersen) where for some there is, using the Senegalese word a *tostan,* or "breaking out of the egg" (Easton, Monkman, and Miles), a deep learning, an experience of personal or social empowerment. Fostering transformative learning is purposeful in the sense that it is about teaching for change, not simply about understanding as a purely cognitive insight, but where there is a desire for learners to act within and on their world in more empowering ways. This change, for instance, is seen in Mandell and Herman's approach to mentoring where students no longer practice "rueful acquiescence" of having to take what is offered at higher education institutions; instead they learn how to make the most of their own interest and curiosity in framing their programs of study. It is also found in Hansman and Wright's popular education Legal Promoter's Course in Bolivia, where participants reached "a point of critical consciousness in which they stopped blaming themselves for their problems and began to look outward at unjust social conditions that oppressed them."

Inherent in the purposefulness of transformative learning is a loosely veiled structure, framework, or even, for some, an explicit heuristic for the educator. For example, Fisher-Yoshida describes a framework, the coordinated management of meaning (CMM), used when coaching clients to help them become more aware of information they do not typically consider in their interpersonal encounters. Similar is Marsick and Maltbia's action learning conversations, which provide a heuristic for coach development. These frameworks as well as others, offer essential practices (for example, problem-based learning, dialogic teaching, meditation, safe environment, rules for listening), core premises (for example, soul work, collaboration, direct experience), or phases (for example, steps, significant markers) to assist the transformative educator and learners in their work.

Ironically this sense of purposefulness and structure on one level seems counterintuitive to transformative learning due to its strong emphasis on a learner-centered orientation, where there is an assumption that transformative learning is not planned or orchestrated, but is left to the direction and will of the learner. However, as Tyler reminds us in her work about storytelling and transformative learning, "Creating opportunities for authentic storytelling requires considerable planning on the front end." It is as if there is an ongoing tension revealed in these chapters between the need for structure in transformative learning and at the same time a need to trust the learners in cofacilitating an engaging and fruitful educational experience. The key seems to rest in the meaning of the term *heuristic,* which is a process designed to solve a problem, although it is often informal in nature, loosely applied, and draws on ways of knowing that are grounded in intuition, educated guesses, and common sense. It is this framework that leads to the "creation of circumstances in which participants learn and find ways to transform themselves" (Easton, Monkman, and Miles).

These heuristics also remind us that fostering transformative learning is a process, naturally occurring, reciprocal, and most often a progressive movement toward change. Characteristically the process is described as "messy," "time-consuming," "emotionally laden," "risky," and replete with "potential potholes" and "ill-structured problems." Furthermore, it "is a process that occurs over time, and at moments within the classroom and much later outside those parameters. Although we can set the stage for potential transformation to occur, we cannot always know what the actual impact of the learning experience has been on our learners" (Butterwick and Lawrence).

Recognizing the challenging and complex nature of fostering transformative learning, educators also face ongoing contradictions among the very premises that guide their purposeful practice. For example, it is imperative that trust be established among the learners and between the educators, as they begin to head down the transformative path. One approach to establishing trust, as Brookfield suggested, is to be "as transparent as possible of one's motives, agenda, and directions." However, he has come to recognize that a measured approach to transparency seems more advisable and not revealing the more difficult tasks until trust has been adequately established. This raises the question of how transformative educators establish trust when they are not entirely forthcoming of the process.

Fostering transformative learning is not a prescriptive or stepwise process. Instead, in the classroom, it involves establishing a collective goal among learners, a process grounded in respect and trust, with an appreciation for the ambiguous and unknown, and a recognition that engaging the contradictions and tensions of life can lead to greater personal and social understanding.

TRANSFORMATIVE LEARNING AS CONFRONTING POWER AND ENGAGING DIFFERENCE

Central to transformative education is developing an acute awareness for power and its relationship to cultural difference. Power is the ability to act and influence events manifest in a variety of ways in the practice of fostering transformative learning. One conception of power not often talked about is associated with learners and the power they have in changing their perspective. Lange, in her work on building sustainable community, sees power not exclusively about individual will "exerting power over" one's future through the construction of a new way of looking at the world. Instead, it is much more about intentionality and choosing to live within the world a particular way and having the courage to "walk the labyrinth" and "live into a new future.'' This seems similar to Fisher-Yoshida's description of coaching, where she finds the learner's commitment to engage in the coaching process essential for a successful learning experience.

In reference to power within the transformative group or classroom, it is essentially about being aware of power relations between and among learners and the educator. Due to power relations (teacher–learner) and in particular positionality (race, culture, gender, class, sexual orientation), the classroom is replete with issues of inequity and diversity that greatly influence and confound the process of transformative learning (Tisdell and Tolliver). Similarly, Alcántara, Hayes, and Yorks struggle with what they refer to as ''power dynamics'' within groups as they engage learners in the practice of collaborative inquiry. In particular, the dynamics are not only challenged by the traditional issues of difference but are further complicated by institutionally formulated groups where ''social change leaders encounter tensions surrounding voice and validation of leadership.''

An example of how power relations have significant implications for fostering transformative learning can be seen in the engagement of artistic activities, such as storytelling. Butterwick and Lawrence discuss at length the dilemma of making participation in storytelling among learners mandatory in the higher education classroom. They remind us that storytelling often unfolds in settings that can be oppressive for some learners. During those ''moments where women who do not occupy powerful locations on hierarchies of privilege and oppression are required to tell their story. These stories are then often interpreted through racist, sexist, classist, ablest, heterosexist frameworks.'' As a result ''the inequities in risk taking . . . can lead to further oppression rather than empowerment. Speaking truth to power can be risky.''

Another way power and positionality challenge the transformative educator is working with learners who have been historically marginalized and oppressed by others. This is found among women in Senegal (Easton, Monkman, and Miles), Bolivia (Hansman and Wright), and Harlem (Meyer), and among farmers in Kenya (Duveskog and Friis-Hansen) and learners in adult basic education programs (King and Heuer). For example, writing about Farmer Field Schools in Kenya, Duveskog and Friis-Hansen found the ''general farming population [had] very little power in relation to other actors in society'' and felt they did not have the wherewithal to make significant changes in their lives. Transformative education in these settings is much more than personal empowerment; it is about developing political consciousness. Framed within critical theory, it is about helping learners develop an awareness of existing power structures in society (such as the dominant ideology) and deeply analyzing ''commonly held ideas and practices for the extent to which they perpetuate economic inequity, deny compassion, foster a culture of silence, and prevent people realizing a sense of common connectedness'' (Brookfield).

How educators engage power and positionality is varied, but all share some core ideas. For example, Easton, Monkman, and Miles, who wrote about a Senegalese nonformal education (*tostan*) concerned with the practice of female genital cutting (FGC) developed a "pedagogy of respect" and an appreciation for the local culture. This involved working directly with women and practitioners, not telling them what to do but letting them share their own stories and make their own decisions and not condemning practitioners of FGC. Similarly, Tisdell and Tolliver worked hard at building community in their higher education classrooms by dealing with positionality directly through fostering cultural imagination—drawing on "the arts to release imagination to facilitate dialogue that helps students experience the multiple ways in which they and others (including those from different cultural groups) relate to the world."

Power and cultural difference are also inherently linked. To truly appreciate and engage the rich diversity found among learners means developing an acute sensitivity of power and how inequity and privilege shape the transformative learning experience. Butterwick and Lawrence offer sound advice; referring specifically to the practice of storytelling, they note its significance to transformative learning and difference in general. They believe that educators "need to understand the dangers and inequalities of risk that exist in any group. [They] need to act with a sense of humility and recognition that [they] cannot know for certain what those dangers are, what stories might emerge, and what the reactions to the stories might be." By appreciating the presence of an unequal playing field, educators can more readily face the risk that comes with the practice of transformative learning.

TRANSFORMATIVE LEARNING AS AN IMAGINATIVE PROCESS

One of the most frequently cited critiques of transformative learning from Mezirow's perspective is its reliance on rationality. This critique is often supported by the premise that learning often goes beyond cognitive dimensions. In turn, alternative perspectives of transformation have emerged that seem to embrace "deeper emotional and spiritual dimensions of learning" and acknowledge "the role of image, symbol, ritual, fantasy, and imagination in transformation" (Dirkx, 2000, para. 1). Despite the fact that this perspective has gained increasing attention in the literature particularly in recent years, Mezirow suggests in Chapter One that "a great deal of additional insight into the role of imagination is needed and overdue." The authors of this book make an important contribution in this regard. They have provided unique perspectives on how they conceptualize transformative learning as an imaginative process and offer insight into how these conceptualizations are turned into practice.

First and foremost, transformative learning as an imaginative process entails engaging images in order to facilitate self-awareness and the development of new perspectives among learners. Tisdell and Tolliver, for instance, drawing on the work of Greene (1995) and Dirkx (2006), discuss imagination as a process of engaging with "images that arise out of one's conscious and unconscious memory." Coupling this definition with Dirkx and Smith's claim that interacting with images becomes a way that "dialogical relationships with one's unconscious" can be mediated, the fostering of transformative learning as an imaginative process can be seen as a process of creating opportunities for engagement with images in order to help students begin to envision new perspectives of the world and "reweave new patterns of meaning" (Tisdell and Tolliver).

Taking this definition into consideration, it is important to note what this means for the theory of transformative learning. In other words, if learning is engaged through the use of images and symbols, then it makes sense that practitioners who foster transformative learning in this way also conceptualize the transformative learning process differently from those who take a more rational approach. This was alluded to by Dirkx and Smith, who provide a depth psychology perspective of fostering transformative learning as doing "soul work" or "inner work." However, others also appear to conceptualize transformative learning in other ways and offer new and telling descriptions of how learning looks and feels from this viewpoint. Lange, for instance, talks about this process as one of immersing ourselves into our own realities where "learning emanates from the living it." This is similar to Tisdell and Tolliver, who suggest that students experience transformative learning through engaging and embodying "new ways of being" and articulate their conception of these experiences as a process of becoming, encouraging students to embrace learning "until it becomes you."

What is particularly interesting about these conceptualizations, along with the engagement of images in order to foster transformative learning, is the variety of ways in which this plays out in practice. For instance, Lange's use of pictorial collage designed to allow students "to begin a social critique of why they feel stress and pressures" promotes a change in perspective as students start to reposition "their experiences within a larger socio-political-historical context." Furthermore, as part of their purpose to promote "self-work and self-change" Dirkx and Smith encourage students to journal about the meaning of "emotion-laden images" and reflect on how these images relate to personal experiences. Although these examples provide an introduction to the engagement of images as a means to foster transformative learning, perhaps the most prevalent example offered by the authors in this book is the use of stories.

Storytelling is frequently referenced as a means to foster transformative learning and for creating opportunities for the "imagining of alternative realities" (Butterwick and Lawrence). Based in language, stories are "highly symbolic," and their "rich texture of images" allows listeners to explore their personal experiences, as well as those of the tellers, thus contributing to the development of alternate perspectives (Tyler). Perhaps the rising popularity of storytelling is related to the numerous ways in which it can be effectively used. For instance, Fisher-Yoshida used storytelling models in order to help her client become aware of her assumptions as well as others' perspectives. Similarly, assisting individuals in learning more about themselves as white people, the European-American Collaborative Challenging Whiteness group uses stories from life histories. In addition, it appears that stories do not necessarily need to be told to be imaginative, as the sharing of stories also appears to be equally symbolic in the written form. For example, women participating in the STRIVE program developed by Meyer were able to imagine new and alternate realities through the use of journaling their life histories. She compares this experience to "constructing a patchwork quilt or creating a mosaic, making something beautiful and valuable out of events that, when viewed discretely, may not seem to have meaning."

Similar to the sharing of stories in its ability to spark the imagination of students, a number of authors also mention the use of role play. Cranton does so by conducting an activity where the "teacher becomes the student." In their Legal Promoter's Course, Hansman and Wright facilitate an activity where students have the "experience of becoming a character, acting out experiences, and exploring stereotypes." And Butterwick and Lawrence incorporate role play and theater, which they conceptualize as "telling stories through embodied or performative activities" that allow us "to reconsider the meaning of our experience."

Butterwick and Lawrence further suggest that "through telling [these] stories, alternate ways of knowing and being become more evident." Numerous other authors share this perspective and suggest that new ways of imagining realities naturally involve the incorporation of other ways of knowing, and an engagement of the emotional and embodied aspects of learning. As Tisdell and Tolliver suggest, "New knowledge cannot 'become you' simply through engaging rationality. It has to get into our hearts, souls, and bodies and into our interactions with others in the world." Lange takes a similar stance, suggesting that her conception of transformation involves going beyond the "rational, cognitive, epistemological process" and instead focuses on "touching the spirit and the body." Likewise, Dirkx and Smith suggest that their intention is to foster "self work and deep learning," entailing a "focus on the emotional and symbolic dimensions of students' experiences."

Authors use a variety of methods in practice to address the creative and imaginative process of transformative learning. For instance, through her sustainability program, Lange uses various relaxation activities, and through "art, creative writing, music, and movement activities, students create a set of principles and intentions they wish to manifest in their lives."

These practical methodologies that engage images and address other ways of knowing point to significant strides in understanding the role of imagination in transformative learning. Imagination, it seems, not only involves the engagement of images; it also values the inclusion of the arts and embodied ways of knowing. Engaging learning in this way also appears to offer new and interesting ways in which to conceptualize transformative learning, as an embodied experience that evokes the soul, and immersing oneself into the experience and becoming one with learning (Dikx and Smith; Lange; Tisdell and Tolliver). These processes of immersion and becoming, as articulated by the authors, thus entail an interconnectedness between learning and living: just as we embody and emotionally engage with images and experiences through deep learning and inner work, essentially we transform by living our way into a new way of thinking (Tisdell and Tolliver).

TRANSFORMATIVE LEARNING AS LEADING LEARNERS TO THE EDGE

While numerous authors suggest a need for creating a safe and trusting environment, a tension seems to exist between establishing a comfortable environment that allows students to explore meaning in their own lives and constructing experiences in order to create feelings often associated with disorienting dilemmas such as discomfort or unrest. This is not to say that this tension is new (Berger, 2004; Lange, 2004). In many ways, there is an innate desire among educators for students to feel challenged to learn and at the same time comfortably express their ideas and feelings. However, this tension becomes particularly relevant in relation to transformative learning, due to its predisposition for learner-centered practice, as does a discussion of ways in which the contributors attempt to create a delicate balance by leading students to the edge in order to foster transformation.

The idea of leading students to a learning edge is most explicitly discussed by Gravett and Petersen. Citing Wlodkowski (1999), the authors suggest that "learners are most susceptible to new learning when they are on the edge of their comfort zones—their 'learning edge.'" Taking this into consideration, it becomes the job of the educator to "create conditions under which learners are pushed to their learning edge" (Gravett and Petersen) and eventually "move participants from resistance to acceptance of new or expanded perspectives" (Marsick and Maltbia). However, once again this presents a challenge for educators who strive for transparency in order to establish trust in the classroom (Brookfield). Thus, from a transformative learning perspective, it is interesting to view what types of activities are conducted that interact with this balance—how various "disruptions" are implemented to "push the learning edge"—as well as how educators go about facilitating the learning process and reconciling the tension in an attempt to "maintain a careful balance between challenge and comfort" (Gravett and Petersen).

Langan, Sheese, and Davidson provide an example of pushing students to the learning edge by using disruptions: the "the introduction of critical texts that impact student consciousness, that present a meaningful challenge to taken-for-granted understandings of societal relations" (Langan, Oliver, & Atkinson, 2007). Their use of disruptions included introducing guest lecturers who brought light to various controversial issues that were then discussed by learners in order to help "bring their views out for examination and reflection." In some ways, there are parallels between "disruptions" and the immersion process Lange described, wherein learners are not only introduced to exemplars of sustainable living, but are also encouraged to immerse themselves "into their own reality creating an opportunity for Freirean problem posing." Likewise, the similarities are present in the experiences of the medical students discussed by MacLeod and Egan, who become immersed in the "realities of caring for a person who is dying." In each of these experiences, learners are confronted with individuals and lifestyles that portray another way of living and provide new perspectives to students. Furthermore, educators need to be aware that direct learning experiences, or processes of immersion, may be "extremely effective in fostering deep learning and transformations in worldviews"; however, implementing such activities can result in "complex, confrontational, and emotional responses from students" and even "offend some class participants" (Langan, Sheese, and Davidson).

Many of these emotional experiences, including student resistance, are not necessarily new to the transformative learning experience. In fact, it appears that such responses are almost inherent when teaching for change. Brookfield, for instance, identifies student resistance as one of the predictable "potholes" educators encounter and argues that "whoever is charged with getting people to question assumptions they have previously been happy embracing is likely to be resented, at least initially." Thus, as long-held beliefs become "challenged and reformed," the ambiguity can create a "state of discomfort" (Fisher-Yoshida) and often lead to resistance and, occasionally, the projection of emotions onto the educator (Brookfield; Lange). However, when educators recognize that these instances of emotions stem from contrived and purposeful practice, indeed a sense of responsibility on their part follows.

In many ways, this sense of responsibility must be owned by the educator and requires some type of action in order to maintain balance. Lange, for example, discusses the need for maintaining "spiritual practice" in order to be "open to the emotional intensity," while for Langan, Sheese, and Davidson, it is about making "relationships an object of importance," and for Dirkx and Smith, it is remembering that "listening is often what is required." And although this often leads to a risky endeavor, Tyler reminds us that risk and possibility are often positively correlated. Thus, by engaging and encouraging students to move beyond their comfort zones in a quest for new meaning, it becomes equally important that as educators, "we function continually on our own learning edge" (Gravett and Petersen).

TRANSFORMATIVE LEARNING AS FOSTERING REFLECTION

Most evident throughout these chapters is the centrality of reflection to transformative learning. Engaging in reflection in concert with experience and for a particular purpose provides the means by which learners transform the way they think about themselves, others, or society. For instance, Langan, Sheese, and Davidson, who teach sociology, see reflection as one of the core values of teaching by "encouraging students to connect the course content with their prior knowledge and lived experience."

Despite the emphasis on reflection in general, there was not much definitive discussion about the role of critical reflection, in particular, in fostering transformative learning. This is not to say that critical reflection was not discussed, for in a few chapters, it was seen as central to the transformative experience. For example, Mandell and Herman, who write about academic mentoring, find "at the heart of both transformative learning and mentoring is critical reflection on customary academic roles. The mentor-student relationship could not exist unless teachers remind themselves that their role is not so much to profess as to facilitate, and equally, students understand that their role is not so much to absorb what is professed but to place their ideas and questions at the center of learning." Similar was Cranton's chapter on helping tradespersons become teachers, where she states: "I essentially follow Mezirow (2000) in seeing critical self-reflection as central to transformative learning, although I also believe that does not preclude intuitive, relational, social, and affective transformative learning."

Instead of critical reflection being referred to directly, the term *reflection* was used much more often, although it was not readily apparent in many chapters whether this term was used as a substitute or meant something different from critical reflection. For example, Brookfield found critical reflection grounded in critical theory, where thinking critically is "being able to identify, and then to challenge and change, the process by which a grossly iniquitous society uses dominant ideology to convince people this is a normal state of affairs." Although Lange does not refer to critical reflection specifically, she seems to share a similar understanding. She discusses the importance of creating opportunities for "Freirean problem posing, a reflection process to position their experiences within a larger socio-political-historical context." For others, critical reflection was less about ideology critique and more about greater personal understanding and revising deeply held assumptions. For example, Gravett and Petersen, in their chapter on faculty development and dialogic teaching, refer to critical reflection as a process whereby faculty "become aware of their beliefs and feelings, are open to revision, and ultimately integrate newly appropriated meanings into an informed and conscious theory of practice." Similar is Marsick and Maltbia's discussion of life history in fostering critical reflection to help make learners "aware of their individually held and collective values, beliefs, and meaning schemes." Despite the variations in meaning of critical reflection, there was much more consensus about factors that fostered reflection. They included such things as the importance of providing a supportive environment (Meyer; Duveskog and Friis-Hansen), dialogue (Brookfield; Alcántara, Hayes, and Yorks) opportunities for action and doing (Tisdell and Tolliver; Hansman and Wright), and exposure to alternative perspectives (Cranton). In addition, a number of educational strategies were identified for promoting reflection, such as working in groups or cohorts (Alcántara, Hayes, and Yorks; Donaldson; King and Heuer), writing and journaling (Dirkx and Smith; Meyer; Marsick and Maltbia), arts-based activities (Cranton; Butterwick and Lawrence), and storytelling (Tyler; Tisdell and Tolliver), to mention a few.

It is apparent that despite the centrality of critical reflection to fostering transformative learning, it is still an illusive concept, often poorly defined, and used with much discrepancy to capture an array of concepts and practices (Kreber, 2004). More work is needed to better identify reflection, its various manifestations (such as self-reflection and critical reflection), and the practices that most directly lead to its development.

TRANSFORMATIVE LEARNING AS MODELING

This final chapter would not be complete without some discussion about how contributors inform the understanding of the role of the transformative educator. Most important for the educator as discussed by the contributors was the importance of modeling the practices of transformative learning. It is modeling, for instance, by clinicians in palliative care that "allows learners to observe the desired behaviors directly" and becomes an "effective method of teaching the human dimensions of care" (MacLeod and Egan). Similarly,

Gravett and Petersen have learned "the importance of consistently serving as a role model for learners by explicitly modeling what is expected from them when they have to enact the teaching methodology in their own teaching settings."

For some educators, modeling is central to their practice. For example, Brookfield states, "The importance of modeling is always at the forefront of my mind. It has long been a tenet of my teaching that before I ask any student to do something, I first show how I am trying to do it." He has even developed a specific activity, the critical incident questionnaire, a "deliberate attempt to model critical reflection in front of students." Others see modeling as not only central to their practice but as a way of living in the world. Lange, who is involved with sustainability education, sees her teaching as organic, "where the themes and experience brought into the educative space derive from the social reality in which we live our lives." From this perspective, teaching is seen "as a 'living practice'... where the learning emanates from the living of it, with the capacity to transform all involved."

The objective of modeling practice is not just about providing students the opportunity to observe the educator in practice; there are other positive outcomes as well. For instance, King and Heuer find modeling "invaluable in assisting them [adult learners] in making connections between theory and practice." They saw as a result of their modeling "expressions of possibility, empowerment, ownership, and new awareness. As one seasoned educator in the alternative high school system exclaimed, 'I get it! You're doing what I can do!'" Similarly, Macleod and Egan found that "modeling behaviors and self-disclosure by teachers can mitigate discomfort or uncertainty the students may feel."

It is important to recognize that it is not possible for the transformative educator to "not model" because the educator is always modeling something. Instead, the question is, What do the educator's actions reflect, and are they consistent with the learner expectations in relationship to transformative learning? Butterwick and Lawrence bring clarification to this point by reminding us that

> we are models for our learners. How we ourselves illustrate respectful listening through our bodies and our words is important. We can create an environment where transformational learning can occur; however, without care and attention to the power we have and the work of creating conditions for respectful speaking and listening, we can also contribute to oppression and silencing.

A way to guide the educator in modeling is to consider the practice of critical humility. It is defined "as the practice of remaining open to discovering that our knowledge is partial and evolving while at the same time being committed and confident about our knowledge and taking action in the world." The European-American Collaborative Challenging Whiteness group sees it as a capacity, a way of being in the world, that leads to greater clarity and understanding.

CONCLUSION

Reflecting back on this analysis, it is apparent that fostering transformative learning is a complex approach to teaching and is replete with many unknowns. We have only scratched the surface at illuminating elements that seem essential to transformative learning. Much is still hidden and inadequately understood about an illusive heuristic to fostering transformative learning. Many questions remain and encourage further exploration. For example, how do we engage in learner-centered teaching within a highly purposeful agenda? Similarly, how do we remain transparent while pushing learners to the edge of their learning? Furthermore, within this purposeful agenda of fostering transformative learning, how do teachers and learners conceptualize and reconcile equity and power in the classroom? Fundamental to this question is better understanding the role of the learner and teachers in relationship to each other. More specifically, and an area often not discussed, is what the responsibility of the learners in the transformative learning process is. For example, is modeling more of an interrelated process, where both the teacher and the learner share accountability in the transformative experience? Answers to these questions and others will emerge only if we continue to share the stories of our experiences with fostering transformative learning. It is the sharing of stories, like those of the authors of the chapters in this book, that provokes reflection, engages our imagination, and encourages others to begin their own journey with teaching for change.

REFERENCES

Berger, J. G. (2004). Dancing on the threshold of meaning. *Journal of Transformative Education, 2*, 336–351.

Dirkx, J. M. (2000). *Transformative learning and the journey of individuation.* ERIC Digest No. 223. Retrieved January 28, 2005, from http://www.ericdigests. org/2001–3/journey.htm.

Dirkx, J. (2006). Authenticity and imagination. In P. Cranton (Ed.), *Authenticity in teaching* (pp. 27–39). San Francisco: Jossey-Bass.

Greene, M. (1995). *Releasing the imagination.* San Francisco: Jossey-Bass.

Kreber, C. (2004). An analysis of two models of reflection and their implications for educational development. *International Journal of Lifelong Education, 9*(1), 29–49.

Langan, D., Oliver, M., & Atkinson, L. (2007). The political is personal: TAs on the front lines of the critical consciousness campaign. *Radical Pedagogy*, *9*(1). Retrieved June 25, 2008, from http://radicalpedagogy.icaap.org.

Lange, E. (2004). Transformative and restorative learning: A vita dialectic for sustainable societies. *Adult Education Quarterly*, *54*, 121–139.

Wlodkowski, R. J. (1999). *Enhancing adult motivation to learning: A comprehensive guide for teaching of all adults*. San Francisco: Jossey-Bass.

INDEX